watching porn

watching porn

And Other Confessions
of an Adult Entertainment Journalist

LYNSEY G.

THE OVERLOOK PRESS
NEW YORK, NY

This edition first published in hardcover in the United States in 2017
The Overlook Press, Peter Mayer Publishers, Inc.

NEW YORK
141 Wooster Street
New York, NY 10012
www.overlookpress.com
For bulk and special sales, please contact sales@overlookny.com,
or write us at the above address.

Cataloging-in-Publication Data is available from the Library of Congress

Book design and typeformatting by Bernard Schleifer
Manufactured in the United States of America
FIRST EDITION
ISBN 978-1-4683-1203-4
2 4 6 8 10 9 7 5 3 1

"It always amuses me that people talk about watching porn like any other form of entertainment. But nobody's watching porn—they're wanking."

—CINDY GALLOP

"I wish more people would take pictures of themselves getting fucked! I feel like it's good for you. It's really, really good for you."

—ORIANA SMALL, a.k.a. ASHLEY BLUE

Contents

INTRODUCTION   9

CHAPTER 1: Before Porn   13

CHAPTER 2: Getting In   23

CHAPTER 3: *East Coast ASSault*   29

CHAPTER 4: The Early Days   41

CHAPTER 5: The Backward Slide   49

CHAPTER 6: *WHACK! Magazine*   59

CHAPTER 7: The Conflicted Existence of the Female Porn Writer   73

CHAPTER 8: In the Flesh   81

CHAPTER 9: The Guys   91

CHAPTER 10: Vegas and the Sex Toy Revelation   103

CHAPTER 11: Creepazoid Territory   113

CHAPTER 12: The New Girl   123

CHAPTER 13: Editor in Chief   139

CHAPTER 14: Racism in the Industry   155

CHAPTER 15: Other "Isms"   171

CHAPTER 16: The Gay Divide & the Condom Wars   185

CHAPTER 17: The Feminist Porn Awards   205

CHAPTER 18: Making It in Miami   219

CHAPTER 19: Losing It to the Tubes   227

CHAPTER 20: Porn, Art, and Obscenity   249

CHAPTER 21: Winner   266

A GLOSSARY OF PORN TERMINOLOGY   283

RECOMMENDED VIEWING FOR THE FEMINIST-MINDED   289

FURTHER READING LIST FOR THE CURIOUS   293

ACKNOWLEDGMENTS   295

BIBLIOGRAPHY   299

Introduction

It was a high-summer night in 2007. I was standing on a friend's rooftop in Hell's Kitchen, basking in the glare from nearby Times Square, which bounced off the glass-sided skyscrapers and lit up the night around me. I was drunk. There was a similarly intoxicated group of old friends surrounding me, wine flowing and music playing, and the sweaty embrace of an August evening in New York cradled me.

I was twenty-four years old. I considered myself a writer, but I hadn't written anything of note except a few poems and some essays that had earned me scholarship money and minor recognition at the undergraduate level. I had a BA in English literature with a minor in philosophy, a year of volunteering experience, and several positions as an administrative assistant under my belt. I had absolutely no plans for the future. Nor did I have a job.

But with the buzzing energy of New York thrumming through my system, I wanted to grab my ambitions by their necks, squeeze out the drops of talent I'd been squandering, and get into the game somehow. I had just returned to the city after two years, having graduated from one of its several universities in 2005 and then wandered off to collect life experiences elsewhere before crawling back, tail between my legs, about a week earlier. I'd left Chicago in a haze of depression and self-medication and landed in a sweltering apartment in a filthy building in Harlem with my boyfriend and two grad-student roommates. I had no prospects, no plan, and nothing to do other than accept whatever cash might deign to come my way. In short, I was a mess.

"Samantha," I slurred to the friend whose shoebox of an apartment downstairs was notable mostly due to its exceptionally well-located roof. "Do you know anybody who's looking for a writer? I need a job."

She cocked her head to one side, evaluating me. We'd known each other since high school, and though we'd never been particularly close, she knew me pretty well: a country girl with a flair for the dramatic, a wide rebellious streak, and a need bordering on compulsion to write.

"Well . . ." she replied slowly, considering each word. "I *do* have a friend who's looking for writers . . ."

I perked up. "Yes! Give them my name!"

"Well . . ." she said again, tilting her head to the other side. "It's at a magazine . . ."

"I can do magazines! Hook me *up*!"

A pause. She straightened her head and looked me dead in the eye. "It's at a *porn* magazine."

I blinked and tilted my cup to my mouth. This required more wine. A vision of what writing for a porn magazine would entail formed hazily in my mind: There would be parties, I thought. Elbow rubbing with sophisticated types, and sexy new friends, surely. I would probably be, within a matter of months, *the coolest person I knew*. Probably the coolest person *anyone* knew. An exotic, interesting, worldly, very, very cool porn journalist.

Little did I know that at that very moment, the porn industry wasn't particularly exotic, worldly, or cool. As a matter of fact, it was just as much of a mess as I was. A hot, sweaty, confused, desperate mess. As I've spent years watching it from my particular vantage point, halfway in and halfway out, I've come to realize that it has always been a mess, and will likely always be a mess. Not because of the literal messes of bodily fluids, or the ethical ambiguity in which it exists, so much, but because it is a mess of an industry. I don't mean that as a put-down, rather as a statement of fact and, really, of wonder that it has clung on as tenaciously and successfully as it has through the near-constant shitstorms that have always plagued it.

Pornography may not really be that exotic or that cool, but it *is* just as interesting as I hoped it would be that night. It is as vast and varied as the City of New York, as disorganized as the mind of a twenty-four-year-old writer. It has no agreed-upon leader, no formalized code of conduct, no entrance exam or standard for advancement. The only rule, really, is to follow the money in as safe a way as possible, with the word "safe" being a very malleable term indeed. Perhaps the only trait its denizens have in common is a genius for finding a way forward—toward the money—through technology, media, and the marriage of the two. That, and a very high libido.

But I knew none of this on that roof in 2007. At the moment in question, with my red Solo cup at my lips, all I saw was unbounded opportunity reflected by the electric skyline.

"Fine by me," I said to Samantha at last, trying to sound as if I weren't mentally foaming at the mouth for the job. "Give him my name! I'm into it."

I didn't want to sound too excited. After all, porn was a shameful kind of thing, in my experience, and I was talking to someone from high school. We'd been raised in the same part of the world, where sex wasn't talked about and the prospect of hobnobbing with degenerates excited nobody. But I was *thrilled*. In my fuzzy dream-vision, my future porn-journalist self was hobnobbing with French art film types and drinking much better wine than the cheapest stuff I'd been able to find at the liquor store on my way here. She was someone I wanted to be.

"Okay," Samantha said. "His name's j. vegas. That's his porn-writing name, but it fits pretty well. I'll give him your info."

"Fantastic! Thank you so much!"

Samantha fiddled with her phone, maybe sending my number to him right then, and I wandered off to refill my cup, then looped my arm around my boyfriend—whom I'd also known since high school. Life was looking extremely rosy.

In that moment, porn was an unexpected godsend. It was something that I, like many young adults, had never spent much time thinking about, aside from the few minutes every day or two I spent getting myself off to it. I'd had moments of doubt and guilt over it, like most of us do, but I'd never gone very far down the rabbit hole of considering its implications on my life, or the world, or the people who made it. Porn just *was*, as unknowable to me as the fashion industry that was currently crowding Bryant Park a half mile away for Fashion Week. As mysterious as whomever lived in the penthouses all around me, looking down on us mortals clustered desperately on a fourth-story rooftop. Impenetrable as the glittering sidewalks.

I've since walked down those sidewalks for ten years longer than I ever planned to, infiltrated the offices of a porn magazine, met a man named j. vegas who would change my life, and though I've looked back many times and wondered why I chose this thorny, often dark, and always fascinating path, I've never turned around. I've learned volumes about the permeability and malleability of one of the most diverse and nebulous—and profitable—industries in the world, about the people who make it what it is, and about what it all means about us as humans. I'm going to try to fit it into this book, if you're willing to come along for the ride.

We're both consenting adults, right?

CHAPTER 1

Before Porn

LET'S START AT THE BEGINNING.

Like most Americans, I grew up deeply, troublingly sexually repressed. And like many Americans, whether in spite of that background or *to* spite it, I have always been obsessed with sex. My parents were not religious, but they were old-fashioned, to put it mildly. Strict about things like table manners, bed-making, social expectations, and anything having to do with sexuality. They were, to be frank, *terrified* of sex. I mean above and beyond the typical discomfort found in most American households. I mean that I was told, as a panicky response to me scratching my crotch when I was six, that I shouldn't touch myself down there because *that's where chicken pox come from.* (I'd already had the chicken pox and knew I wouldn't get them again, so I kept at it, just privately.)

In typical sex-fearing fashion, my parents presented me with a "How Babies Are Made" sort of book when I was quite young. And I, in typical sex-obsessed fashion, was captivated by it. I asked my mother to read it to me almost every night, and my undisguised interest in its subject matter frightened both her and my father. They began refusing to read it, capitulating maybe once a week to my persistent requests.

We moved to a farm in the country when I was six, and after we'd settled into the old, tree-shaded house, I recall asking my mom to read me the "mating" book again. (I called it "mating" because it felt grown-up to use what I considered the technical term.) It had gotten lost in the move, she told me. I'd have to pick another book. But some years later, I discovered the mating book tucked away in a little-used bookshelf in a back room. She'd *hidden* it from me, a six-year-old curious about her body and urges! The subject matter in that book, I deduced, was *bad.* And that made my unbridled interest in it *also* bad.

This conclusion, however, did nothing to cool my interest in sex. I've never been one to do what authority figures want.

Sometime in middle school, I discovered a little-used copy of *The Joy of Sex* buried in my mother's pajama drawer. What I was doing digging around in there, I don't know, but the drawings I discovered within changed my world. I'd done my share of imagining what "mating" might look like, of course, but this was before the Internet, and the closest I'd gotten were a few Renaissance paintings of nudes a friend had shown me in the encyclopedia in the second grade. But these drawings were entirely different. Not only were the people in them fully naked, but they were *doing it*. In imaginative ways *with names*. And there was so much *hair*! I found the book mesmerizing. For a while, every time my mother left the house for more than twenty minutes, I would sneak in for a peek at the book—at the reproductions of old Japanese prints in which the men's penises were oversized and turgid; at the dark, florid bushes of the women and the confusing squiggles of lines beneath them.

When I was maybe fifteen, a friend was housesitting, and she invited a few friends over. One of those friends (the same one who'd shown me the nudie pics in the encyclopedia) produced a pilfered VHS tape from her bag. She'd found it on her parents' shelf, and though the label was cryptic, she knew damn well what it was. The five of us settled down with snacks in front of the homeowners' big-screen TV, giggling, to watch our first-ever porno.

The movie was fuzzy (ah, VHS!), confusing, and generally awful. We laughed our way through an hour or so of what we now, decades later, fondly refer to as "Boner Beach." The scene was supposedly set at a beach house, though the "beach" scenes were clearly filmed in a warehouse against fake-as-hell backdrops. The conceit was that several friends were vacationing together in various stages of horniness and undress. I recall few details, aside from the extreme hairiness of the male star, which inspired howls of laughter and many jokes about Sasquatch. I remember one scene in which a woman was making a salad while overhearing some friends fucking in another room. As she surveyed the vegetables at her disposal, growing more turned on by the second, I shouted, "Use the carrot!" But she went for the celery instead, much to my confusion—at least the carrot was *round*.

Sadly, "Boner Beach" was my only experience with outright pornography until college. I went to high school in the days of the Internet's infancy, when rudimentary porn in the form of photos and dirty stories *was* available online, but most houses had one desktop computer shared by the entire family. Said desktop inevitably had a dial-up connection, which meant that downloading JPEGs of boobies was excruciatingly slow, and accessing the Internet in the middle of the night to find them was loud and obvious. I learned to occasionally find sexual content online, but I was honestly too scared of getting caught to risk much more than a passing glance. And, besides, boobies were really all I needed—although I hadn't yet wrapped my brain around my queerness, my body knew damn well that breasts interested me just as much as, if not more than, penises.

At any rate, it wasn't until I learned to masturbate in college in New York City that I came back to pornography. Maybe "learned" isn't the right word; it might be more accurate to say that I'd *tried* it in high school, but having never had an orgasm, I didn't understand exactly what it was that I was trying to accomplish. It wasn't until one crystal-clear afternoon with my first college boyfriend—a very attractive young man who, in hindsight, would probably have made an excellent submissive if I'd known what that meant—that I had the revelation. I can still remember the shock of it. There I was, enjoying myself as always but, as usual, a tad indifferent to the experience, when *BLAM!* My field of vision went white for a few seconds and my body exploded with pleasure. When I came to, collapsed face-first into the pillow, my lifelong obsession with sex had finally come home to roost with my first real orgasm. I *got* it now.

When I got back to my dorm room that Sunday night, inspired and still aroused, I immediately found porn on my fancy new laptop. With an Internet hookup built into the wall of my dorm and file-sharing sites like Napster and LimeWire exploding, literally nothing could stop me from my exploration of ecstasy. And nothing did. Not even my two roommates, who seemed to *always* be hovering. But I was sneaky, and determined. I persisted in my devotion to getting off, and by the time I returned to New York six years later, having lived in three different states since I'd graduated, I'd been through a succession of relationships, hookups, and sex toys. I'd earned money as both a go-go dancer and as a nude model. I'd inched closer to understanding my own sexuality, and for the most part I'd enjoyed the process.

But I'd also been sexually assaulted, an event from which it took me years to claw my way back to a semblance of sexual health. Many of my explorations, both with partners and alone with the porn I'd come to enjoy, were attempts to relocate the pleasure I'd found that day in college when I'd discovered that sex and bliss could go together. But my shame-filled upbringing combined with PTSD to deliver one hell of a blow to my ability to experience ecstasy. Along with the occasional fits of violent terror that accompanied a partner saying or doing the wrong thing during intimacy, I had developed a mental and emotional barrier to reaching orgasm when anyone else was around. This meant that, though I threw myself into sexual situations in attempts to return to my pre-assault orgasmic capabilities, I couldn't climax with whomever shared my bed for years. Even after my orgasm returned to me, it was hit or miss as to whether it would make an appearance when I was with someone. And, since my libido had gotten more complicated but not less active, I found myself alone with my computer even more often than I had before.

A helpful factor in this solo activity was that, as my young adulthood had progressed, so had the Internet. And with the Internet, as we all know, came a deluge of smut that has yet to recede. By the time I asked Samantha to pass along my contact information to a porno mag editor in 2007, I was an old pro at online smut. But, despite my fluency in porn, my relationship with it mirrored those of many people I've spoken to since: Although it was a recurring motif in my life—a standard part of my weekly (okay, maybe daily) routine—I managed not to think about it very often, if at all. One of the greatest advantages, and also drawbacks, of free online porn (the kind I was watching) is that it can be accessed quickly and easily, with neither forethought *nor* afterthought. At the drop of one's pants, it can be cued up and enjoyed. When the viewer is sated, it can be closed and the browser history purged in a matter of seconds. *Et voilà!* We can walk out the door with a clear mind, a spring in our step, and virtually no mental or emotional connection to what we just watched remaining in our minds.

That's pretty much how I related to porn as a young adult. My repressed upbringing, and my trauma from being assaulted, stood the test of time just as steadfastly as did my high sex drive, and though I frequently told myself I would give up the porn to appease my guilt, I wound up alone in my room with a laptop and a vibrator more often than I wanted to admit. So I didn't admit it, even to myself. I allowed Internet porn to comfort me when I was lonely, bored, or depressed, but I didn't give it the time of day in my normal waking thoughts.

But the catch was that most of what I was finding online kind of freaked me out. As an overworked and underpaid administrative assistant just out of college, I couldn't imagine being able to afford a porn site subscription, so I was left with the free stuff—for the most part, short clips of badly pixelated boning. Like, really hardcore boning. One of the signatures of the "gonzo" style of shooting that dominated the industry at the time was low production value (at least for many studios), so much of what I was seeing looked like it could have been filmed in some weirdo's basement in a suburb in Ohio. For all I knew from the pirated clips I streamed, the actors could have been unpaid or non-consenting—the latter of these being a big issue for me, given my personal experiences.

The ambiguity of the circumstances under which these clips were filmed compounded the guilt I already experienced every time I engaged in sexual activity. I wasn't sure whether the things I was seeing were normal, but my upbringing told me that they could not possibly be okay. I'd been raised to feel *bad* for being interested in "normal" sex between two people behind closed doors, so gangbangs and dirty talk and bondage couldn't be healthy. Could they? The question plagued me, but I was young and broke. I didn't have many options for taking in higher-quality entertainment. And it bears mentioning that I have always nurtured a deep and abiding attraction to the forbidden. So I watched porn a few times a week, at least. Online. For free. And I felt terrible about it.

I was just like thousands, probably millions, of other Americans. We almost all watch porn for free online, but we try not to think about it because we're remorseful, and because we don't really understand what we're seeing. But no matter whether we regret our decisions or not, we keep going back to it. After all—*really*—how could we *not* watch porn? It's everywhere.

While the statistics on Internet porn vary wildly from source to source and remain unreliable due to a paucity of serious research on the subject, estimates range from four to nearly thirty percent of the Internet currently being devoted to pornographic content. Somewhere in the neighborhood of twenty-five percent of Internet searches are for porn,

and popular porn tube site Pornhub reported twenty-three *billion* visits
in 2016. That's billion with a B. In other words, given our ever-increasing
dependence upon the Web and the still-evolving prevalence of technology
in our daily routines, ignoring the siren song of free porn is becoming
more difficult all the time.

ALTHOUGH OUR ACCESS TO pornography has exploded in the new millennium, there's no use in taking an alarmist approach about it or wallowing
in guilt over our prurient tendencies. Porn, after all, has always been
available. And I do mean *always*. Ever since we became *Homo sapiens*,
and arguably even before, we've been into pornographic depictions of
naked people doing sexy stuff. Some of the earliest artwork known to
have been produced by human hands are the small carvings of volup-
tuous and luridly detailed female figures called "Venus figurines," which
date back as far as the Aurignacian period some thirty-five thousand
years ago. Ancient cave paintings the world over (from China's Kangji-
ashimenji Petroglyphs to England's Creswell Crags) depict sexual content
ranging from stylized genitals to bisexual, bestial orgies. According to
Shira Tarrant, author of *The Pornography Industry*, "The Turin Erotic
Papyrus was an ancient scroll painted during Egypt's Ramesside period
(1292–1075 BCE), two-thirds of which includes explicit depictions of
sexual acts."

Erotic artwork and inscriptions were so rampant in pre-volcano
Pompeii that modern archeologists restricted access to large portions of
the preserved city until quite recently, fearing an adverse reaction to the
amatory murals. When researchers from Oxford deciphered a gigantic
collection of two-thousand-year-old papyrus from a garbage dump in
Egypt, they found themselves reading copies of a wildly popular book of
erotica—the *Fifty Shades of Grey* of Alexandria. The Moche people of
what is now Peru were painting scenes of anal sex on their pottery in the
first centuries AD. Temples in India from the tenth century sport graph-
ically-carved orgies. Japanese wood-block prints in the *shunga* style depicted explicit sexual liaisons from the thirteenth century on. In the
fifteenth century, no sooner had the printing press concluded its Bible-
printing duties than it got to work on porn. In 1749, *Memoirs of a
Woman of Pleasure* (commonly known as *Fanny Hill*) caused a sensation

in England and throughout Europe, and the book was first banned then collected by smut-hungry noblemen, with the debauched writings of the Marquis de Sade only a few decades away.

It hardly needs to be said that photography's invention in the early 1840s was nearly immediately put to dirty use—some historians consider pornographic photos of prostitutes and dancers called "French cards" major contributors to the explosive popularity of the new medium. (Despite the popularity of these nudie pics, however, the term "pornography" wasn't coined until 1857 in the UK, and didn't come into common use in America until the late nineteenth century. So while we might call the Venus figurines pornographic, they wouldn't have been considered so by their makers.)

The first porn films were produced in the mid-1890s, more or less simultaneously with the advent of the moving picture. The earliest known surviving explicitly pornographic film, *À L'Écu d'Or ou la Bonne Auberge*, dates from 1908, and though that may sound quaint to us today, it's worth noting that these films were *not* much tamer than what we're used to. The filming techniques may have been less sophisticated, but Ye Olde Pornographers were into some kinky shit. The oldest surviving American porno flick, *A Free Ride*, for instance, features a raunchy *al fresco* threesome that's spurred by two women getting excited by watching a man urinate. Water sports, anyone?

"Stag films," as they came to be called, were men's club institutions, presented by their producers for small groups of men at Elks lodges, bachelor parties, brothels, and the like, well into the twentieth century. The 1960s saw an increase in legalized hardcore porn from Europe in magazines and on 8mm film, which was often looped and played in adult bookstores' popular peep-show booths. American filmmakers soon followed suit, giving rise to a budding porn industry on this side of the pond. As the decades wore on and the Supreme Court passed down a number of rulings that more closely pinpointed the definition of prosecutable obscenity, full-scale adult theaters began to pop up, and big-budget, full-length feature films showing explicit sex were played on the silver screen. The "porno chic" films of the 1970s, like *Deep Throat* (1972), *The Devil in Miss Jones* (1973), and *The Opening of Misty Beethoven* (1976), saw pornography emerging as big business, often bankrolled by organized crime.

When the Supreme Court's 1973 *Miller v. California* ruling made the definition of obscenity reliant upon local "community standards," the Golden Age of Porn was curtailed, but the advent of home video was not far behind. Porn workers continued doing business with lower budgets and less refined technology, skulking around without explicit legal protection. By the release of Reagan-backed Meese Commission's report on pornography in 1986, many Americans were investing in home viewing systems to consume their sexy films in private, and the market expanded accordingly.

Since the establishment of an explicitly legal and wildly profitable industry in California in the late eighties, our voracious appetites for smut haven't let up. The nineties witnessed a proliferation in the medium, with hundreds of independent companies springing up in the San Fernando Valley. And, with the emergence of the Internet, pornographic websites were some of the first to make money from selling products online—a move that revolutionized the way consumers shop . . . and masturbate.

It's been argued that porn—or at least our never-ending desire for it—is one of the major forces, if not *the* primary driving force, behind almost every major technological advancement in our species' history, and I tend to believe the hype. HD video was popularized by the porn industry just as much as by IMAX films. Virtual reality tech was adopted by pornographers long before mainstream producers took it on. Text messaging may never have become the go-to short-form communication of the new millennium if photos and videos had not been thrown into the mix, enabling "sexting." Virtually every media-sharing platform and app must grapple with the masses' wont to use it for sending, receiving, or watching sexy media. And, as far as anyone can tell, the cycle will continue for as long as we keep inventing things.

In short, we love our porn. We have always loved it. As of 2016, CNN reported that between fifty and ninety-nine percent of American men, and thirty to eighty-six percent of American women, consume pornography. Yet, especially in America where our repression breeds obsession, we are ashamed of our proclivities. We keep porn carefully contained behind our locked bedroom doors, except for those few times a month, a week, or a day when we take it out to play before slamming the door shut again, leaving our shameful partner untended to do what it will in the dark. And, like many things that exist in the dark, it scares us to imagine seeing it in the glaring light of day.

I had been downplaying my own relationship with pornography for years when, in the late summer of 2007, I was offered a chance to take a good, long look at the monster lurking in my closet. I reflected on the few years I'd spent out of college and noted that I had written nothing worth a damn since I'd earned my BA. I had to face the fact that, at this point in my life, I didn't really have anything to write *about*. And here was porn itself—my greatest source of shame and satisfaction— knocking from the other side of the bedroom door, offering me a chance to face my lifelong struggle against the horny nature with which I'd been born.

A photo of me taken during my pre-porn journalism days, feeling carefree in the New York City subway system   (PHOTO COURTESY OF THE AUTHOR)

CHAPTER 2

Getting In

A FEW DAYS AFTER THAT rooftop party, I made my first visit to the offices of a publishing company that put out several "jizz rags," as Samantha's friend, the editor in chief who went by the pen name j. vegas, had called them on the phone. They were looking for a DVD reviewer, and I wanted the job.

After a confusing series of events that left me trapped in a fire stairwell due to construction in the lobby of a nondescript office building in midtown Manhattan, I was greeted at the emergency exit by one of the tallest, skinniest white guys I'd ever seen. He was fresh faced and wearing thick black plastic-rimmed glasses, a punk T-shirt beneath a plaid button-up, cuffed and torn blue jeans, and a pair of black Converse All Stars. He stuck out a heavily tattooed arm for a handshake. "Hi, I'm vegas. I take it you're Lynsey?"

"Yes!" I wheezed, winded from climbing the emergency staircase.

"Great!" he said, grinning. "Follow me, if you please!" After a few twists and turns through a maze of perfectly normal hallways hung with large prints of magazine covers featuring all manner of tits and ass, we arrived at a modestly sized office with windows looking out onto the sweltering city. A large desk was piled high with glossy magazines, photos, and notebook paper filled with illegible scribbling in red pen. A small plaque on his desk featured his name over the words "Editor in Chief." I was impressed; he didn't look much older than I was, and here he was with his own office, a fancy job title, and a plaque. Maybe this porn stuff was a bandwagon worth jumping on.

I don't remember much about our initial conversation. My nerves were in such a state that I skated through it with only part of my brain dedicated to the task. I recall that he showed me a few copies of the magazine, making it clear that this was a hardcore magazine—no *FHM*-style tasteful nudes here. With glee reminiscent of a child repeating all the bad words he's overheard his parents using, j. vegas informed me that this magazine was about filthy sex, gaping holes, and close-ups of penetration. It was placed on high shelves behind all the other magazines, and it came wrapped in plastic.

I was unfazed by this litany at the time, but I realize now that he was trying to warn me. My bright eyes and smiling optimism were red flags, I'm sure, that I had no clue what I was getting into. But I didn't take his speech as the caution sign it was—I instead looked into his friendly eyes and noticed how happy he seemed, and I unconsciously decided that this couldn't be as "bad" as my sex-phobic upbringing would have me believe.

After he'd vetted me well enough for his liking, the two of us headed over to his boss's office. When we entered Charles's office, the graying editorial director had a set of photographs in hand and was examining them closely with one of those tiny magnifying glasses that you hold right up to the paper. I'd never seen anyone actually use one before, so I considered this impressive. He was looking, *very closely*, at anatomy-textbook-grade close-ups of anal penetration.

As we waited for Charles's attention, I noticed a small sculpture atop a stack of papers on his desk. I'd never seen anything like the shapely, shiny piece of contemporary art, which had some sort of disk balanced on top of it. It was large—the bulbous part must have had a diameter of three or four inches at least. Driven by curiosity, I reached out and touched the disk, which promptly fell off and revealed the "sculpture" to have been a blank CD balanced atop a massive black butt plug.

I can't imagine that I *hadn't* been blushing before committing this faux pas—I've been blessed with that type of redheaded complexion that flushes if I so much as meet someone's eyes—but I'm sure I was at high crimson when that butt plug revealed itself to me.

At any rate, I left the magazine offices that afternoon with copies of several magazines to study, and one double-disc DVD set called *East Coast ASSault*. Charles wanted a sample DVD review and some set copy within a few days, which he'd review before deciding whether or not to hire me.

I went home, had some lunch, and popped in the first of the two

DVDs. My roommates were at school, my boyfriend was at work, the sun was shining, and I had my first-ever freelance writing assignment for a print publication. I was *so* ready for this.

IT'S IMPORTANT TO NOTE THAT, in mid-2007, I had landed in a strange situation. Moving in with my boyfriend, I had assumed, would rid me of my desire to watch porn. I'd be getting laid so much, I assumed, that my desires would be satisfied and I'd be able to forget all about my shameful secret.

But, perhaps unsurprisingly to those with more life experience, I'd been disappointed in myself when I discovered that, despite the lots of sex that I was indeed having, I still wanted to watch porn. And I did. I told myself it was because I was oversexed and unemployed, and after I'd gotten a job and acclimated myself to having regular access to a willing partner, everything would calm down. But I was watching a *lot* of Internet porn, reliably getting off to it when I couldn't always do so with my partner, and I didn't approve of the trend.

So when porn reviewing came to me, I saw it as a way out of my nasty habit. Sure, I'd be developing a new habit to replace it, but it would be sanctioned by the income it would bring, and it would provide me, I assumed, with *better* porn than the stuff I'd been finding online. In that quaint way that children often arrive at imaginative but wildly inaccurate conclusions about matters for which they have no guidance, I had gotten it into my head that, because I considered much of it distasteful, my usual Internet fare was not *real*, professionally made porn. I thought it must be the work of bottom-feeding amateurs, and that "real" porn made by professionals didn't end up on the Internet. "Real" porn would be fancier, I imagined, and look prettier than my Internet porn. Because they would be higher-end fare, I thought, the movies I got for review wouldn't make me feel so bad for watching them.

I could hardly have been further off target. The truth was that Internet porn as I knew it was just your standard, ho-hum American porn of the day, which had been illegally reproduced and put up for free on the Internet. Because people just like me were watching pirated material so damn much, the porn industry was losing millions. In fact, money was evaporating so fast that porn producers had entered into a terrified frenzy in which they filmed as much cheap content as possible and put it out into the market as fast as they could in order to make a few bucks before the pirates got around to stealing it.

Thus, in the mid-2000s, a genre of porn called "gonzo" rose to prominence. The majority of gonzo produced in those days spent very little time, money, or effort on production value, and required no scripting, costuming, plot, or really anything else. It was what Wicked Pictures director Brad Armstrong called "the make-it-for-as-cheap-as-you-can, throw-it-out-there, sell-it-for-as-little-as-you-can stuff" in an interview with me a few years later. (Certainly not all gonzo porn fit this mold—some studios did, and still do, produce gonzo porn with high production value and beautiful cinematography, but there are several boatloads more of the cheapo stuff in existence.) The genre's "in the action" filming style, often using Point of View (POV) camera angles without dialogue, scripting, or setup, embraced an "erasure of the so-called fourth wall where there is no pretense of separation between the performers and the viewers," according to Shira Tarrant. It was named after Hunter S. Thompson's infamous immersive style of journalism, and though in many cases it may have been a miscarriage of a literary legacy, the name stuck.

In keeping with its breakneck speed and pared-down production style, gonzo porn often prioritized shock value in the hopes of baiting consumers into paying for something they hadn't seen before. One company would offer a brand-new performer's first-ever blowjob, but then another would up the ante by offering that performer's first-ever blowbang (think gangbang, but with oral sex only). A third company would then enter the fray, showing a first-time model's debut blow-bang, but then another company would release an even-newer newbie deep-throating the biggest cock in the biz while taking the second-biggest anally. This of course would give rise to a different company releasing video of another newbie drinking semen out of a shoe, which would lead to a different company grilling up a multiple-man semen omelet and feeding it to the woman who'd just been gangbanged. (I'm not making that one up. And there's actually a word for semen-feeding content, which is perhaps unsurprisingly Japanese: *gokkun*. Not to be confused with *bukkake*—also Japanese—in which multiple men ejaculate on one person. But *bukkake*, in turn, is not to be confused with a simple gangbang, during which men *may* ejaculate on someone's face, but they may do so elsewhere, and in which no semen consumption is required.)

You get the gist. The name of the game was to shock in order to sell as much as possible, at as little cost as possible—whatever it took to make a quick buck, even if that meant grossing out ninety percent of the audience.

Let me be clear. I'm talking about more than hair-pulling and getting the occasional spurt of semen in someone's eye. I'm talking about rigorous double, triple penetrations. Fishhooking and smacking and choking, retching and swearing and spitting. Close-ups of holes gaping so wide a viewer could question what they were looking at. Acts that may have been exciting and even intensely pleasurable for the actors, but which might have just as easily been painful, dangerous, or traumatizing, if conditions were wrong. Sitting at home watching, I had no way of knowing, and the uncertainty made me squirm.

Let me also state that most of these sex acts were not considered specialties or fetishes. They were just run-of-the-mill samples of the adult entertainment being filmed primarily in California at the time. Most of them were scenes that had been filmed randomly, then grouped together according to a theme and packaged under a somewhat upsetting name like *Throat Yogurt*. (Yes. That's a real title. So is *Sperm Receptacles*.)

The gonzo period was when edgy became normal in adult film. The now-standard deep-throat, gagging blowjob scene became mainstream in the mid-2000s; anal sex became a matter of course rather than an exotic side dish; behavior that some might find degrading and borderline violent was normalized in porn. Sure, this kind of hardcore fare had been made for decades, largely in low-budget fringe films, but the gonzo era pushed it as far into the mainstream as possible. And now it was being produced and marketed aggressively to an audience that had such a glut of choices that the weirder the content, the more intriguing it seemed, and the more likely it became that anyone would spend money on it.

Danny Wylde, a now-retired porn star, artist, author, and big fan of horror and grindhouse entertainment, made an excellent point in our 2011 interview: "A great deal of contemporary audiences get off on degradation," he said. "It's in our films, television, and magazines all the time." I suppose there is something to that—gonzo porn may be another arm of our already-existing tendencies toward degeneracy. But I've never overly enjoyed the horror genre, and there may be an element of this kind of media that passed right over my earnest little head.

In 2007, it shocked and concerned me, and I really hoped that the DVD reviewing gig would buoy me above the dregs I'd been floating around in online.

CHAPTER 3

East Coast ASSault

As I popped *East Coast ASSault* into the shared DVD player in the living room in my apartment in Harlem, I envisioned myself in a few months' time, wearing a beret and black turtleneck with a cigarette holder (never mind that I've never been a smoker) and a glass of wine in hand, telling my rapt friends about my first film reviewing experience. "This film asked some important questions about what butt stuff really *means*," I'd drawl, receiving impressed nods in response.

But *East Coast ASSault* did not open my eyes to a new existential contemplation of filmed sex acts. It did, however, deepen my understanding of the reality of the porn industry, and inspire in me a line of questioning that to this day has not ended.

The conceit of the film was that a tired, oversexed porn actor (also the film's director and producer) was trying to get away from his grueling schedule in Los Angeles by vacationing on the drearier side of the country, but everywhere he went, some voracious acquaintance (or several) would seduce him (and sometimes his friend, too). And so, on video, he fucked his way through Baltimore, Philadelphia, New York, Montreal, and maybe Toronto. Or Providence? I don't remember. Anyway, it was a solid five-hour marathon that contained the same kind of hardcore, frill-free, pared-down boning I'd been watching on the Internet for years, but with slightly better production quality than I'd been accustomed to online.

I remember being confused—this was not what I'd thought I was signing up for. But then again, some of my ethical qualms were allayed. I knew where it came from, for instance—there were credits all over the place, a notice of where the legal records were being kept, and professional editing to indicate that somebody gave a damn about the product.

I knew that everyone in the film had been paid for their work, that the women involved had consented to do what they were doing and had signed papers to that effect.

And, for all my dismay over the bursting of my Internet porn bubble, *East Coast ASSault* didn't exactly disappoint me.

In fact, the scene filmed in New York was exceptionally arousing. It was a threesome shot in a hotel room, and the two women involved were extremely, vocally, voraciously enthusiastic. I don't just mean that they seemed to enjoy themselves; I mean that they *loved* it. They were smiling and laughing and squealing and clearly getting off, again and again. For sex-shamed little me, it was hugely erotic to see women so into the sex they were having, and I didn't feel bad about enjoying myself as I watched their pleasure. True, there was a lot of slapping and spitting that I didn't find erotic, per se, but it was made sexy by the sheer enjoyment of the participants. Their excitement obliterated my queasiness.

But, as I soldiered on through hours two, three, and four of the double-disc set, my qualms came roaring back. There was a scene filmed in Montreal in which the woman seemed uninterested at best, deeply intoxicated at worst. Whatever the case may have been, she did not look aroused or even really *there* for most of the forty-five-minute scene. I wanted to skip it, but I had to review the entire film, so I stuck it out, wincing the whole way through as I was blearily reminded of one of the worst moments of my own life—being sexually assaulted while I wasn't fully conscious. Her placid face and lethargic movements felt deeply wrong, and I wondered if the fact that she had signed the same papers and been paid the same as the other women in the film made her clearly uninspired performance, strictly speaking, okay.

In a way, the big questions I'd hoped to find buried in the artistic subtext of the film were here, writ large and less than artsy: Why had this model signed up to do the scene if she didn't really *want* to? Was she just there for the money? Did she hate what she was doing? Was she being exploited? Was the act of watching her exploitative in itself? Or was she exploiting my willingness to watch her, no matter what state she was in? How did this work?

I'd gone into this first review strong in my belief that the women I would be watching were as empowered as anybody else and that I would be supporting them in their choice of profession by viewing their work. But the Montreal scene made me question that resolve and the principles upon which it had been based. If their profession involved them having sex that upset me personally, would I stand by their decision to pursue it? And more than that, *should* I?

Now that the imaginary veil between "real" and "Internet" porn had been ripped down, I had to grapple with issues I'd been sweeping under the rug of my latent, lazy feminism. The gross Internet porn I'd been watching for years had largely flown under my radar. For the reasons I've already mentioned, I tried to avoid thinking about it, outside of a few post-orgasm moments of contemplation. My participation in this kind of ambiguity should have indicted me to my own conscience, but I told myself that I didn't know the truth of any of it, so I had no right to judge.

I had considered myself a feminist ever since the question arose sometime in high school, but I had never really examined what that meant to me. I attended a tiny rural public high school that offered neither AP classes nor any philosophy outside of what was necessary to get through literature courses, and then went on to college at a Catholic university that I liked because the buildings looked like castles, not because I was Catholic. (I wasn't.) Sex was just as taboo at my undergrad institution as it had always been for me, and though I thought often, long, and hard (hah!) about the topic, I had received zero formal education on the intersection of sex and feminism. I eagerly participated in the scant few feminist and sex-positive activities available to me there, from a few hotly protested productions of *The Vagina Monologues* to *The Rocky Horror Show*, but they didn't exactly round up to a strong background in feminist theory.

I knew nothing of the feminist porn activists of the eighties and nineties: Candida Royalle, Annie Sprinkle, Nina Hartley (all of whom I would go on to meet). But I was familiar with the anti-porn feminists who had started the feminist "sex wars" that raged through the late seventies and early eighties: Andrea Dworkin, Catharine McKinnon, and their ilk, for whom female empowerment could not possibly be tied up with sex work. Those rabid activists whose "men-are-pigs-and-women-are-victims" theories (as summed up by Nina Hartley in a 2011 interview) had gained enough traction internationally to have become the most recognizable face of modern feminism in the nineties. I knew of them, and I knew that I vehemently disagreed with them.

Even with my copious intake of borderline-scary gonzo smut on the Internet, I recognized that one couldn't reduce the vast landscape of pornography into the "evil" category. It felt small-minded and reductive to try to pigeonhole the thousands of people who made it, or the hundreds of thousands of films they'd made, into any one box. Surely not all pornography is wholly empowering to women, and some of it absolutely *can* feed into an attitude of misogyny and the larger patriarchy that mindset serves. But is all porn, then, by definition, bad for women? Certainly not. The logic doesn't follow well enough, in my mind, to even bother pursuing. And so, for the most part, I hadn't.

It is an interesting phenomenon that I've seen in other places, however. In conversations with anti-porn activists at industry conventions and protesting outside film festivals, with consumers in their homes, and even with some pornographers, I have heard all manner of generalizations made about "porn" as if it is one monolithic entity, usually with a single clear aim in mind—be it to destroy American morality, or to drive humanity to Onanistic damnation, or whatever other doom these crusaders have read in the tea leaves. It's never been clear to me how one industry could be so single-minded; in my experience, pornography is a massive and varied organism that some refuse to even call an "industry." Tim von Swine, a long-standing male performer and director, for instance, told me once, "I don't like saying 'industry' because porno's *not* an industry. When you have an industry, there are protocols and standards that you adhere to and regulate . . . There's not that regulation in porn. It's a bunch of free enterprises. A bunch of pirate ships."

Pornography in America is spread out, decentralized, and fiercely individualistic. Basically, even if there are slimy, evil, rape-y pornographers out there seeking to exert control over women in heinous ways—and don't get me wrong, there certainly are—they don't speak for all pornographers everywhere. For every one of the outright skeezy porn makers I've met, there is at least one beautiful human being who sees porn as a way to express the beauty of sex through art.

But when I started writing for porn magazines, I hadn't thought much about any of this. My solitary contemplations of sex-positive feminism had left me with a few basic stances: I believed that women should be afforded the same rights and opportunities as men, and that they should be free to make their own decisions about their lives and their bodies. Ostensibly, this led me to support the women who made porn or did any other form of work that involved them using their bodies at their discretion. Like legendary performer Nina Hartley told *Rolling Stone* in 2016, "If I have the right to choose birth control, to choose abortion, then I have the right to choose to fuck for a living." End of story.

Now I had to start thinking about who the people I supposedly supported actually were, who they'd been all along, and what we were all participating in.

For instance, I had never entered into contemplations of capitalism and feminism, but porn brought me around to them quickly. Like many others of my generation who had been familiar with the porn superstars of the nineties and early 2000s—Jenna Jameson, Asia Carrera, Ron Jeremy—I went into my new job in adult entertainment thinking that performers were making oodles of money from their work, which made their choices easy to understand. It wasn't until some time into reviewing that I realized that the good old days in which production companies contracted porn performers and then dumped money, time, and energy into their careers to produce "stars" were nearing an end. Most of the industry talent was comprised of independent contractors hired for one-off gigs, for which they were typically paid at the completion of a scene and then sent on their way. Porn stars did not (and still do not) earn royalties on their work. No matter how much money a scene makes for a producer, non-contracted performers earn a flat fee. (Performers who are under exclusive contract with one production company earn a salary that's usually more generous, but they don't pull in extra money on royalties.) In other words, porn was not the lucrative career that many of us had always thought.

For those entering the industry without a game plan or the means to take their careers by the horns, many would-be porn "stars" end up disillusioned by the relatively low profit margins versus the amount of hard physical labor the job requires, and summarily drop out of the race. Given that these short-lived, not-very-profitable stints come along with a side helping of Internet infamy and the scorn of millions who look down on sex workers, I began to wonder what motivated performers to do this kind of work. Especially when the current ambiance in the field was over-the-top pseudo-violence that looked painful at times and gross at others.

It's important to note that from a more enlightened (or possibly world-weary) vantage point, now I can recognize much of the gonzo frenzy of the mid-aughts as an unbridled take on freedom of sexual expression. For reasons that are unique to every individual, lots of people enjoy hardcore porn of this kind, as well as sex that looks like it. As French performer Katsuni put it to me a few years later, "There are many taboos in the USA, and this is also why porn is so extreme . . . Porn is a reflection of society. People are extreme because they are frustrated and need to express their compulsions. Porn has a real function of catharsis." Certainly, in the first decade of the twenty-first century, with the War on Terror at a fever pitch and the tensions running high in America, more of us may have felt a pull toward the porn equivalent of action movies, and I am loath to blame them for dealing with stress by watching or making smut instead of getting into fistfights.

Exhibitionism is not my personal kink, but it is a legitimate and common one that motivates many porn actors. I acknowledge and respect that. When I was twenty-four, what I couldn't respect, because I couldn't fathom it at the time, was why anyone would choose to do these things on camera. An actress allowing her mouth to be held open so that two men could ejaculate inside it, for instance: Obviously there's a certain shock value to an act like that, and in the gonzo-heavy climate of that period, it fit right in. But could I really be a feminist and not only watch this type of sexual behavior—but profit on it?

I had good reason to hesitate, but I also had good reason to jump right in—namely that I hadn't yet landed a job and my meager two months' worth of rent money was disappearing fast. I had no safety net to fall back on. I was interviewing for full-time jobs, but even if I landed one and started working immediately, I'd barely have my first paycheck in hand by the time my savings ran out. I needed some kind of cushion, and thus feminism met capitalism in the form pornography yet again.

So I decided to let the fates decide whether I had a future in the porn industry and got to work on my first review. If Charles and j. vegas decreed that I had what it took to review smut, then I would figure out how to make my feminism square with what I reviewed. I tried to work within the parameters of the magazine's existing review model: a wry tone, a bold dedication to alliteration and puns, and as much shameless double entendre as I could manage.

Reading over my *East Coast ASSault* review now, I can see that I had not exactly mastered the technique. But I sent it and some set copy describing photos from a previous magazine, along with my résumé, to Charles and vegas.

"Nice work. You're hired!" Charles wrote in an e-mail four days later. He offered me seventy-five dollars per review to start and asked me to come to the office soon to pick up a bunch of DVDs. And just like that, I was a part of the porn industry.

LET ME TELL YOU SOMETHING about making money as a writer in the twenty-first century. What with the fancy binding, colorful cover, and nice paper stock of the volume you're reading now, you might not realize that money for writers these days is, basically, not actually *a thing*. It does not exist. Of course there are a lucky few who survive as authors, big-name novelists and biographers and thinkers, and some celebrities who have a thriving side business in print. There are journalists who write and pitch and get bylines in *The New York Times* and its ilk, who eke out solid earnings for their reporterly merit. But for the vast majority of us who write, making a living on our words is a dream very much akin to the fantasy of a Little Leaguer who wants to play in the World Series. The best we are likely to achieve is an editorial position on the high school paper, then a few publications in our undergraduate lit mag, followed by an online publication or two for no pay. Some of us will keep it up and pitch our way into positions as staff writers for websites with real payrolls, but most will eventually succumb to a salaried desk job where we can copyedit the office's monthly newsletter.

To earn a real living as a writer is nigh unthinkable. And, while I knew that a few reviews a month at seventy-five dollars each wouldn't exactly pay for a loft in SoHo, that kind of scratch for a lousy five-hundred-word review of a movie I could fast-forward through was the stuff of my wildest writerly dreams. I could not, and did not, turn it down.

I went to the magazine's offices again, where I smiled a lot and was sent on my way with a FedEx shipping box packed to nearly bursting with porn. I had been promised payment for each review I completed, and I was now, officially, a Paid Writer. I walked across town to Penn Station, where my boyfriend, who we'll call Matthew, held down a job as a shipping coordinator at a big store in the area. I demanded he break for lunch so we could celebrate my new gig as the Coolest Person He Knew, and dragged him to the nearest sushi restaurant and ordered a bottle of sake with our meal.

After a few maki rolls and two bottles of sake had been ordered and dispatched, my cell phone rang. It was an employment agency back across town, to which I had apparently submitted a résumé for a position as an art gallery receptionist. My memory called up a fuzzy association with a Craigslist ad, so I agreed to drop by the agency later that afternoon. I was in flip-flops and a tank top, but the woman on the phone assured me that it would not be a problem.

I was gleeful. A box of porn, a job offer, and another interview, all in one day! But when I hung up, Matthew had one eyebrow raised.

"What?" I demanded. He kept quiet, and I took stock of my situation for the first time since I'd left the magazine office. I was toasted.

"You really *ready* for an interview right now?" Matthew asked.

"You shut your face. I already got one job today! I'm on a roll." I laughed, because I was holding a piece of eel and avocado roll. The irony!

He shook his head but didn't argue. I might be too shnookered for an interview, but that walk back across town in the heat would sober me right up. And hey, I already had one *very* cool job, so if I blew this interview it wouldn't hurt too much.

Matthew and I ran a few errands together—post office, key copying, and some shopping—before I started the cross-town trek again. Halfway to the interview, I decided to grab a cup of iced coffee to help me sober up. I stayed in Starbucks for a little while, nursing my coffee and waiting for my head to clear, before skipping over to the agency's building. It was one of those über-modern lobbies with a gigantic front desk guarding an elevator bank that seemed to be made entirely of glass and shiny metal surfaces. I signed in, got directions, and proceeded to open an alarmed door into an emergency stairwell. The coffee had, apparently, not sobered me up.

But, after passing my typing and computer skill tests with flying colors, I wowed my interviewer, tipsy or not. By the time I left, I had gained numerous phone numbers within the agency, promises of calls back, and certainty that I was both charming *and* employable, particularly when I'd been day-drinking.

I was strutting toward the subway, my head spinning with alcohol, coffee, and confidence, when I realized, suddenly, that my hands were empty. I was *supposed* to be holding a rather large box filled with pornography that was worth at least a hundred dollars, and which was my only promise of a paycheck in the near future.

I stopped dead. Had I left the FedEx box propped against Tanya's desk at the agency? And if I had, should I go back for it? Clearly not. But if I didn't, there went my job at the magazine. The only one I had actually *gotten* so far. Would it be worth it to destroy my newly sparkling reputation at the employment agency in order to keep my job at the jizz rag? After what I'd seen so far, did I even *want* to keep it?

I heard thunder rumbling as I turned back toward the agency, but then I distinctly recalled walking into Tanya's cubicle and sitting down, *empty-handed*. Relief washed over me, but then my panic resurged. If I hadn't brought it into the agency, then where was it? I attempted a mental rewind of my afternoon: Everything between the restaurant and leaving the agency was fuzzy, but now that I thought about it, I was pretty sure I hadn't had the box when I got to Starbucks, either. Or walking across town to get there.

I must have left it at the restaurant. How embarrassing. Well, it was the only sushi restaurant near Penn Station and Madison Square Garden; they'd probably seen a lot worse than an abandoned box of porn. I started walking across town once again. What a day.

By the time I got to Broadway, it was raining. I was slipping around in my flip-flops and little pieces of grit were digging into the undersides of my feet. As I waited for a light to change just north of Herald Square, I experienced a clear memory of getting up from my table at the restaurant and *picking up the box of porn*. I was certain that I'd walked out of the restaurant with it in my hand.

Thunder clapped overhead, and for the first time in hours I remembered that I'd also gone to the post office. The James Farley United States Federal Post Office, the giant stone historic landmark taking up two city blocks at 32nd Street and 8th Avenue.

Shit.

This was only six years after the 9/11 attacks, and paranoia was still running high. Police and soldiers dotted public places, particularly federal buildings, and unattended packages of any kind were often marked as terrorist threats.

As I attempted to run in my soggy flip-flops through crowds of businesspeople with their umbrellas raised, I blearily recalled approaching one of the automated postage machines and setting my box-o-perversion on top of the unit. I could vaguely remember a sign near the exit warning that unattended packages were subject to inspection by NYPD or federal forces. Shit, shit, shit.

My brain conjured images of the postage machine surrounded by police in riot gear, leaning back against the straining leashes of their leaping, slobbering canines. One of the men would step forward—after doing whatever they do to check boxes for bombs—and look inside, pulling out filthy DVD after filthy DVD, then smutty magazine after smutty magazine, before getting to the photocopies of tax paperwork I'd filled out at the office. In slow motion, he'd scan it, then address the crowd: "Is there a Lynsey of 147th Street here?" The crowd would part as everyone turned to me, standing pale, sodden, and finally sober near the door.

I stopped on 33rd Street, just north of the post office. I was right next to an entrance to the 8th Avenue subway line that would take me straight home. Maybe I'd get the gallery job and not need the porn gig, anyway. Maybe I should turn tail. Maybe *this* was the hand of fate, making its decision known.

But at last I knew: Deep down, I really wanted that porn gig. It was possibly the coolest thing I'd ever do.

I walked, very slowly, up the stairs to the post office, taking one of the less-used side entrances to be inconspicuous. There was no obvious police activity inside. No dogs. No flashing lights or tear gas.

There it was! I broke into a jog, right past an armed police officer who paid me no mind. There was a woman using the postage machine atop which my box of smut was perched. She saw me coming, and as I rushed up to the machine and grabbed my prize, she turned to stare.

I grinned, hugging it to my heart. "I can't believe it's still here!" I told her breathlessly.

"Congratulations," she said. Her smile was genuine, if bemused. I smiled back, and I would have skipped the whole way to the subway if my flip-flops weren't so wet.

A stack of porno DVDs I'd received for review as of early 2012

CHAPTER 4

The Early Days

A WEEK LATER, I LANDED the gallery job. So I took my place as the receptionist at an elite art gallery in midtown Manhattan that catered to the artistic tastes of millionaires. I manned the phones, greeted customers, provided informative materials on exhibits, and turned prospective buyers over to salespeople. And in down time between duties, I wrote porn reviews.

I elected to take a "nom de porn," as j. vegas called it, from one of my favorite cult films—an easy decision that I didn't spend much time on, which at that point more or less reflected my involvement with the porn industry as a whole. It didn't require much brainpower, aside from that pesky feminism issue, with which I continued to wrestle.

I tried to play it cool, though, for the sake of my poker face at the gallery and in order to keep making the money that came rolling in. I wrote about the films as if their contents came as no surprise. As if they served only to turn me on, or better yet, to make me laugh. The magazine's line was to take everything with many grains of salt, so I cracked jokes as much as I could, and endeavored to keep in the forefront of my mind the fact that every person involved in these situations was a consenting adult. It was a challenge for me, but it paid well enough to make it worthwhile.

My editor, j. vegas, on the other hand, seemed to have been born for his job. He had a half dozen pen names, and he got a sort of childlike glee out of coming up with colorful new terminology for sex acts and the people who practiced them. And he was *good* at it. If there were some kind of award system for excellence in witty porn journalism, I'm sure he'd have gone home with the trophy for "Most Inventive Use of 'Jerk-Off' in an Alliterative Sentence," and several others. He saw the porn industry as the pinnacle of humanity's capacity for dark, self-deprecating humor, and his role was to point out and capitalize on the ridiculousness of it all.

But even with his enthusiasm and the magazine's more general lais-sez-faire attitude toward most things pornographic, there were still rules in place to remind me that this business wasn't all fun and filthy games. For instance, we could not use the word "kid" or "child" anywhere for fear of setting off child-porn alarms. And I was prohibited from men-tioning female ejaculation, even if it happened in a movie I reviewed.

I was told that any mention of squirting was prohibited because in some places where the magazine was distributed, this could be considered urination, which could in turn be considered obscenity, and which could lead to any number of negative consequences for the magazine and the makers of the film in question. I assumed at the time that the places vaguely referred to in this prohibition must be some backwaters where women were not allowed to vote, but it later became clear that the back-water in question was, incredibly, the UK. The epicenter of the "civilized" world is, apparently, not enlightened enough to admit that women squirt-ing in ecstasy is not, in fact, the same as women peeing.

Female ejaculation, or "squirting" (considered two different phenom-ena in scientific circles but synonymous in porn) has been recognized as a pre-orgasmic or orgasmic occurrence for centuries the world over, basi-cally up until the Victorian period when preexisting notions of women having anything like sex drives or real arousal seems to have been squashed. In moments of great sexual excitement, fluid gushes forth from two small ducts to the sides of the urethra in many women and other peo-ple with vulvas. These ducts are attached to the Skene's gland—a very re-cently discovered gland that is thought to be linked to the G-spot on the anterior wall of the vagina—which becomes engorged during arousal. The fluid they expel is sometimes copious enough in volume to be mistaken for urination. (Note: The amount of liquid expelled is limited, however; many squirting videos in porn are faked—those streams shooting all the way across rooms are usually the result of douching during a cut in the action, then expelling the liquid during filming. If you look very closely, you can usually see that it's coming out of the vagina, not the urethra, which means it's not really squirting.) Though the liquid is usually clear, with very little odor or taste (hey, sometimes somebody's face is down there when it happens!), it's more similar to urine than any other bodily fluid, and until very recently, the scientific community refused to consider that it could be anything else. But thousands, nay millions, of people with firsthand experience attest that squirting is *not* peeing. Numbers are hard to come by, but most studies attest that somewhere between ten and forty percent of people with vulvas are able to squirt, with some folks I've spoken to in the porn industry claiming that the ability is universal.

Nevertheless, the scientific community has remained skeptical of the notion that anything that looks like pee could be anything else—actual female experiences be damned. And so, in the UK in particular, squirting was considered close enough to urination to rule it out from any and all film reviews I wrote. Oddly, it wasn't until 2014 that female ejaculation was officially banned in adult films in the UK, along with spanking that leaves visible marks, facesitting, and the use of restraints, to much protestation and rebellion from British pornographers. Nobody can put their finger on *why*, exactly, these and a number of other benign and extremely widespread acts were deemed obscene by the Brits, but even if they could, they'd have to be careful not to finger too hard, lest somebody squirt on camera.

But the biggest and hardest (teehee!) rule at the magazine was that if I didn't have anything positive to say about a film, I could choose not to review it, but I could *not* choose to give it a bad review. The relationship the magazine had established with certain production companies did not allow for less-than-glowing words about those companies' work. If I wanted to make my hundred bucks (my rate per review had increased after a few months), I had to come up with ways to gloss over the things I didn't like.

So I settled into a sort of benevolent numbness in my viewing habits, in order to facilitate benign reviews. After the initial excitement about the novelty of it all had faded, I spent a lot of time holding down the fast-forward button. I would press play every so often, of course, to take note of the soundtrack, dirty talk, and so on, but if I'd watched every film at normal speed I would have had very little time left over to spend all the money my reviews were earning me. And I would have been bored absolutely to tears. I'd often review five films in a month, each of which stretched on for four to six long hours of hardcore fucking. Who could *possibly* be interested enough to watch all of that? And who would pay the forty or fifty dollars that these jumbo packs of porn were retailing for? No matter how gleaming a review I wrote for *Anal Creampies #7*, I just couldn't imagine who was buying all this smut.

The answer came to me in a roundabout way through the business of working for a dirty magazine.

About a month into my reviewing career, the editorial director told me he could give my name to an editor at another magazine. One that *wasn't* about to go bankrupt.

Oh. *Nobody* was buying all that smut.

It began clicking into place that the industry that supported these magazines—the same one responsible for *Elastic Assholes*—wasn't just hyperventilating over the threat of Internet piracy. It was failing.

THE PORN INDUSTRY BASICALLY went through a turbulent adolescence in the seventies, blossomed into young adulthood in the eighties, and settled into a corpulent, self-satisfied routine in the nineties. It kept on top of new technology, but it got a bit round in the middle, secure in its status as the "recession-proof" industry. Production companies fattened themselves on easy profits and let their business models languish, unaware that they would be harshly yanked from their stupor early in the new millennium. When the Internet exploded onto the capitalist playing field, pornography was naturally the first to exploit its promise, but it was also one of the first to fall.

In the early days of the World Wide Web, as most industries were trying to figure out how to make this new technology work for them, pornography jumped into the fray feet-first, as it always had before. In their book about modern sexual desire, *A Billion Wicked Thoughts*, Dr. Ogi Ogas and Dr. Sai Gaddam state that there were fewer than ninety adult magazines published in America when the Web went online in 1991, but by 1997 there were nine hundred pornographic websites. The adult industry took to the new technology like fish to water, establishing new models for payment and distribution that everyone else followed. Streaming video, membership websites, credit card verification systems, encryption coding, and nearly every advancement in file sharing and video display were pioneered by porn, then taken up by the rest of the world.

Third-party payment processors like PayPal are particularly deep in debt to the porn industry; when opportunists realized the ease of making money on porn in the early days of the Internet, they jumped on the bandwagon and proceeded to make a mess of things by laundering money. There were affiliate click-through systems that collected money on falsely generated traffic, porn sites used as fronts for less-legal money-making strategies, and so on. Some sites would charge sky-high fees for website membership cancellations, which unsurprisingly took place quite frequently. Since no one had figured out yet that the name of a porn site showing up on someone's credit card statement might cause blowback for people whose significant others looked askance at smut, membership cancellations were routine. And so were chargebacks—people denying outright that they had made a purchase from a porn site in the first place and demanding their money back. Due to rampant chargeback rates and fraud, credit card companies started to turn down online porn business—to this day, American Express will not work with the industry at all. Unable to process payments at reasonable rates with the remaining credit card companies, porn companies were bereft until third-party payment processing companies came to their rescue, taking on the risk that their clients' businesses posed and charging through the nose for the privilege. In short, PayPal might not have come to be unless the adult industry had paved its way.

In an ironic twist, the industry that birthed online payment solutions is now a victim of online finance's scorn. Pornographers—and a variety of other businesspeople who deal in sex—are prohibited from using most major payment platforms online. Overall, the finance industry has, astoundingly, not yet gotten over the sting of the first few years of Internet craziness and is still convinced that porn, despite its almost ludicrous financial promise, must be lumped in with other "high-risk" companies—like loan consolidation and online gambling. Never mind that pornographers have gotten savvy to the idea that nobody wants their credit card statement to read "BigTitsXXX.com," or that as society adapts, chargeback rates have gone down for porn purchases. Never mind that, as Cindy Gallop, founder of the real-world-sex porn alternative site MakeLoveNotPorn.tv told me in 2014, "The bank that welcomes ventures like ours, designed to change the world through sex, will make a fucking shedload of money" when sex-oriented companies inevitably flock to it. Most banks still flat-out refuse to do business with porn companies, citing outdated morality clauses or the Puritanical interests of their investors.

Compounding the existing squeamishness of the finance industry regarding online porn money, in 2012 the Department of Justice launched Operation Choke Point, an initiative that encouraged banks to restrict service to businesses that pose a "reputational risk," like pornography, online gambling, and payday loans, according to *The Washington Post*. Operation Choke Point was behind a 2013 rash of porn stars' personal bank accounts being shut down and sex workers being refused service at financial institutions, for no given reason. The operation was exposed to public scorn, but to date there's no evidence that it has been shut down, and it certainly didn't encourage banks, or the credit card companies and payment processors that depend upon their largesse, to work with adult companies online.

In sum, porn may have gotten a heady start on the Internet, but its kerfuffle with online finance was an early indication of how quickly cyberspace could turn. Though porn initially made huge financial gains online, hackers and pirates were not far behind. Whereas the jizz biz, as j. vegas liked to call it, had learned to think quickly to keep up with the pace of innovation, it had never before had to deal with anything quite as fast as the Web and its legions of faceless thieves.

In the words of veteran performer Tim von Swine, "Technology has always been the midwife of destruction in porno." Porn used to make its bread and butter selling *things* that had smut *on* them, like DVDs and VHS tapes and magazines, but with the advent of the Internet, pornography became available as *information* that was easily reproducible, easily distributable, and, when hackers caught up with it, entirely free to whomever wanted it.

The porn industry, like others, reeled. Brad Armstrong—one of the most decorated directors in porn history—once told me that the Internet hurt porn from every angle. "People can even shoot movies on their two-hundred-dollar . . . phone and throw it up on the Internet," he said. "If any business had to deal with that kind of saturation and overflow, there's no way they'd be operating. Thankfully, everybody's horny. That's the only thing that keeps us going!" He was right; unlike many other industries, pornography didn't have powerful protectors to buoy it in its time of need. Nobody cared enough about porn to publicly stand up for it. Armstrong told me he sometimes found himself wondering, "If we stopped tomorrow, there's still so much of it out there, would anybody really care?"

It appeared, at times, that they wouldn't. And the industry stumbled. It got desperate. It started paying performers less, doing away with the bells and whistles as the ship began to sink. The sex scenes I was watching in the late 2000s were products of fear, anger, and desperation, acted out in the language of lust. The industry was thrashing out its own death throes, flailing and clutching at its throat, certain the end was nigh. And as ridiculous as it seems, given the direness of the situation, much of the industry was refusing to do much to help itself. Porn, having earned a reputation for paving the way forward with technology since the beginning of technology, was falling behind.

Case in point: As recently as 2012, I was reviewing DVDs instead of video files for magazine reviews, waiting for them to arrive in the mail instead of downloading them. Meanwhile, a video file with no cover or packaging could have been e-mailed in hardly a fraction of the time and at literally zero cost. It was incredible. The adult industry may have invented the Internet as we know it in many ways, but in plenty of others, it likes to cling to the past. Director Ivan summarized the situation for me in an interview in 2010: "Many companies didn't evolve with the times, and that's why they are dying off. The smart guys behind the Internet porn boom capitalized on it. Years back, DVD people smirked at Web guys, saying stuff like, 'Oh, it's just Internet—quicker scenes with lower rates because it's *just Internet* content.' Whoa, did they get a dick slap of reality a few years later."

In other words, the old world order of the porn industry, which had come into being by way of innovation and rule-breaking, had calcified itself into an immovable leviathan that was all too easy to topple. The industry was in decline not because of one great failing, but because it was too bloated and proud to acknowledge that thousands of seemingly insignificant ruffians were picking away at it, bit by bit. Stealing a scene, reproducing it, sending it off elsewhere, and removing profits brick by brick.

By the time the problem was recognized as a crisis, porn companies scrambled to counter the damage, but nobody knew how. There was no clear way forward, no new technology to save them or fresh business model waiting to take over. New video technologies like HD and 3D were adopted by high rollers, but for most in the industry, cheaper and quicker seemed the only way forward. Profits weren't just dwindling, they were evaporating. Porn mags and companies were crumbling left and right, and the magazine I was writing for appeared to be the next to go.

With the venerable, world-changing, and incredibly hot Cindy Gallop at the AVN Awards in Vegas, January 2011 (PHOTO COURTESY OF THE AUTHOR)

CHAPTER 5

The Backward Slide

IN EARLY OCTOBER OF 2007, I landed a gig at a second dirty magazine, for which I wrote the set copy for photographic spreads of ladies with large bosoms. You know, "This is Sally and she likes long walks on the beach, frozen daiquiris, and cradling big boners between her double F cups." That kind of thing. I concocted five hundred words about each woman in the magazine, often according to some theme: big-titted tramps of the UK, for instance. The money was almost as good as what I got for reviews, and I didn't have to fast-forward through hours of hardcore porn to get it. In fact, I rarely even saw the photos I was supposed to be writing about. I'd just make up a name and a story, let my imagination run, and allow the editors to pair my words with a model. Months later I'd get a copy of the magazine and stare in disbelief at "Maisey's" smiling face and boobies, unbelieving—"How could they think *that* was Maisey? Maisey would *never* wear that bra and panty set!"

Thus set up with a second gig, I was prepared to take the financial hit when the first magazine went bankrupt at the end of 2007. It had been a short run, but it had come through for me when I needed it. I wasn't, however, exactly heartbroken to give up reviewing titles like *Breast Meat* and *Teens Like It Big #4*. I'd already amassed an alarming repertoire of silly names for body parts, become aware of positions and activities I'd never have dreamed up on my own, and developed a knack for alliterating jokes about all of them. Words like "slut" and "cock-hungry holes" took up too much of my written vocabulary for my own comfort, but at the magazine I'd been writing for they fit right in.

The editorial director, Charles, assured me that if another publishing company bought out the magazine, I would be reviewing for him again as soon as possible. But j. vegas was made no such promises. He was given full unemployment benefits, however, and relegated to his apartment in Washington Heights not much worse for the wear. We'd developed a close friendship, partly aided by alcohol and marijuana, so he included me in his plans to write a satirical web series about working in the smut business—a lifelong dream, he told me, that had been realized more comically than he'd expected. As an aspiring filmmaker, he felt the experience had to be memorialized.

AS MONTHS PASSED, I surreptitiously praised the gigantic jugs that dominated Lizzy's life and got Pauline kicked out of boarding school for distracting the Sapphic nuns, all while assisting with the sales of extremely expensive contemporary art. And I slid right back into my Internet porn habit. It was surreal: I now knew the names of the actors and their oeuvres, their preferences, even their dirty-talk styles. I appreciated them, at least more than I had before, as human beings. And yet I gravitated back to the free, pirated clips of their material, fully aware that I was stealing from them and contributing to the industry-wide collapse that had cost me my first paid writing gig.

As Lux Alptraum, a porn critic and journalist, summed it up for me, "It can be really, really difficult to negotiate ethics when orgasms are concerned . . . Sometimes your orgasm is not concerned with whether somebody got paid for that day."

In a lot of ways, *I* was concerned about people getting paid, but like Lux said, my orgasms were not. I had a boyfriend who was ready to go at the drop of a hat. I had stacks of porn DVDs under the bed, which I could have watched anytime I wanted. Most of them were filmed in HD and featured behind-the-scenes footage, cum shot compilations, and lots of other goodies that the streaming video clips on free websites couldn't match. Yet I kept reverting to the same crappy websites I'd frequented for years. I was still more assured of getting my orgasms there than anywhere else, and something about the surreptitious scrolling I was doing met a deep-set need in me that I couldn't quite name.

I felt like an anomaly: aware of the harm my habit was doing, getting laid but nevertheless gravitating back to pirated porn, and being a woman, to boot. I'd heard the old platitude that women don't like porn because they are not visual—that porn is for men.* Women, the thinking popularized by

---

*I don't like to use such binary language in writing about sex and desire. Particularly when it comes to brains and genitals and their interactions, there is such a massive range of experiences, preferences, gender identities, body types, brain types, and so

Alfred Kinsey in the 1950s goes, are more complicated creatures than their male counterparts and require a more complex series of switches to be flipped in our brains before we can get aroused. The authors of *A Billion Wicked Thoughts* write, "The male brain is designed to be more visually responsive to sexual stimuli than the female brain," which they dub "the most sophisticated neural structure on earth." And they back these claims up with investigative journalism, citing study after study claiming that, whereas men get a rise from looking at a pair of boobs, women don't find much eroticism in those boobs unless they also know whom they belong to, why they're being displayed, who else can see them, and whether the set dresser knows that that lamp on the bedside table isn't plugged in.

The desire for context, this conventional wisdom tells us, is the reason that women gravitate toward romance novels and erotica, written works that provide them with all the background information they crave, while men enjoy the direct visual stimulation that porn provides. I can't deny the allure of a good romance paperback—when I was in middle school, my friends and I passed one novel around, rereading it until the spine broke and the book split in half. And we were part of a much larger trend: According to *A Billion Wicked Thoughts*, the romance novel industry pulled in $1.37 *billion* in 2008, and ninety percent of its readers were women. Since the advent of *Fifty Shades of Grey*, erotica readership has skyrocketed, making the so-called "porn for women" genre an even bigger seller.

But I still liked "porn for men" just as much, and probably more. And it wasn't just me. Women are far from immune to the visual cues that erotic films provide. In a 2004 study conducted by Meredith Chivers of Queens University in Canada, women were hooked up to a plethysmograph—a device that tests the blood flow to the vaginal walls—and shown photos of a wide range of erotic and non-erotic photos. Afterward, they were asked about how aroused they had felt, and their answers were compared to the plethysmograph's findings. The results were stunning: Physically,

---

on that it feels disingenuous to me to pretend as if "male" and "female" are the only two categories upon which to draw. Unfortunately, the vast majority of scientific inquiry into these matters so far has broken subjects of study down in these binary terms, focusing on the experiences of cisgender (people whose gender identity doesn't conflict with the genitals they were born with) people with fairly typical sexual function. I hope that changes soon, because there is so much to be learned from the rest of the wide world of human sexuality!

the women were aroused by literally *all* of the erotic images, regardless of their sexual orientation . . . or even their species (some photos showed apes going at it). But psychologically? Not so much. Most women only reported *feeling* turned on by the type of smut that tickled their particular fancies—heterosexual women said they responded most to heterosexual sex, and so on. *None* reported feeling any psychological response to the ape sex. But the proof was in the pussy, as they say. These women's bodies did react to pornographic images of literally all kinds, whether their conscious minds picked up on it or not. It's not much of a stretch to say, based on this research, that women are just as aroused by porn as anybody else—they may just not be aware, or willing to own up to it.

And there I was, with the bedroom door locked and my laptop fired up, to prove it. I didn't seem to much care for context; I was turned on by just about any pairing of human genitals, whether it was straight, gay, or something else entirely, even if the images were supposedly made for men by men. I wanted hot, visual stimuli that would turn me on easily, without complications. There was something about being able to get off without noticing the credits, the lighting, the music, the company logo, that I appreciated. It was all painlessly simple. As director Ivan told me, "I think one of the reasons the Internet is so popular is you can find what you want, watch it, stroke it, and off you go."

He was onto something. Particularly for women, the Internet has become a haven for the exploration of taboo fantasies. As the authors of *A Billion Wicked Thoughts* put it, "Women who previously felt too mortified to be seen in the back room of the local video rental store are finally empowered to explore their erotic interests in privacy and comfort" in the Internet age. The freedom of online porn viewing isn't just exciting, it's foundational: After years of experience talking to people about pornography, I know I'm not alone in my proclivity for easy orgasms—especially when it comes to people my age and younger—regardless of gender identity. There is something incredibly seductive about the quick and almost mechanical payoff of the disembodied clip or animated GIF showing just the best few moments of a porn scene. It is delightfully, and damningly, easy for even my (female) body to get aroused by the simple mechanics of sex without involving the difficult moral baggage of real human beings, their stories, or their motivations. Prevailing wisdom about women's preference for context be damned: Online pornography's devastatingly simple format and nonexistent price tag prove alluring enough to bring millions of women to the Internet seeking quick and easy orgasms.

With every passing year, women are viewing porn in greater numbers and getting more vocal about their habits. In the last quarter of 2015, *Marie Claire* reported that a whopping thirty percent of women they'd surveyed declared that they viewed porn at least once a week. And Pornhub reported in its 2016 year-end review that just over a quarter of its viewers, worldwide, were women. As discourse around the subject of pornography opens up, some of the stigma once attached to watching blue movies has been lifted, and more of us are poking our heads out of our shame dungeons to talk about our habits. More than that—whereas porn used to be a veritable desert for women who wanted an alternative to the standard made-by-men-for-men fare, the past decade has seen a huge spike in porn made for women, by women, as well as porn made for queer and nonbinary folks, with viewers in mind who aren't necessarily straight, white men. These companies clearly give female viewers—and viewers of any other gender identity—a case of the ol' warm fuzzies, as well as the wet and slipperies.

It's not only out of self-interest that I implore you to believe that people aren't depraved sex maniacs if they tend toward a simplified version of pornography, but I do find some relief in asserting I *am* normal. Free, fast, and easy can also be called "efficient," and I'm a sucker for practicality. Yet, as 2008 began, I worried about the effects of masturbatory efficiency on myself, and on the rest of us. Was I—were *we*—sacrificing the experience of fantasy for the simple mechanics of sex?

It's certainly no revelation that easy is, well, *easier* than intimate. But it's less obvious that our penchant for what's easy over what's meaningful could be reflected in our porn viewing habits, or that those habits might extend into our personal sex lives. And it's certainly far beyond my singular ability to prove that this might be the case. But a staggering amount of anecdotal evidence amassed by myself and others points to a developing trend in which young people who have been watching hardcore pornography from an early age take that hardcore pornography to heart.

There's nothing wrong, per se, with trying out a move you learned from porn in the bedroom. But when the totality of one's sexual experience is downloaded directly from porn, there may be reason to pause.

"Porn operates as default sex ed," sex-tech disruptor Cindy Gallop told me in an interview several years after I began writing about porn, "in the complete absence of a counterpoint of an open, healthy discussion of parents feeling able to teach their kids about sex as opposed to feeling utterly embarrassed about it, in the absence of schools and colleges operating an open, honest sex ed curriculum."

The scarcity of reliable sex education available to young people in America makes online pornography an easy substitute; as of the time I'm writing this, only twenty-three states mandate sex education at all, and only thirteen require it to be medically accurate. Most sex ed in this country focuses on the male external anatomy and discusses erections and ejaculation, but girls are taught about menstruation and pregnancy risks instead of their anatomies or orgasmic potential.

School isn't educating the youth about sex, and it seems that neither are parents. *The Pornography Industry* author Shira Tarrant writes, "Between 1998 and 2005, there was a tenfold increase in the number of porn videos produced (13,000 vs. 1,300). Yet a survey of teenagers conducted by *Psychology* magazine found that during this same time period, seventy-five percent of parents never talked with their children about pornography."

There is a vacuum being created, and it's not difficult to see why many young people turn to the mountains of smut on the Internet to find out about sex. For instance, if I'd had access to videos on my parents' home computer when I was in middle school, my crippling anxiety about the mechanics of the pelvic thrust would have been put to rest, likely along with any other questions I had about what the human body is capable of in the bedroom. And these days, there aren't many ways to get information as trustworthy as what we can see people doing on Pornhub. As Mike Stabile, a spokesperson for Kink.com and the director of communications for the Free Speech Coalition, said in an interview with Mark Hay, "Sexuality has always operated in tandem with pornography. Pornography tends to crystallize desires that you might not have articulated." And for those whose desires haven't even fully formed yet, it can be a system of guidance that easily jumps off the rails.

Even porn stars I've spoken to learned about sex from the industry they would one day enter, and the lessons they learned were often of a particular nature. At AVN in 2010, performer Andy San Dimas told me,

"I started watching porn in high school because I wanted to suck dick better. So I studied how to give a really nasty blowjob, like really intense and gross."

There's no reason that a nasty, intense, and gross blowjob is any better or worse than a polite, discreet blowjob, of course. And I don't mean to cast aspersions on anyone who genuinely prefers athletic sex over candles, R&B, and rose petals. Or anyone who enjoys athletic sex *along with* said romantic accompaniment. It's of dire importance, I believe, that nobody with an interest in or relationship with the adult industry (which is to say, *everyone*) judges the sex lives or fantasies of others, whether onscreen or off. We're all in this mess together, and nobody's preferences are better than anybody else's. Fantasies are personal, private, and innocuous—unless they are acted out on an unwilling partner. But when fantasies are derived from pornography, a few things can get lost in translation—things that can cause problems.

As many porn actors have told me, and as many sex-positive thinkers have echoed, fantasy is *not* the same as reality, and porn is only a fantasy acted out for the gratification of the masses. Porn sex is not *real* sex, though there's real danger in conflating the two. As now-retired performer Kelly Shibari told me in a 2012 interview, "It's *sex* because there's actually penetration, and a guy ejaculates at the end. Besides that, it is *so* not sex. Sex, to me, in real life involves a lot of tenderness that you really don't see a lot of in porn . . . a lot of close tenderness that you can't get a camera inside."

The camera's presence on a porn set doesn't just change the level of intimacy between partners, it physically alters the way that sex is choreographed. On most sets, performers must "open up" to the camera with plenty of room for light and a camera lens in between bodies. This results in sex that not only looks very different from what many of us find physically pleasurable, but also sex that is difficult to perform. Porn actors are professionals in their field and are often capable of feats of strength and endurance that the rest of us could never match. These superhuman acts are performed in controlled environments under the watchful eyes of directors and camera crews who are ready to call "Cut!" at a moment's notice if things go wrong. And things *do* go wrong—ask any porn model about mishaps on set, and you'll get an earful. (I once wrote a whole article about what happens when performers fart on camera, and what didn't make it into the finished product were the tales of, shall we say, *more* than farts that almost everyone I interviewed told me about.)

But we don't see these faux pas in the edited cuts that make their way onto the Internet, or the mountains of preparation that performers go through to avoid those slip-ups. Feminist pornographer and performance artist Madison Young said something once that really stuck with me: "You're not going to see, necessarily, the enema in the bathroom, or the *five* enemas that you did in the bathroom before being anally fisted." (The mental image is striking, no?)

Nor do viewers witness the cuts between positions, the reapplication of lube, or the ten minutes it often takes between the sometimes very long cut and the male performer reaching orgasm. Danny Wylde told me once that, "In most porn you see a facial. I think it's just a matter of convenience, almost. It's like, we get her to that point, then we cut, now the guy gets ready to ejaculate, however he does that, then he comes over and does his thing . . . I don't think most consumers have any idea how bizarre that whole process is."

What I'm trying to say is that we, as consumers, are not privy to the realities of the fantasy sex we may be trying to reenact at home. What we see is a heavily edited, hand-picked series of video pieces that leads us to believe that this superhuman sex is easy, natural, and satisfying. And we can take that message to heart.

Compounding the blurry line between porn fantasy and honest-to-goodness reality is the fact that, while Hollywood can revert to stunt people, smoke, mirrors, and CGI for action sequences, pornography uses flesh-and-blood *Homo sapiens* honest-to-god banging. (Or blowbanging, or gangbanging, as the case may be.) In porn, it's not *really* real sex happening naturally for its own sake, but it *is* showing really real human beings engaged in real sex acts. Retired performer Oriana Small told me in an interview that on her hardcore sets, "I cried a bunch of times. There was a time when I would cry in every scene, because I would get so overwhelmed and it was so emotional. It was so *real*."

This realness complicates the impulse to give porn a pass for its status as fantasy. Particularly when the fantasy in question is hardcore gonzo porn that depicts gagging, asphyxiation, slapping, spitting, and the like as standard, sans disclaimer that, while many people may engage in these activities for their own pleasure, they are not everyone's cup of tea and are best attempted by those with a lot of experience.

As the months went by without a noticeable change in my online habits, I caught myself thinking more about the people in the clips I was watching. I'd been able to pull the wool over my own eyes before, my ignorance of the industry giving me a lame but still convincing excuse to divest myself of responsibility. But my months of reviewing had given me a peek into where all this fantasy material I was bootlegging came from, and I couldn't quash my conscience so easily anymore.

But I was in a unique position from which this train of thought was almost unavoidable. For the tens of millions who visit Pornhub every day, it's very easy to avoid thinking about the people who make pornography or the differences between real-world sex and porn sex. There's been a lot of talk in recent years about the "mainstreaming" of porn, but I believe that the actual effect of porn on most lives is nearly as silent a topic as it's ever been. Be honest. When's the last time that you had a *real* conversation with a friend about the porn you watch? Maybe you've talked from time to time about your thoughts on pornography as a medium, or about a porn star whose name was in the news (usually accompanied by some illegal activity, A-list celebrity whose name is being dragged through the mud, or another negative spin). But can you remember a time you talked to anyone about your personal preferences or how your consumption of pornography has affected your sex life? When's the last time you leveled with someone about your *feelings* on adult entertainment? The real shit. The juicy stuff.

If you're like most of us, your answer was probably "never."

Which is all a way to explain why, when the first magazine was purchased by a new parent company and reopened, I was happy to accept my reviewing job back in May of 2008. I'd spent a lot of time and energy grappling with the ways in which I didn't like my relationship with online, pirated pornography. I had a lot of questions I still wanted to ask. They were messy, and many of them implicated me for my past, as well as the not-entirely-healthy way I'd been processing my personal trauma by watching emotionless, context-less clips for the sake of purely physical gratification. But it was starting to seem that facing those questions head-on might be better for my peace of mind than continuing to look for answers in a vacuum.

Holding a printout of an early WHACK! Magazine *prototype, probably in 2009*

CHAPTER 6

WHACK! Magazine

FOR THE NEXT YEAR, I kept myself busy with my day job while I came up with increasingly creative descriptions for copulation and delivered glowing praise of oversized breasts I'd never laid eyes on. I had also begun research to ghostwrite a book about swingers in New York City for a couple in that lifestyle, so I was attending swing parties to observe their carousing on weekends. In short, I was drenched in sex twenty-four-seven, even while watching blue bloods peruse sculptures worth more than my apartment. Whether watching it on video or in person, imagining it for set copy, or remembering what I'd seen that weekend at a party, sex was my main occupation for most of 2008 and into 2009.

After the requisite New York City bedbug infestation hit our cramped Harlem apartment, Matthew and I moved into a small flat in the south Bronx. My former editor, j. vegas, was surviving on unemployment in Washington Heights and sending me regular updates on his web series. As expected, he hadn't been offered his old job back when the magazine started up again; I felt slimy for earning extra money when vegas didn't have that option, but he seemed content to write in peace in his uptown digs.

The idea behind the script, which he was calling *pornocracy* (which is, incidentally, now the title of a documentary by erotic filmmaker Ovidie, about the porn conglomerate MindGeek's effects on the world), followed the exploits of a smarmy, happy-go-lucky writer with a penchant for sleaze and satire, along with his best friend—a more earnest young woman who played the straight man. (Any of this sounding familiar?) They both worked at *WHACK! Magazine*, an odd-world version of the publication we'd written for. It was all fairly straightforward satire, with a manageably sized cast and what felt like a not-too-ambitious series of shooting locations. He asked for my help with casting and filming, and I, having no experience with that kind of thing, agreed.

It became quickly apparent that we did not have the resources to make the series happen. Between the two of us, we had about zero dollars to feed into it and few options to find any more. He enlisted the help of a friend to oversee casting and crew on the condition that she would play the role of the best friend. We cobbled together the rest of the cast and crew on the promise of "exposure" but without pay. But costuming, props, sets, lights, editing, post-production . . . all of these were beyond the reach of our bootstrap budget. And remember, this was before Kickstarter campaigns were de rigueur in the making of indie films.

Over discounted Bloody Marys at a bar near vegas's apartment where we held semi-regular "meetings," Matthew, vegas, and I tried to brainstorm funding options in the early summer of 2009. After a few hours, we'd come up with more empty glasses than ideas, but slowly, a concept took shape in my mind: Why not raise awareness about the web series by creating an online version of the magazine that the characters worked for? Make it *feel* real until it *is* real. We could write in an overblown parody fashion, using *pornocracy*'s characters' names as pseudonyms. Do fake interviews with the imaginary porn stars in the make-believe films they watched. If we played our cards right, we could leverage the site into some notoriety for the web series and eventually turn the project into money.

After another round of Bloody Marys, we set about purchasing www.whackmagazine.com and setting up a free Blogspot platform. (It was 2009; don't judge!) We took on the names of the show's characters and invented a few other pseudonyms to flesh out the magazine's "staff." I invented the moniker "Miss Lagsalot" off the cuff: My initials spell "LAG," and "Sir Lagsalot" jumped to mind. "Sir" seemed a bit confusing, though, given the fact that I was born female and present that way, so I tacked the "Miss" on instead, and off I went into the land of satirical porn journalism. Little did I know how much that "Miss Lagsalot" designation would come to mean, or how tenaciously it would cling to me.

We settled early on j. vegas applying his skill at Photoshop to original porno-litical cartoons, a monthly horoscopes column tailored specifically toward porn stars and fans, and op-eds on all things porn and sex. These carried us for a while, and I was thrilled to be writing op-ed pieces. I had free range to tackle issues I thought were important, champion causes, and eviscerate problems I saw in porn. My feminist colors began to show in a rosy rainbow hue; one month out of the gate, I'd already written impassioned articles on the female ejaculation controversy, the necessity of accessible healthcare for porn actors, and the importance of legalizing more forms of sex work.

Despite my enthusiasm for anonymity, however, it soon became clear that these real-world segments made no sense next to profiles of fictional porn stars and films. In the current piracy-happy online climate, in which most people weren't thinking about porn stars' careers, the difference between a real porn model and a fictional one might sail right over our readers' heads. And how exactly did we intend to find still shots from imaginary pornos to run with our reviews, anyway? Besides, j. vegas pointed out, he had a lot of contacts in the real porn world. We may as well get some *real* films to review, and see if we couldn't rustle up a few interviews with real, live porn stars. If we leveraged their fan bases, we'd have a much larger audience to beg for funding for *pornocracy* when the time was right. The real world of smut, he argued, was crazy enough to meet our weirdest needs. Why invent anything?

I was skeptical about our chances of convincing real pornographers to work with us. The idea felt far more "legit" than our little blog could ever be. But we wrote a few e-mails to a few porn companies and PR outfits, and soon enough I was receiving screeners of DVDs, addressed to "Miss Lagsalot," at my home address.

This was my first exposure to the fact that the porn industry does not set a particularly high bar for entry. This might sound self-evident, but having grown up on a farm in the countryside, *any* real industry had always felt unattainable to me. But one important quality that has long allowed the porn industry to maintain its "recession-proof" status is its openness to newcomers. It makes sense: In a business in which technological advancement is a constant and fresh faces are lifeblood, a lax attitude toward who gets to participate is vital. Retention of high-level performers is all well and good, but a high turnover rate that keeps the carousel of novelty spinning is just as useful, if not more so.

This applies to journalists, but it is far easier to see in performers. The human sexual brain is highly motivated by novelty, as our collective obsession with porn and the longstanding prevalence of extramarital affairs in monogamous cultures will attest. Whether we like to admit it or not, we are suckers for variety in our sex lives, and pornographers have learned to capitalize on our insatiable appetites for new faces by providing them—along with other body parts.

The phenomenon of "the new girl" is a well-worn trope familiar to anyone with a passing familiarity with the porn industry. When a new female performer appears on the straight porn scene, she (or, in the gay industry, he, and in the queer industry, any number of pronouns) is likely to find work *very* easily. Depending upon her appearance, demeanor, and the set of skills she's willing to put to use on camera, there will almost certainly be a filmmaker looking for just her type. There is no proficiency test, no background check, and very few hoops to jump through, aside from an industry-approved STI test, proof of age and identity, and a smile. It's relatively rare for a new actor to have spent a lot of time researching or preparing to enter the business, though in a recent interview, Nina Hartley told me that this has been changing after the Great Recession: "More women come to porn with real-world experience [or] college degrees, so the level of professionalism has risen," she said. Still, many of my acquaintances in the biz decided to try it on a whim, or just to make some quick money, then decided they liked it and stayed.

April Flores, a performer whose presence has played a large part in the rapid evolution and popularity of plus-size porn, told me that for her first scene, "I wore a wig to hide my identity because I really thought that it was just this one-time thing, having sex on film. I did it because I was curious." But she loved the experience and, over a decade later, she's still performing.

Many who have spent a significant amount of time in the industry advocate for a more formal set of requirements for newcomers—mentorship, a how-the-industry-works curriculum, and so on. And the Adult Performers Advocacy Committee (APAC) in Los Angeles is now providing these things for its members. But the truth is that pornography is so spread out, so decentralized, and so relatively open to outsiders that it's impossible to regulate who gets involved and what level of education they receive about the industry. Particularly now that almost anyone with a cell phone could, technically, make a porno, it's impossible to require everyone to fill out standardized forms or complete a certification course. And many pornographers wouldn't have it any other way—new faces are money. As such, there's not a lot of time or interest in showing someone the ropes before they take the plunge, and their naivety can serve the industry well, as their series of on-camera "firsts" brings in viewers whose appetite for novelty translates into cash.

I may not have been interested in putting myself in front of the camera, but as an open-minded young woman looking to dip a toe in the shallow end, I was welcomed with open arms in the hopes that I could contribute, even as a journalist, to the industry as a whole.

It was only a few months after starting *WHACK!* that I lined up my first-ever porn star interview with Mr. Marcus, a performer whose name and image were attached to a clothing line and a few sex toys— one of which was, incidentally, the go-to vibrator I kept in my drawer. When I'd purchased it, I hadn't known who Mr. Marcus was, but by the time I scheduled a phone call with him in September 2009, I had reviewed plenty of his scenes, become intimately familiar with the toy he'd branded, and would have been able to identify him by his penis alone. Yet the idea of *calling* him petrified me. I had no idea what I was doing.

But, just like the industry at large, he was fine with giving me a chance. When I called the number he'd sent me, I told him that I'd never done this before. Clearly accustomed to hearing these words from young women, he laughed and set me at ease with a mellifluous cadence that soothed me into a fantastic conversation that lasted for almost an hour. He was kind, gracious, and intelligent. He didn't think my questions were silly, instead treating my naivety as an opportunity to educate me and my readers. "We can affect a lot of people," he told me of porn stars. "And you know, there's something to that, there's a power to that. To sexually inspire people . . . across the planet."

And suddenly, I was a real jizz journalist. I transcribed my interview with Mr. Marcus, breathlessly attached several photographs of his warm, handsome face—and plenty of the rest of his well-muscled body—and published my first porn interview. And then *WHACK! Magazine* was on the porn industry's map in a real way.

• • •

ONE THING I DIDN'T REALLY understand at the time is that the porn industry can use all the *good* publicity it can get. For decades it's been the scourge of American entertainment; porn is routinely blamed for an astonishingly wide variety of social ills. If you can think of a "bad" thing that exists in the world, especially if it's tied to a vice that Americans don't like admitting to, there's a good chance that pornographers have at some point been implicated in it. As professor Mireille Miller-Young put it in her foreword to *Coming Out Like a Porn Star*, "Porn is perceived as the cause of our modern cultural decline, the trafficker of thousands of innocent women and girls, and the purveyor of rampant and misogynist prurience that is infecting the minds of our youth."

The mainstream media is most concerned with porn when it can be paired with other inflammatory words in headlines—violence of any kind, drugs, and pretty much anything involving children. (Although "child porn" and the actual porn industry have literally *zero* mutual ties, the word "porn" is used when describing both legal adult entertainment and a horrific crime perpetrated against the most vulnerable people in our society. It's awful that the legal porn industry is so readily lumped in with such horrendous crime, given that pornographers follow very strict rules on age verification to a T or face dire consequences.)

In a *WHACK!* interview in 2010, actress Kristina Rose noted, "Anytime the adult industry is mentioned in mainstream media it's always some awful story. No one ever talks about when a girl or company does major charity work. America only wants to hear horror stories." And she was right. If a former porn star robs a convenience store and shoots someone in the process, it's likely the national news will be all over the story, and you can bet the word "porn star" will be included, even if the person has been out of the industry for years. Meanwhile, if a former bank teller does the same thing, a local paper might deign it worthy of a police blotter mention.

So when we started *WHACK! Magazine* as an independent entity, with no money on the table, no ties to anyone in particular, no distribution deals in the works, and no *reason* to share porn news with the world except for the hope of one day funding our web series, the porn industry was happy to oblige. We weren't lauded as heroes by any stretch, but we were certainly welcomed.

The same can be said for most aspects of the porn industry, both to its credit and its detriment. For all the flak it takes for giving porn consumers a distorted view of what human bodies and sex look like, the porn industry itself might be one of the most welcoming in the world. While it's true that many in the porn industry have augmented their appearances with surgery and Botox, it's increasingly true that there is room for all manner of natural beauty, too. Although many of us picture a bleached-blond, spray-tanned, long-legged, double-D Amazon when we're asked to envision a porn star, this is an outdated stereotype. In fact, a 2013 study of ten thousand female porn stars in America found that the "average" porn star was a five-foot-five brunette with B cups, with the stage name Nikki Lee. Not so "exotic," when it comes down to it.

And despite its reputation for sexism, racism, and homophobia— much of which isn't misplaced—there's still, arguably, more diversity in porn than in most entertainment. The work force comes from nearly every imaginable background, race, socioeconomic status, level of education, and personal credo. People of multiple sizes, shapes, and levels of physical ability can find companies with an interest in shooting them, and those who work behind the camera rarely object to diversity on set. No high school diploma? Generally not a drawback. Have tiny breasts, a giant butt, and a PhD? Fabulous! Come one, come all. Just come.

A lot of people I've talked to believe that those who go into pornography do so for a reason. They've failed at everything they've ever done, for instance, or were abused as children, or are trying to get revenge on parents or exes. A friend I interviewed in 2012 about her thoughts on porn asked, "Why would that woman put herself in that position? Something happened along the way that made that woman decide to do that. Something happened. Someone wasn't good to her at some point." We've all heard this line of thinking: People who make porn for a living are *damaged*.

The story goes that nobody in their right mind could decide to fuck on camera (or film people fucking, or edit the footage, or whatever). If you look at the comments section of nearly any online article about porn (and wade through the glut of abusive language that I guarantee lives there), I bet you'll find at least one comment claiming that female porn stars were sexually abused as children, that these people don't respect themselves, that they need to be "rescued," that they are all addicted to drugs. These are the tired battle cries of sex-negative second-wave feminism and also—tellingly—of paternalism, seeking to paint women in porn as hapless victims of the patriarchy, refusing to consider that they could have decided to go into the business for their own perfectly valid reasons, much less find satisfaction in their work.

And I can tell you that it is a big load of hooey. A big, steaming pile of crap.

While it's certainly true that some people in adult entertainment do drugs, I wouldn't say that there are more of them per square mile than in other populations. While a 2012 study by James D. Griffith of Shippensburg University showed that porn performers tend to have tried more *types* of recreational drugs than people in the rest of the population, their rates of use and addiction were not statistically higher.

Furthermore, although it is true that some porn stars are in fact "damaged"—as are many, many of us in the rest of the population—it's just as true that many of them are not. There will always be people who gravitate toward the relatively "easy" money and the notoriety of porn due to some mental or emotional instability. But if you'll take a moment to reflect on the people you work with now, and your friends in other industries, I'd wager that you'll come upon more than a few who would qualify as damaged or unstable who would never dream of making smut. Pornography may put some of these traits on display more visibly than other lines of work would, but porn stars are frequently asked about their pasts and their emotional states in a much more direct way than, say, accountants. Yet that isn't any reason to think that there *aren't* thousands of CPAs with histories of abuse, bullying, and other horrors. We just don't hear about them because their industry isn't constantly under fire for what the outside world calls immorality.

I agree with director and performer Nica Noelle, who told me, "There are men and women from all walks of life performing in adult films by choice; not out of 'desperation' or because they lack the skill set to do anything else. The notion that every performer is a drug addict, a sex addict, a victim, or just a confused and exploited person, is patently false."

What baffles me further about the allegations that porn is a home for tragic pasts is that this line of thinking is usually deployed to delegitimize the choices that porn stars make. If so-and-so was molested as a child, the logic goes, then her decision to do porn is somehow made invalid. Through some mystical set of circumstances, her history has made her incapable of using her brain. But I just don't understand how a shitty past makes one less capable of being human. Let's be honest: *Lots* of people have shitty pasts. If someone had a horribly abusive father, then left home to work as a waiter in another town, do we assume they're making bad decisions because of their past? Nope. Same goes for most career choices. So why is that that people who do sex work for a living are "broken" while anybody else with a similar history is not?

Kristina Rose gave a magnanimous reading of the situation in our interview: "I think generalizing a group of people as damaged just because we have sex on camera is just dumb," she told me, but then continued, "I think people are afraid of things they can't understand and labeling us as damaged makes it easier for the person labeling us to understand how we can do what we do." I suppose she's right, that it's a way of understanding people whose choices baffle us, but the infantilization inherent in the concept bothers me to no end.

There are, absolutely, plenty of examples of people who have made the opposite statement, telling stories of horrible working conditions, coercion, drugs, and worse on set. There's no need for me to pretend mishaps and bad situations don't happen in the adult entertainment industry. But after years of interviewing porn stars about their experiences, I have to tell you that the horror stories aren't more prevalent than the tales of success and satisfaction. And scientific inquiry says I'm right about that. The aforementioned Shippensburg University study set out to test the "damaged goods hypothesis, [which] posits that female performers in the adult entertainment industry have higher rates of childhood sexual abuse, psychological problems, and drug use compared to the typical woman." Researchers compared a group of 177 American female porn actresses with the same number of "civilians" (as those in porn refer to the rest of the world) matched in age, ethnicity, and marital status. The study found *no* differences between the two groups in the prevalence of childhood sexual abuse or mental health disorders. It *did* find that porn actresses had significantly higher self-esteem, better body image, more social support, and a higher level of spirituality than the control group. The study's abstract concludes with a simple statement: "These findings did not provide support for the damaged goods hypothesis."

Arguments have been made that the sample was too small for these findings to be significant, and that the self-reporting aspect of the study may have skewed the results. But I'm skeptical of skeptics, especially with regards to both groups of women having the same rates of childhood sexual abuse. Although statistics in this arena are slippery because sexual abuse is so rarely reported, according to the National Sex Offender Public Website, one in four girls and one in six boys are sexually abused before the age of eighteen. Given that a full twenty-five percent of American women aren't currently working in the sex industry, I think it's safe to assume that most industries are home to many victims of abuse, and porn is just one of them.

The point being that there are plenty of people in the porn industry, and around it (like myself) that simply enjoy it. Their reasons for being involved with sex on video run the gamut: I've spoken with pornographers who considered and researched porn from afar before diving in (jessica drake), went into nude modeling after injury left them unable to do other work (Cadence St. John), made the transition from fetish modeling (Nikki Darling) or mainstream modeling (Nina Mercedez), started an art gallery with profits from porn (Madison Young), started porn as a form of activism (Sophia St. James), and dozens more. There is no one-size-fits-all "reason" why people do porn.

Performer Misti Dawn told me, "Nobody has sex on camera without being wired a little off"—but I think that the wiring is really only a matter of sex drive. With few exceptions, my adult entertainer interviewees have reported that they love their jobs because they love sex, and always have. In a 2012 interview, model and PR wiz Kelly Shibari backed up my take on the situation. "We're actually real women who just have a really high sex drive," she said. And a high sex drive, most doctors will tell you, is nothing to be worried about unless it's causing you significant difficulty in the rest of your life. But how could it cause problems if you're making a legal, profitable, satisfying career out of it?

That high libido unites many in the porn industry, as well as, I thought back in 2008, a sense of humor. At least, I'd been led to believe as much because of the way delicate matters were handled at the print magazine—which is to say, not delicately at all. *WHACK!* had assumed a similar outlook on all things porn: This is fun. This is ridiculous. Let's make fun of it.

I was more heavy-handed with my interviews, reviews, and op-eds than vegas or Matthew, but when it came to researching the month's astrological information and applying it to the denizens of the porn world, I let myself have some fun. I'd predict that, based on the alignment of Saturn and Mercury, a herpes outbreak was headed your way, or that before your anal shoot on the fourth, it would be best not to have those beets for dinner, and so on.

Matthew tended toward high-minded philosophical rants in his op-eds and reviews, which would degenerate to hyperbolic statements that were intended to pinion the sex-terrified masses and often the performers themselves. They were frequently spot-on, but I'd venture to say that they went right over the heads of most readers in a manner that could be described as "inflammatory."

And j. vegas took things further with his porno-litical cartoons, in which he ragged mercilessly on still photos from porn shoots. He'd doctor the photos according to his whim and insert thought or speech bubbles over the actors' heads, delivering satire that was raunchy, irreverent, and often downright offensive. When some industry people got upset with us, vegas was astonished. It was *satire*, he said. Didn't anybody understand that? Didn't they get that, as a publication that supported and publicized the porn industry, we were on their side?

While it's arguable that many Americans actually *don't* understand the line between satire and outright meanness, it's also arguable that some of those cartoons had a toe on both sides of that line. For as long as I've known him, vegas's sense of humor has gone straight for the jugular, and I couldn't blame people for being offended by it. If I'd found myself parodied in one of his cartoons, I'd have been upset, but I was still surprised when others got pissed off. I had been going along my merry way thinking that everyone who made porn saw it as the same kind of dark, humorous commentary on the human condition that vegas took it to be, since he had ushered me into this industry with his biting wit and dark sensibility.

But if I was being honest with myself, which I decided to try now that the industry that had welcomed me was calling for my colleague's head, I'd always been a tad suspicious of this devious humor. As someone who grew up with the idea that sex was pretty much the most evil act a human being could engage in, I took porn quite seriously. I tended toward showing the human side of the industry, trying to understand it rather than make jokes about it.

But I'd let myself assume that I was a loner in that respect. Of course, I hadn't *met* anyone in the industry aside from vegas and his former bosses (the second magazine gig had come along solely through e-mails), so this was really an excuse for going along with the cartoons that landed us in hot water. Even as I was beginning to do respectful, insightful interviews with porn stars, I'd let myself be cajoled into supporting nasty caricatures lambasting the self-same people whose words I'd clung to over the phone, in which we used photographs they'd given permission for someone else to take, divested them of their context and thus of the performers' consent, and mocked them. Of *course* they were pissed off.

A giant kerfuffle eventually broke out between a big-name star we'll call Bee Hanson and j. vegas, who had made a series of pointedly nasty cartoons about her after she'd flaked out on a number of scheduled interviews with us. Bee had slandered vegas all over social media, and things had gotten ugly. But after much grousing about satire and freedom of the press, vegas finally backed down and took the cartoons off the website.

Personally, I felt awful about the Bee Hanson situation. I didn't apologize personally for the cartoons, since I hadn't made them, but I *did* branch out on my own.

A friend alerted me to an essay contest for a year-long column for *McSweeney's Internet Tendency* in 2009. The online arm of Dave Eggars's publishing company was looking for personal columns on any topic. *McSweeney's* had a tone I liked—a dry sense of self-deprecating humor that felt right to me. A bit of self-flagellation could go a long way for my conscience, and also provide a significantly larger audience than the few hundred people who were starting to look up *WHACK!* on the regular.

So I pitched a column about my weird life as a feminist and a porn journalist to *McSweeney's* in 2009, considering it a practice run for pitching the idea to other, more attainable, publications. But my column was accepted. I got a small cash prize, but the real reward came in the form of tens of thousands of readers that "The Conflicted Existence of the Female Porn Writer" eventually attracted.

Interviewing the legendary feminist performer Nina Hartley at the New York Sex Bloggers calendar release party in 2010   (PHOTO COURTESY J. VEGAS)

CHAPTER 7

The Conflicted Existence
of the Female Porn Writer

WITH THE BIGGEST OPPORTUNITY of my professional life bearing down upon me, I had to face the most daunting task of my *personal* life: telling my parents what I'd been up to since I'd moved back to New York. I knew that their response would be shock and likely horror, but I was proud of my accomplishment. *McSweeney's* was, and still is, a big freaking deal. I hoped that when they read the column, it might be a source of non-confrontational information on my career. Explaining to them the finer points of my thinking about orgy scenes might be difficult over the phone, but the deep (pun sort-of intended) thoughts I had to offer on the subject were intelligent, forward-thinking, usually feminist, and sometimes even poignant. They were worth reading. At least I thought so, and now someone at *McSweeney's* agreed with me.

It would be a relief to come clean, anyway. It had become increasingly difficult to answer questions about my career at family functions. My sisters and cousins were accomplishing things: getting promotions and research grants, graduating with honors, traveling abroad. Meanwhile, I looked like the typical family "creative" type—a receptionist with little to show for her work—to those who didn't know I'd actually been writing quite a lot. It was time for me to unburden myself, and now that my name would be plastered on the front page of a renowned literary outlet on the Web, even my tech un-savvy family would likely hear about what I'd been up to, one way or another.

And so, one night, I called my parents. I pep-talked myself into hoping that the years between my childhood and this phone call might have mellowed their perspectives on the immorality of sex, or at least given them some perspective. But I doubted it.

I barreled through my rehearsed monologue in a breathless jumble of words that I don't recall clearly; the adrenaline overwhelmed my memory. I know that I couched it all in lemons-into-lemonade terms: "I've been doing this job you'll find very icky, but I'm getting paid and leveraging it into something that will be great for my writing career! Hooray!" When I stopped talking, they both stayed silent for a long, long time, while I pictured them on the other end of the line, wide-eyed and open-mouthed.

My father eventually spoke up. "So, this *McSweeney's* . . . Is that also an *adult* publication?"

"No!" I warbled, breaking into a panicky grin. "Not at all! *McSweeney's* is a prestigious publisher of literature. *Real* writers publish with them all the time! It's a very big deal for me!"

Another silence. I could picture him working his jaw, trying to find words. "Well," he intoned carefully, "I'm glad to hear that you're making the best of the situation."

I felt my smile falter.

"I'm going to take a shower," he said, and hung up. To date, that is the only conversation I've had with my father on the subject of the adult entertainment industry and my involvement with it.

I think that trauma-processing mechanisms in my brain must have been set off during the conversation I had with my mother after Dad hung up, because I can't remember any details. I was impressed that she handled it as well as she did, which was likely the result of our shared Northeastern Protestant upbringing, in which emotional reactions are sanctioned only in the direst of situations. I walked away with a glimmer of hope that perhaps, someday in the future, my mother and I could have a conversation about sex that didn't involve shaming tactics, long silences, or suppressed tears.

In the years since, I have attempted to start that dialogue. As I've moved through reviewing porn films, writing set copy for naughty pictures, interviewing porn stars, interviewing consumers, making documentary films, moderating panel discussions, reviewing books, publicizing adult industry events, blogging about all these things, and now writing this book, I've tried to bring up my work without forcing details upon her. But her engagement with the subject matter has been grudging at best. She told me once that she'd read a few things I'd written online, and was unable to sleep for days afterward.

In the spirit of good daughterhood, I asked my editor at *McSweeney's* to remove my last name from the column. I would henceforth publish my explorations of pornographic matters as Lynsey G. or Miss Lagsalot so that my parents could claim that the sex-crazed deviant on the Internet just *happened* to spell her first name the same way as their daughter. *Isn't that so strange, what are the chances!*

For quite a while, I kept the Lynsey G. identity separate from my Miss Lagsalot pseudonym, which was in turn distinct from the other pseudonym I utilized at the print magazines. To be honest, I was becoming increasingly embarrassed by the stuff I was writing for the old-school jizz rags; although I was doing my best to be witty and quietly feminist, there's only so much you can do with five hundred words about the surprising perkiness of a pair of E cups or the orgasmic expressions in *Anal Acrobats*. And, because much of my work involved searching for sexiness in films or images that didn't exactly inspire me, I needed a place to speak more freely and more seriously as Lynsey G. I felt a certain weight lift when I assumed the alliterative, bad-joke-making mien of Miss Lagsalot, and a different burden disappear when I sat down as Lynsey G. to relieve my mind of my conflicted thoughts as a porn writer. And I had lots of them.

From where I spent my days at my oversized desk in midtown, I couldn't see anyone trying to bridge the gap between pornographers and porn consumers. There was writing about porn out there: magazines like the ones I wrote for, which glorified yet often degraded porn stars in pursuit of the consumer dollar; industry trade publications, which ran press releases about directors' vanity projects; online review sites that pandered to whichever companies provided their review fodder; and a smattering of scholarly articles tackling snooze-worthy subjects like the significance of eye contact during gangbangs vis-à-vis some philosopher or another's writings. But none of it felt accessible to someone like me, or to the people I was interested in: consumers of pornography who might want to think more deeply about what they were watching. I knew they had to be out there in the thousands, but nobody had found a platform from which to speak to them.

In her 2016 book *The Pornography Industry*, Shira Tarrant wrote, "Its ubiquitous presence in so many aspects of our lives means that pornography is a rich source for studying the ways in which ideas about gender, race, class, beauty, and sex are constructed, conveyed, and maintained." In 2009, I felt exactly the same way. I'd been attempting to cultivate a space for this discussion at *WHACK!* in my op-eds, where I reported on matters like STI screening in the adult industry and legislative attempts at enforcing the use of barrier protection on set. But although I had complete creative freedom at *WHACK!* I also found myself facing a largely empty room. Our audience was heavily skewed toward the industry itself. As it turned out, convincing consumers to spend more than a few seconds on a website that *talks* about pornography but doesn't actually *show* pornography was not so easy to pull off. Consumers weren't looking for a place to find out what their favorite porn star thought about *Star Trek*; times were tough for Americans during the Great Recession, and most were more interested in seeing what that porn star thought about ejaculate on her face.

And thus the paradoxical middle ground I hoped my *McSweeney's* column could begin to inhabit: the space between the industry itself and the public's consumption of the products it sold. Between making porn and masturbating to it. The chasm that few people spend time lingering in after they've gotten what they wanted.

I considered this expanse confusing, fascinating, and scary all at once, and I was standing squarely within it, as neither a creator of porn nor a typical consumer of it. I knew more than your average bear about what was happening on both sides of the fence, and I felt that this was an important place for someone to stand in—someone who wanted to talk about it.

I was mostly alone in this space not only in my writing life, but also socially. The crowd I ran with was a mix of young professionals, artists, and graduate students—a fertile field in which to reap some interesting perspectives on porn, I had hoped, yet I found myself standing in a self-made echo chamber when I brought up the subject. People would seem charmed to find out that I wrote about porn, but also standoffish. Shira Tarrant summed up the experience of being "the porn girl" at the party in a 2016 interview with *The Atlantic*: "I've had this experience so many times, where people, colleagues or what have you, aren't even listening to what I'm saying about the industry or the politics or the financial aspects of what's going on. They're just thinking about whether or not I'm watching porn." I know exactly how she felt.

Nobody knew what to make of me in social situations. I liked to think it was because I was doing something new and different—challenging people to have real conversations with me about their thoughts on smut —but more likely it was simple discomfort. For my generation (those not quite young enough to be considered millennials, but too young to be Generation X), porn is a type of entertainment usually viewed privately and in the dark; it has never been something one talks about at a party with a stranger, much less a bright-eyed female stranger who's earnestly inquiring about what websites you frequent and why.

I discovered that most of my acquaintances had never spoken to anyone on these topics, and—more to the point—they didn't *want* to. The one answer I often could eke out of a conversation before the person I was talking to squirmed away to get another drink (and then forgot to come back) further solidified my belief in this empty space of silence between the adult film industry and its consumers: Almost none of the people I spoke to had *ever* paid for pornography. Not even once. When I asked them if they had, I'd often get a series of confused blinks in response, as if the concept had never crossed their minds. And it probably hadn't. As Tim von Swine once pointed out to me, "Ten years ago, someone who was fourteen is now twenty-four . . . If you've been jerking off since you were fourteen to free porno, you *expect* it to be free."

In a capitalist culture where dollars are stand-ins for voicing approval, this lack of communication between a customer base and the industry attempting to cater to its desires was, quite literally, hurting everyone in 2009. Porn was getting weirder by the day, and the few who would speak openly about their habits often said that they didn't like the violent and misogynist stuff they saw online. But none of them were willing to pitch in the dollars to support the kind of porn they *liked*. From what I was hearing, most of them didn't even bother looking very hard to find things that didn't make them feel so icky. They kind of just watched whatever they found easily and for free, then complained about it. I tried to lure them out into the middle area with me by encouraging them to look harder, giving them the names of a few companies to support, and engaging them in meaningful conversation, but my attempts were largely fruitless.

I also exhorted people to *talk* to pornographers via their many available social media channels. Most porn actors and directors are very active on social media, and they want to know what you want to see so that they can make it. In an interview, when I asked groundbreaking trans superstar Buck Angel how consumers can help pornographers, he said, "They should speak up and be vocal about what they want to watch. I get lots of specific requests, which I love. And I always try to accommodate them whenever possible." Buck was far from an outlier in that respect; especially in the trying days of the late 2000s, when pornographers were fearing that their industry would be dead in a year, if consumers expressed a serious interest in seeing something, it was very likely that someone would make it in hopes of turning a profit. As more porn stars were building their own websites and filming content for themselves, the space between fans and producers was shrinking, and turnaround time disappearing. Porn made on spec was no longer a thing of the past, and finding someone to make it was getting easier. (Hint: It's even easier now. A lot of performers make custom videos or do cam shows where you can make requests! Get on it!)

This all seemed obvious to me, but I began to realize that other people my age didn't always see porn as an industry made of human beings with whom interaction was possible. It was viewed as more akin to Hollywood, which makes what it feels like based on some metric that none of us are privy to. But porn is more like an open book, willing to be rewritten by its fans, and leaving the space between the industry and the rest of us empty was dragging everyone down.

So I tried to start the conversations I wasn't having at parties in my column at *McSweeney's*. I wrote about the dangers I saw in leaving this space empty—the inherent inequality in the drastic separation between "them" and "us." In a culture that already mistrusts and mistreats what Danny Wylde once called the "very visible, but somewhat ostracized minority" of sex workers, a chasm between those who do and those who don't is a fertile breeding ground for prejudice and dangerous lapses in understanding. "A bridge is what we need," I wrote in my *McSweeney's* column, which gave me the opportunity to invite more people to consider crossing the rickety one we currently had.

I had been learning, and now I was ready to open that learning up to asking big questions, hypothesize their answers, and make some room for a discussion about them. Although there wasn't a whole lot in the way of feedback—no comments section, and not much going on just yet on Facebook, which was only a few years old—it felt good to shout those ideas of mine into space. And I *was* onto something. By the midpoint of my yearlong column, my editor told me that more people were reading my column than anything else on the site.

CHAPTER 8

In the Flesh

THE BEAUTIFUL THING ABOUt this middle ground into which I'd stepped between porn industry and porn consumer was the freedom it afforded me to walk back and forth between the two sides. At least, hypothetically. But two years into my work as a porn journalist, I had never actually met any of the people I spent my time watching, talking to, or thinking and writing about. Although I was imploring my *McSweeney's* readers to close the gap between themselves and their porn heroes, I myself had yet to step outside my comfort zone.

It wasn't until late September of 2009, almost a year after I'd done my first porn star interview, that I took the real-life plunge into industry waters. The *WHACK!* team had secured press passes to the Exxxotica Adult Entertainment Expo in Edison, New Jersey, booked a hotel room, and prepped ourselves mentally for what would be my first adult industry event.

Exxxotica, now a mainstay of the porn calendar year with several events held annually in a variety of locations, was just a wee bairn of a convention at the time. It had started in 2006 and was still getting its legs under it in 2009, trying out venues from Miami Beach to Los Angeles to Edison. My inaugural expo was a decidedly porn-centric affair, but in latter years it has opened up to sex toys, webcammers, lingerie, kink, exotic dance venues, head shops and other 420-friendly vendors, and—peculiarly—novelty car shows. It draws crowds numbering into the tens of thousands to the suburban New Jersey expo center every fall and is an excellent source of revenue for the porn personalities who rent booth space.

The expo circuit was a latecomer to the adult industry, but it proved a vital one in the twenty-first-century financial climate. True, the Adult Entertainment Expo (AEE) in Las Vegas had been a fixture for years as a gathering place and sister event to the Adult Video News (AVN)

Awards—also known as the "Oscars of Porn." But that was only one convention, available only to vendors and fans able to make it to Sin City, and though it still attracted crowds in 2009, the recession had put a dent in its numbers. So the advent of multi-location expos like Exxxotica proved a godsend for American pornographers, who could now more conveniently bring themselves and their wares to consumers all over the country.

In a way, the bring-the-smut-to-the-masses approach speaks to my "middle space" theory. The past decade has seen adult industry denizens making more frequent public appearances at conventions, strip clubs, public speaking venues, and even college classrooms, bringing them face-to-face with members of the public who may otherwise have never dreamed of shaking hands with their favorite adult star. But, when that star more or less comes *to* them, there's no harm in leaving the comfort of one's own side of the us/them divide and saying hi. Meanwhile, an endless parade of social media platforms has transformed the public's ability to get to know porn personalities from afar. In the age of free porn for all, providing the public with digital access to the lives and times of porn stars has proven invaluable to the industry. Without tethering themselves to their fan bases in ways that solidify both loyalty and cash flow, many pornographers may have seen their careers crash and burn.

Despite its importance, however, all this human interaction with fans can be rather humdrum in practice. The Raritan Center in Edison is one gigantic open space, and in 2009, the Exxxotica convention hadn't yet managed to cover more than half of that space with booths, giving the expo a sadly small look. Go-go dancers gyrated lazily on poles and in cages set up around the show floor while much-too-loud hard rock music blared from somewhere high overhead. Someone at the far end of the show floor shouted into a microphone on a temporary stage, trying to attract a crowd to some booty-shaking contest or giveaway. Awkward fans laden with goodie bags, lanyards, and expensive cameras goggled at the scantily clad dancers, graphic depictions of sex splattered on DVD covers, posters, and other promo items, and performers clattering around in mile-high platforms. It was at once disappointing in its fluorescent lighting and ho-hum tackiness, and awe-inspiring in its sensory overload.

But the convention also exceeded many of my expectations. Thus far in my career, the particular subset of porn insiders I'd been running with had viewed the industry as a delightfully disgusting source of sleazy entertainment, in which they could delightedly abandon the trappings of "civilized" behavior. Case in point: Our tag line at *WHACK!* was "A Provocative Periodical for the Cultured Degenerate." When we started up, j. vegas had made it known that our tone was to be one of sly camaraderie with the industry, so long as everyone involved recognized that we were all swimming in the shallow end of the morality pool. In other words, my experiences with professionals in the adult entertainment sector thus far had reinforced the idea that nobody was going to take any of this seriously. Porn was for miscreants and malfeasance, and we were there to party.

I met Chet, my editor at the second of the two print magazines, for the very first time at Exxxotica. We'd corresponded up until then entirely by e-mail, and I'd developed a mental picture of him as grumpy old man with bushy eyebrows and a deeply embedded scowl. I had been spot-on: Chet was younger than I'd imagined, probably in his late forties when I met him, but he was as jaded a man as I'd ever met. He and Charles— brothers of a sort in their simultaneous adoration of and contempt for pornographers—had both been in this business for decades, and they'd been to more than a few rodeos. As the elders of my little corner of the industry, I'd looked to them as the bearers of wisdom.

As I put it in a later *McSweeney's* column: "These jaded folks paint a picture of porn performers as broken-down human beings with deep-seated emotional issues whose only love is for degrading themselves and each other . . . Who would do this willingly but broken-down delinquents?" With this understanding of our industry in mind, I went into the convention expecting a menagerie of debauched cretins swilling booze, snorting drugs, and throwing clothing and dignity to the wind. To be honest, all the while I'd been exhorting my readers to think of porn stars as people and to cross the middle ground between "them" and "us," I'd been pretty damn comfortable thinking of "them" as fundamentally different from *me*.

But, as the day wore on and the *WHACK!* crew made the rounds of performers' booths for introductions, autographs, and video interviews, I realized that most of the models were different from me in only one striking way: They were businesspeople. Focused, effective businesspeople. Pros who were willing and able to plaster on their fake eyelashes and enough makeup to balance out the terrible lighting at the convention center, spill themselves into undergarments that squeezed in all the right places, and dazzle onlookers with radiant, rehearsed smiles for hours on end. Specialists in batting those fluffy fake lashes in just such a way as to inspire adulation, self-confidence, and the desire to spend money on the spot—and well into the future. Crack practitioners at styling, maintaining, and promoting their own brands.

And make no mistake: Branding is as much a part of the porn industry as it is anywhere else. As we barreled along through the early years of the Information Age, porn stars caught on to the power of their own personal styles and sexual proclivities in selling their work. As Christina Cicchelli told me once in an interview, "My brand as a sex worker is important because I have to compete with so many other ladies." With thousands of women active in the adult entertainment industry at any given time, it's important to stand out.

For the porn fan with an affinity for bubbly Southern blondes with big butts, Alexis Texas was happy to offer herself as a brand distinct from, say, Kelly Shibari's variety of curvy, kinky, nerdy, Japanese intelligence. Just as Joanna Angel catered to an alternative punk-rock crowd that enjoyed tattoos and quirky senses of humor, Misty Stone fed the desires of a more mainstream audience with a penchant for a lithe body and raw sensuality.

A heightened awareness of one's strengths and a recognition of the demographic that enjoyed those strengths enabled savvy models to make the most of their fan bases, and to keep adding to them. In short, most of the porn stars I met at Exxxotica had actively developed themselves and their public personas to fit their fans' desires. These were people who had decided to trek from Los Angeles (or Las Vegas or Phoenix or Tampa or Miami) to the suburbs of New Jersey because they meant business. And they were great at it.

As a young adult who majored in English and minored in philosophy, then spent her few post-collegiate years messing around in a variety of odd jobs, I was flabbergasted by the level of professional focus I saw in these porn stars. But watching Jenna Haze in a skintight minidress and six-inch platforms as she effectively seduced a fan without even touching him—and then performed the same feat over and over, all day long—I was awestruck. She told me a few years later in an interview that her convention demeanor was just as meticulously planned as I suspected: "I've always believed that if you carry yourself like a star, and if you carry yourself with respect, then people will respect you and treat you like a star . . . I go all-out on my signing outfits. I always wear something that's very sexy but that's really classy and fashionable. I think that kind of sets me apart." Given that the line for her signing booth stretched around the "block" of her section at the expo, clearly her strategy was paying off.

Nyomi Banxxx, a hugely popular performer who headed her own mainstream production company, adult production company, and clothing line, told me in a 2011 interview that her best advice for aspiring female stars was this: "Your name is your company, your body is the assets and stock in that company. Trademark, copyright. Do your research on who's the hottest in the industry and where you fit in. Know your markets! And never sell yourself short! Know your worth!" Nyomi took her own advice and became highly successful, transitioning out of the adult industry gracefully and on her own terms years later, with no regrets.

Ever hear someone express awe over a bootstrap start-up selling for billions? Of course you have; it's a tech-age fairy tale we all know and love. But here's a challenge: Try achieving success with a business in which your body is your capital and you are selling it in an industry in which royalties are nonexistent, job security is elusive at best, and there are no formal pay standards. Add to this equation the fact that the rest of the world looks at this industry with contempt, fear, and sometimes outright hatred. Do all of this in the face of outside forces attempting to legislate what you are permitted to do with your body, protestors arriving at most of your public appearances, and the media waiting to pounce on any whisper of negativity in your industry. And do it all in stilettos.

What I'm saying is: Successful porn stars are not the flighty bimbos many of us expect. They are successful because they work hard at succeeding in conditions that aren't conducive to success. Not only do many porn stars turn a profit as freelance contractors on the above dreadful terms, but a growing number of them also take the reins of production, go on to start their own companies, and expand their personal brands to encompass the performances of their colleagues while negotiating distribution deals, merchandising opportunities, and—at last—residuals. So, when I met Joanna Angel in September of 2009, she wasn't just a porn star. She was an entrepreneur, and one whose star has continued to rise steadily in the time I've known her, despite astronomically high odds against success. Please don't try to tell me she doesn't deserve the cover of *Businessweek*. I disagree.

I WAS, IN SHORT, IMPRESSED by the women I met in New Jersey. In some cases, perhaps too impressed. I formed a crush on one star in particular, who I'll dub Jennie Hart. Sometime in the wee hours of Sunday morning, at the after-after-party back at the hotel, where my *WHACK!* cohorts and I, with a group of porn actors, had taken over a lounge on the top floor after the bar downstairs closed, I slurred a proposition to her. I thought myself quite savvy for phrasing my come-on in the form of a drug reference as we passed a joint around, but she just smiled and told me that, though she thought I was "really cute," she couldn't go around kissing people outside the performer talent pool, since she hadn't seen any of my STI testing paperwork and couldn't be sure it was safe.

In the cold, sober light of the next day I realized that Jennie's refusal made no sense—kissing wasn't dangerous to her sexual health. But she'd had her wits about her enough, even at three a.m. and after numerous drinks and a puff or two of the aforementioned joint, to turn me down in a way that showed she valued me as a future consumer of her products, but which conferred that, as a professional, she simply had to act in her own best interest. Smooth, indeed. Of course I was disappointed not to have landed a make-out session with my porn crush, but I came away from the experience with a whole new appreciation for her business acumen. And a hangover.

Speaking of hangovers, I'd be remiss if I didn't mention here that not all the female porn stars in Edison that weekend were cut form the same cloth. As a journalist who's let into the VIP section of the party might be expected to do, I gravitated toward the most famous people in the room. And I got very lucky; while there was a small but vocal media presence at Exxxotica in 2009, I was the only female journalist for an industry-specific publication in attendance. And that got me much further into the fold than I could have hoped.

This may seem incredible now, with the Internet having changed the landscape of media and journalism so drastically, but believe me when I tell you that in 2009 there were very few publications that covered adult entertainment with any degree of seriousness. Whereas today the porn industry is often the subject of journalistic scrutiny and celebration at outlets as varied as *Marie Claire*, *The Atlantic*, *Vice*, and even CNN, in the first decade of the new millennium, *WHACK!* was pretty damn unique in talking about pornography as an industry instead of a punch line (although we were obviously not above punch lines, either). And I was unique in that I was near the helm *and* female, which seemed to put many of the models at ease; after being "on" for their mostly male fans all day, they were able to relax around me. Although there may have been a number of women I would have accepted a proposition from— most notably Jennie—I was likely the only reporter they spoke to that weekend who wasn't obviously hoping to sleep with them. I try to be discreet, after all.

But I digress. While I was enjoying the heady scent of success as a porn industry journalist, I also bore witness to a fair share of what my elders at the magazines had led me to expect from a porn convention. There were, naturally, drinkers and pill-poppers exhibiting their addictions at the after-party. Ghosts of humans with vacant eyes and too much makeup. Washed-up elders who seemed to have nowhere else to be. Hopefuls with no idea how to go about realizing their dreams. Even a few young, attractive Jersey girls hoping to catch the eye of a casting agent for a quick scene that night at the hotel.

In short, the after-parties that weekend displayed a cross-section of humanity you might find at just about any crowded bar in New Jersey that charges a cover on Friday and Saturday nights. Just, maybe, with higher platform heels and more stringently enforced VIP entry criteria.

I've said it before, and I'm sure I will say it again, but I simply cannot stress this enough: Porn stars are not much different from anybody else. As Nikki Darling put it in an interview I did with her in 2016, "At the end of the day, you're dealing with different individuals of different backgrounds and different beliefs, just like in the real world. We just all happen to be having sex with each other for money."

There's little holding the group together as a universal characteristic, except for maybe one salient feature. Former industry scriptwriter and producer Dan Reilly told me in an interview that porn stars "seriously get off on the attention. They get off on the act of shooting it. That's really the equalizer that I see . . . That's the universal thing."

It's true: Exhibitionism must enter into the personality of any porn actor who has a shot at success. Without the desire to show oneself off to the world, nobody in any entertainment industry can survive. But particularly in pornography, where so very *much* of oneself is shown on camera and also as a branded commodity on social media and in public appearances, a yearning for attention is necessary. Prominent performer and now two-time author Asa Akira wrote in her first book, *Insatiable: Porn—A Love Story*, "Almost every time I shoot a sex scene, I feel a little bit in love. It's the only way I can describe it. Not necessarily with my partner, but just in general. With the situation. In love with being watched. In love with being on display." These exhibitionist tendencies and a relatively high sex drive, really, are the only differences I could pinpoint between porn stars at the Exxxotica conference in 2009 and the rest of "us," and they are to date the only differences I have ever found.

Holding up my first-ever media pass as a porn journalist at Exxxotica New Jersey—with my first-ever porn-convention hangover—in 2009

(PHOTO COURTESY J. VEGAS)

Ron Jeremy signing Miss Lagsalot's shirt at Exxxotica New Jersey in 2009

CHAPTER 9

The Guys

OF COURSE, THERE WEREN'T only female performers representing themselves at Exxxotica New Jersey in 2009. Though women comprised easily ninety percent of the talent there, a healthy contingent of their male counterparts was also on hand to represent its equally important role in the straight porn industry. (Gay male pornography didn't have a presence at the expo; the gay industry and the straight industry maintain a fairly strict separation, which I'll address later.)

The male talent pool in straight porn is notably smaller than the female for reasons both numerous and complicated. To name a few, and to skirt their many implications in favor of brevity: (1) The consumer demand for female models is far greater than the demand for males. (2) Porn is likely the only industry in which women typically out-earn men by *three times*, which makes men less likely to jump into the game than women. (3) There are astonishingly few men both psychologically and physically able to achieve and maintain erections on camera in front of film crews, and even fewer are able to ejaculate on command as the job requires. With all of these obstacles set up to bar entry, it's rare for a man to decide to go into porn and actually prosper in the field—and it's just as rare for a director to give new guys a chance.

Ryan Driller, the Superman of many a porn parody and a talented actor to boot, laid it out for me. "Most producers, most directors do not want to take a chance on a new guy. I shouldn't say they don't *want* to, but they're hesitant, because a guy can't fake it," he said. On set, "if you're waiting and hoping that the guy is going to be able to perform . . . every minute is money lost [if] he's not going to be able to do the job. So once a studio usually finds a guy or a group of guys that they like and they're comfortable with, and they're getting the performances they want specifically from them, they'll latch on to them and keep them because it's more of a sure thing."

Even once they've gotten started, suffice it to say that straight male porn actors don't have it easy, so many careers don't last, making straight male porn *stars* quite the rare breed. At any given time, there are maybe a few dozen (and that may be a generous estimate) guys in the industry who get regular work from big studios, a few dozen lower-tier performers who work for smaller companies (often websites that deal in more extreme content, located in far-flung hubs outside LA and Vegas), and a few dozen more who appear in group scenes for low pay. These guys are not-so-lovingly referred to by some in the industry as "mopes"—a term that j. vegas enjoyed using.

It's safe to assume that any male actor you see in a well-produced straight porno probably works *a lot*. The upper crust of male talent shoots almost constantly with the hundreds of female models active in the industry at all times. I've heard lots of people complain about how unattractive they find male porn stars (which I find mystifying—I mean, have you *seen* Ryan Driller or Manuel Ferrara?), but their purpose in the skin biz isn't to be attractive, it's to perform. Moe Johnson, also known as "Moe the Monster" on set, told me that the impression he often gets from directors is, "You're a tool. Be what you're supposed to be." The men who excel in this role are those who can establish their personalities *along* with their cocks strongly enough to attract a following. That requires charisma, as well as a strict mastery of one's body that requires practice and self-discipline of a very specific kind.

In short, straight male porn stars doing well enough to fly to New Jersey for a convention are hardened professionals (sorry, not sorry!) with oodles of experience and often a fair amount of pull in the industry. Most of the male performers at my first Exxxotica were professionals in a business in which they were highly successful and confident as hell. And it showed.

You may be thinking that this sounds a bit gross. That these dudes swaggered around, pounding each other on the back and smashing beer cans on their foreheads to display their virility. Given the dispiriting nature of heteronormative maleness in America, particularly in 2009, I also assumed that egregious displays of dominance would be their modus operandi. But I was pleasantly surprised to find that the majority of male performers at Exxxotica were possessed of a quiet, smooth, and sane self-assuredness that was far more inviting.

I saw MR. MARCUS FROM across the expo and made a beeline for the subject of my first interview. He was dressed simply in dark jeans, a navy-blue T-shirt, and his trademark baseball cap, smiling at the fans and coworkers who greeted him. He wasn't as tall as I'd expected, but he was just as heavily muscled as he looked in the movies, and he exuded a laid-back confidence that drew me in. When I introduced myself, he smiled warmly and came out from behind his signing podium to wrap a very large arm around my waist in a surprisingly soft embrace. He shook my hand gently, his dark brown eyes never leaving mine.

I automatically turned bright red. I had expected him to be attractive, but I was unprepared for his magnetism, and I felt myself responding to his maleness the way I thought only naïfs in romance novels did: I may have actually swooned. He told me he hoped to see me later in the weekend, and I stammered a response before tottering away like a turned-on ninny.

Over the course of the weekend, our paths crossed multiple times on the show floor and at after-hours parties. Each encounter grew friendlier until, on the last day of the convention, I sought him out at his signing booth to say good-bye. He stepped away from his booth, ignoring the line of fans, and placed a hand on the small of my back with expert precision. He drew me close and whispered into my ear: "You're leaving? But I was looking forward to seeing you running around my hotel room naked tonight."

My jaw dropped. I felt myself flush from head to toe. I stepped out of the hug and stared at him with saucer eyes while his face crinkled into a broad smile. At a loss for words or appropriate behavior, I turned on my heel and giggled my way out of the convention.

THE *WHACK!* CREW ALSO crossed paths with Sean Michaels, an industry veteran whose work spans decades of hardcore films. Michaels is often cast as the male "bull" who humiliates less masculine husbands, a dominant and sexually insatiable force of nature. But in real life he is courteous, articulate, and immaculately dressed. When we met him at the hotel bar, he was wearing a three-piece black pinstripe suit with an impeccably starched white button-up and a black bow tie, a matching black pinstripe fedora, and black dress shoes—with spats. He looked every inch the gentleman, and when we introduced ourselves as the *WHACK!* crew, he followed through on that first impression. We expressed our excitement at meeting him, and asked if he would like to adjourn to our room for some pre-gaming before the party started.

And so we found ourselves stuffed into our cramped hotel room with one of porn's greatest legends and a few hangers-on from smaller production companies in the NYC area, engaged in a heady conversation that ranged over topics as vast as the Buddhist outlook on life, to those as trivial as the choice of carpet color on the expo show floor. I was captivated by Sean.

After an hour, he raised his beer bottle in a toast and told the room at large that he hoped he wasn't offending anyone by saying so, but that he was honored to be in my presence because I was "a truly beautiful woman, inside and out." Then he leveled a look of the most serious sexual intention I have ever seen right at me. Again, I went scarlet—damn my Irish heritage!—while I mumbled something about being my own woman. Then I added that I was actually in a relationship with Matthew, who was sitting right next to Sean.

Without batting an eye, Sean turned to Matthew and raised his glass again in congratulations, and offering apologies if he'd offended either of us. Then he turned back to me and smiled. "Keep on being a lady," he said. The lust was still apparent in his eyes, and I squirmed at its delicious intensity.

When Sean eventually left, one of the hangers-on who'd watched the scene unfold burst into laughter. "Holy shit, Lynsey!" he gasped. "Do you know what would have happened if you'd gone back to his room?"

The guys around me (I was the only female present) snickered.

"No . . ." I replied, confused. "What do you mean?"

"Have you ever seen any of Sean's movies?" He arched his eyebrow.

"Actually, no," I admitted.

"It would have been like this," he said. He balled up his fist in front of his face, then mimicked the lowering of a zipper and dropped his forearm with a "thunk" onto the dresser. The implication was that Sean's penis was the size of John's forearm.

Since then I *have* seen a few of Sean's films. He was right.

MOST OF THE SUCCESSFUL male porn stars I've met since that first Exxxotica convention fit the kind-and-confident mold. But it must be said that not every guy who has sex on camera for a living exudes the same warm, gracious presence as my two paramours in Edison that weekend. Every kind of person you meet outside the porn industry is also represented within it. And that applies to creepers whose self-confidence is higher than it needs to be.

If you're thinking Ron Jeremy, you're right.

On the first day of the expo, my cohorts and I spotted The Hedgehog signing autographs nearby, and I jumped into his signing line immediately. A picture of me with Ron Jeremy would be great for our budding magazine, and maybe I could schedule an interview. The white *WHACK! Magazine* T-shirts we'd had printed were perfectly suited for signing, so I whipped out a Sharpie and stood at the ready while I waited for his attention.

When it was my turn, I approached Ron with a smile that faltered before we even said hi. After years of occupying the throne as porn's most recognizable star, Ron didn't place too much importance on maintaining a strictly professional demeanor. He was wearing a stained T-shirt, sweatpants, and Crocs. His thinning hair and mustache were both in disarray, and his stomach jutted out into the space between us as I offered my hand and introduced myself. Ron ignored my proffered handshake and slipped his arm around my waist, pulling me into a close embrace around his gut and grinning lasciviously.

"Hi, baby," he said. Then he kissed me on the lips.

The kiss was pretty chaste, but in the second that it lasted I experienced a riot of shock, embarrassment, and annoyance. But I told myself I couldn't be too angry that Ron Jeremy's mustache was scratching my upper lip; I had been waiting patiently in a long line of fans who probably had hoped for a kiss, after all. Ron was in his natural habitat, and he had no idea that I was approaching him in a professional capacity. His professional capacity was having sex with women. All things considered, a kiss wasn't *so* bad, even though I wasn't happy about it.

As Ron pulled back, I could hear my comrades from *WHACK!* giggling and snapping photos of my bright-red face. I ignored them and tried my best to forge ahead, asking Ron if he would sign my *WHACK!* T-shirt. He leaned in with the Sharpie I offered and made a small "RJ" with a little heart that took only a few seconds to complete. I mugged a faux-shocked expression for the cameras gathering nearby as he leaned over my chest, but then, egged on by the onlookers and my smiling face, Ron grasped my shoulder, turned me away from the crowd, lifted my shirt, grasped my left bra cup, and proceeded to sign my breast—all without missing a beat.

"Mortification" doesn't adequately describe my emotional state at that moment. "Revulsion" might be closer. And horror that Ron Jeremy was gripping my bosom in such a way that, though nobody else could see, he was able to view my entire breast, nipple and all, *without my consent*. And rage that my boyfriend and my editor were standing by, laughing and snapping photos from the sidelines as I was manhandled by a gross old man in front of a crowd.

In my memory, this signature took a *long* time—significantly longer than the one on my T-shirt—but it probably wasn't more than a few awful seconds. At least, I hope it didn't take long, because the uproar of emotions inside me left me so stunned that I couldn't summon a reaction before he dropped my breast and pulled my shirt back down. I'd like to think that if more than a few seconds had elapsed, I'd have come up with an appropriate reaction, like slapping him in the face.

As it was, I just plowed ahead with my sales pitch as if nothing had happened. I introduced myself and the magazine, gave him one of my business cards, and told him I'd love to get an interview sometime. He grabbed a stack of business cards held together by a rubber band, riffled through it for a moment, and, when he found the appropriate card, handed it to me while leaning in for another kiss.

I endured it, then staggered away from the scene of the groping to collect myself and assess the situation. I looked down at the card he'd given me: a business card for the hotel we were both staying at, with his room number scrawled at the top beside his standard "RJ"-and-heart signature. No need to carry cards of your own when your face is synonymous with sex, I supposed. *Groan.*

That night at the after-party, j. vegas, Matthew, and I had been let

into the VIP section by Teagan Presley, a multiple award-winning performer (and former ballerina and gymnast) with a sweet smile and a
sleeve of gorgeous tattoos. We were having a few drinks and watching
the industry royalty interact when we saw Ron, this time in more party-
appropriate attire—I believe he had on a suit jacket and jeans. Immediately, vegas made a show of pointing him out. "Hey, Lyns, it's your
buddy! You should say hi!"

I threw a few swear words and a glare his way before turning to look
pointedly in the other direction. A few minutes later, however, Ron had
worked his way around the room. I looked away to avoid any recognition, but vegas stepped forward. "Hey, Ron!" he yelled over the thump-
ing music. "Check it out! Your signature's still there!" He pointed at me,
indicating the shirt-dress I was now wearing, and what lay beneath it.

Ron smiled at me, the memory of our earlier rendezvous twinkling
in his eye, and said something to vegas that I couldn't make out over the
music. Then he stepped toward me, intoning, "This won't take long."

Without ascertaining my consent *at all*, Ron Jeremy moved behind
me, his stomach pressing into my back. He grasped me firmly around the
waist, and, without so much as a "How do you do," he began to . . . sort
of . . . *gnaw* on my neck. I'm not sure what he was aiming for, sensation-
wise, but I'm confident he was trying to show off his sensual prowess by
making my knees buckle under the wave of overwhelming lust he was
sure I would experience.

That's not the reaction I had, though. I think "horror" would be the
most fitting term.

For the few seconds that this humiliating scene lasted, I fought an internal war between shrieking, slapping, and running away . . . and gritting my teeth and bearing it. The atmosphere didn't seem to lend itself to
a freak-out: I was very much in Ron's territory here, surrounded by industry folks, many of whom had been far more intimate with Ron than
a mere neck-gnawing—but their encounters with him were consented to,
pre-negotiated, and paid for. Would any of his coworkers have looked
kindly upon me screaming and flailing at one of their elder statesmen?
After all, I was here willingly, with the specific intention of interacting
with porn stars. Would showing my true colors as a dyed-in-the-wool
prude do me any favors? Would it be better to just let it happen and live
with the embarrassment?

Honestly, I just froze while all of this went through my head. My autonomic nervous system's response was to play dead, like an opossum.

He finally drew back and cheerily noted the crimson cast of my face before nodding at vegas, whose eyes had bugged out behind his thick glasses. "Gets 'em every time," Ron said before turning to me. "I'll see *you* later." He grinned, waggling his bushy eyebrows. And then he was gone.

Both vegas and Matthew burst into laughter.

I gave them what can only be described as a death look. "You threw me to the fucking wolves, you rotten bastards!" I ground out.

Teagan, sitting nearby, motioned me over to her table. "Did you just get attacked by Ron?"

I nodded sadly. The group of performers at the table all shook their heads in understanding.

Teagan put her hand on my arm reassuringly. "I'm sorry. He does that."

I gulped, uncertain if I was going to scream, cry, or laugh. "I don't know what to do right now," I told the group.

Teagan lifted an eyebrow. "Get a penicillin shot!"

The rest of the evening passed in an increasingly drunken haze. I busied myself with downing vodka, chatting with performers, watching the fans outside the VIP section, and eventually ending up in an after-after-party in the penthouse lounge of the hotel. The memories of Ron's mouth and mustache on my skin were receding in the face of the beverages I had consumed, and by the time we were unceremoniously kicked out of the lounge by hotel security around 3:30 a.m., I'd nearly blocked it out.

That's when I noticed a missed call from a number I didn't recognize, which had come in around the time the official after-party had shut down at 2:00 a.m. A text message had popped up about a minute after a voicemail had been left.

"Hi, Lynsey," the text read. "This is Ron Jeremy. Please give me a call when you have a chance." I refused to think about it further, found my hotel room, and passed out.

The next morning I checked the voicemail. "Hi, Lynsey, it's Ron Jeremy. I noticed that we're staying in the same hotel tonight. Why don't you give me a call or stop by my room later? I'd love to see you."

I wasn't surprised, exactly. But it was mystifying to me that a man who was literally world famous for having sex with thousands of women for pay was so keen to get into my pants on his time off. Didn't he get enough play without stalking the hotel bar? Weren't there enough adoring fans and professional acquaintances in attendance with whom his chances might have been better? Did he see me as some kind of challenge since I hadn't melted in my panties when he'd chewed on my neck without my consent?

I worked hard at avoiding Ron for the rest of the weekend. Our paths crossed a few times, but he showed no special recognition, either because he had actually forgotten who I was or because he took my silence as a slight. Either way, I was fine with the arrangement. And in the years since that first Exxxotica Expo, I've never spoken to him again.

IT'S STRANGE TO THINK about after so many years, and after writing thousands of words on the topic of sexual consent. Today, I am appalled by my behavior with Ron. I wish I'd pushed him away, screamed bloody murder, accused him publicly of assault, and stormed away after the first kiss. It would have been a good idea to take vegas and Matthew aside and rip them apart for their complicity in both the show-floor spectacle and the after-party debacle. A complete freak-out would have actually been the mature, responsible, correct thing to do.

But, as a rape survivor who has done a lot of work in the time since to understand the complicated intersections of assault and shame, I don't want to put too much pressure on myself. As do most women who are sexually assaulted, I'd blamed myself completely for my own experience when it happened—I spent far too many hours obsessing over the nausea-inducing memories of the incident, telling myself I should have done something different, that I could have stopped it from happening if I'd just done this, that, or the other thing. The anger and guilt over a situation that I couldn't have controlled hung over me for years, hurting me just as surely as did the man who victimized me. It took me years of soul searching to understand that I wasn't at fault for what had happened to me, and even more years to forgive myself for a crime I hadn't committed. And I have no interest in blaming myself further for what Ron Jeremy did to me—the infraction isn't nearly so grave, but my immediate desire to implicate myself in its root says volumes about how upsetting it was.

As is so often the case, hindsight is far clearer than the cloud of conflicting emotions experienced in the moment. Writing about it now, I'm feeling that too-familiar mixture of nervous energy, sweaty palms, and general greasiness that comes over me when I recall trauma. It may sound trivial to some, given that I was never in dire physical danger, but I can't state strongly enough how having one's agency forcibly removed can leave a person with a piercing sense of violation. My body hadn't really been harmed, but my dignity was bruised, along with my sense of physical autonomy. And my budding respect for porn stars was battered—not to mention my feelings for my friend and boyfriend, who'd stood by and watched.

And this is where it's important to note that the charges of second-wave, anti-porn feminism are not always wildly off target. Don't misunderstand me: The idea that all pornography is rape is patently ridiculous. I absolutely and unreservedly support any adult human being's participation in whatever non-harmful, consensual, sexual behavior they wish, and I do not think that the medium of pornography is inherently demeaning to women. At all.

But I *do* recognize that within the historically male-dominated culture of the porn industry, where performers are quite literally selling their sexual bodies as commodities for consumption, the slope down to seeing human beings as sexual commodities can get slippery. Male privilege in the social contract that allows pornography to place monetary value on female bodies *is* the same male privilege that allows certain members of the porn industry to see women as things to be used. Clearly not all of the men in the industry see the world this way: I don't believe that Sean Michaels, for instance, would *ever* have treated me with such disrespect. But I do think that, in my interactions with Mr. Jeremy, the male-privileged, female-objectifying mindset presented itself clearly. I was a thing to him—a thing that he could use to remind everyone present of his status. In his mind, my being there was reason enough to assume I wanted it.

Gross.

I do believe, however, that in the years between the Ron incident and the publication of this book, the landscape has changed significantly—both within the porn industry and without—when it comes to sexual misconduct. There has been a huge growth in public discourse about the difficult gray area in which I found myself with Ron that weekend: Issues like male privilege, slut-shaming, victim-blaming, and sexual autonomy have been discussed publicly and debated hotly in America and around the world.

Especially within the adult entertainment industry, efforts to highlight actor consent in everything from gonzo scenes to kink films have become more prevalent. Although porn has been maligned for teaching young men that "women always want it," the past few years have seen the industry taking pains to demonstrate otherwise. The fantasy aspect of pornography has been discussed in interviews, books, lectures, academic inquiries, panel discussions, and elsewhere as performers and consumers learn to tease apart the differences between what an edited porn scene shows an audience (what Seymore Butts described to me as "cut up and glorified and perfect"), versus the intense negotiations, heavy editing, and nitty-gritty reality of the performances. Many companies now shoot pre- and post-scene interviews to accompany sex scenes, featuring actors talking about what they're about to do, negotiating sex acts with each other, and enjoying the afterglow.

I think that if Ron Jeremy tried to gnaw on my neck without my consent today, I'd have the fortitude to rebuke him. And I think that I'd have the support of many people in the room if I did.

But back then? I tried to laugh it off. After all, it *was* a funny story, even if I broke into a sweat when I told it.

CHAPTER 10

Vegas and the Sex Toy Revelation

EXXXOTICA WENT SO WELL—my personal feelings about Ron Jeremy notwithstanding—that the *WHACK!* crew decided to go to Vegas for the Adult Entertainment Expo and the Adult Video News Awards. The porn industry's time-honored annual gathering was held every January at the Sands Expo Center at the Venetian Hotel and Casino in Sin City (though in recent years it has moved to the Hard Rock Casino, off the Strip) and 2010 seemed like the perfect time for *WHACK!* to make an appearance.

We talked the two lead actors from *pornocracy*, which we had continued to film on a shoestring budget, into paying for their flights in exchange for a free room in Vegas and a chance to hobnob with porn royalty on camera. The lead actress cashed in a long-standing offer from her grandmother for a free weekend stay at the Flamingo. We packed up our actors in an overcrowded taxi from Manhattan, shoved j. vegas's six-foot-four frame into an economy seat, and crammed all five of us into a two-queen room that smelled of cigarettes from the seventies. It wasn't glamorous, but it worked.

Our plan was simple: Use the two press passes we'd finagled for the expo on a rolling basis. We'd get two people in with the passes, then send one person back out with both passes, hand one off to another member of our crew, and sneak back in at a different entry point, until all five of us were wandering the show floor, looking for interviews to put in the magazine, porn stars to do cameo appearances for the show, and secluded corners quiet enough to film a few scripted scenes we'd planned for the trip. It was a racket, to be sure, but for a bunch of broke hopefuls squeaking by in New York, it was exhilarating. And, hey, nabbing the dubious title of skeeviest group at the porn expo? No small achievement.

The Adult Entertainment Expo was similar to Exxxotica in many ways—very loud, badly lit, and packed with every manner of perversion. But the booths were bigger, and there were considerably more of them. The premier producers had pulled out all the stops at their booths, with floor-to-ceiling banners sporting photos of their top stars and latest films. Early 2010 saw an upswing in big-budget adult film features, so there were themed booths and swag everywhere you looked. Porn parodies were on their way to the fore of the industry as well, so performers were wandering the show floor in costumes appropriate to their roles as pop culture icons. There were go-go dancers at every turn, a giant penis in the style of a mechanical bull, and even a few sex dolls modeled after porn stars hanging *Mission Impossible*-style from the ceiling. Several stages were set up throughout the hall, from which a parade of adult personalities drew crowds. Roving camera crews bumped into one another, camera equipment tangling. It was a veritable wall of sensory overload, making every pass through the show to find and interview a performer a complicated, tiring, and lengthy affair.

Our best bet was roaming the show floor without a clear target, then pouncing on unsuspecting porn talent at their signing booths. We quickly and happily discovered that with our press passes around our necks and cameras at the ready, we were rarely rebuked for cutting in front of signing lines. Taking full advantage of our credentials, we nabbed camera time with Andy San Dimas, Asa Akira, and Kaylani Lei, among others. I'd reviewed films starring most of my interviewees already, so I was able to ask pertinent and timely questions about recent performances. Most of the interviewees responded positively to my knowledge and were more than happy to talk. After two days of hitting the show hard, I felt pretty proud of myself. Well, proud and exhausted.

By the third day of our stay in Vegas, I was burned out on yapping with porn stars over the loud music, over-tired from late nights partying and long walks along the Strip, and completely *over* the convention. I left the show floor with our extra press pass in hand to go find Matthew. When we decided to take a previously untried door back in, we found ourselves in a smaller exhibition hall near the main show floor that I hadn't realized was there. And it was filled with sex toys. I had unwittingly stumbled into the Adult Novelty Expo, an affiliated sub-expo to the one I was there for and a free bonus in a weekend where free bonuses were basically feeding and housing me.

As we moved through the show floor, ogling the vibrators and butt plugs and whips and gags and paddles, a light bulb went off in my noggin. Free bonuses. Adult novelties. Adult industry *magazine* . . . that I wrote *reviews* for. *Free bonus adult novelties!*

I marched right up to the first booth I saw and started talking. I told the guy behind the table about the industry magazine I was writing for and my own expertise at reviewing sex toys and by the way would he be interested in getting a *free* review *from me*, Miss Lagsalot?

There's something about Vegas that can inspire even the least self-aggrandizing novices to become boldfaced braggadocios, and it had hit me. Little did I realize at the time that I was at the base of a swelling tidal wave of the adult industry's shift in the new millennium.

ALTHOUGH ARCHEOLOGISTS HAD BEEN collecting "ice-age batons" from dig sites for years and delicately avoiding publicizing their intended uses, a 2005 dig in a cave near Ulm, Germany caused too much of a stir to keep prehistoric phalluses under wraps any longer. In the Hohle Fels Cave, an eight-inch-long, inch-wide siltstone "baton" in the shape of a penis—with carvings near the wider tip that made its primary use obvious—forced the scientists in charge to admit that they had found the world's oldest confirmed dildo. The dildo (please excuse me while I gleefully overuse this term to counter all that "baton" nonsense) is estimated to be around twenty-eight thousand years old. That's the Paleolithic era, folks. Pieced together from fourteen separate fragments found around the cave, the dildo appears to have been abandoned after it shattered—one hopes not during use. Its ground and polished veneer was enough to convince researchers that, while it may have also been used to knap flint, it was most definitely meant for insertion into body cavities. For fun. Like a *dildo*.

This Stone Age diddling device was made in the same time period as the Venus figures that proliferated in Europe in the Paleolithic period (one of the earliest examples of which was actually found in the same cave), but whereas those were mere visual turn-ons, this was meant to complete the job. Other similar "batons" from later periods have been found worldwide made from antler, bone, leather, ivory, camel dung (coated in resin, but still . . . ew), and wood, as well.

And the phallic novelty train didn't stop in pre-recorded history—
not by a long shot. In ancient Greece, dildos, called *olisbos*, were standard issue for wives whose husbands were away at war, to prevent
female hysteria. The Greeks, you see, thought that women expelled
sperm-like "seed" at orgasm, like men. This was likely a misinterpreta-
tion of the common thick, milky vaginal excretion (lovingly dubbed
"cream" in modern parlance, and considered the only *confirmed* female
ejaculation by the scientific community—none of that "squirting" nonsense!) that often accompanies orgasm in women, and it was thought to
comingle with male ejaculate at conception. In ancient Greece, the theory was that if women did not expel their seed regularly, it would turn
toxic and lead to "hysteria," a dreadful ailment that could result in all
manner of symptoms. (A contradictory theory held that, if unused for
too long, the uterus could wander throughout the body, perhaps in
search of satisfaction, and cause blockages and disruptions. The word
"hysteria," as a result, has its roots in the Greek word for uterus.)
"Treatment" for this condition could be self-administered with an *olisbos*, or by a doctor stimulating a woman's pelvic region—usually by
hand, but sometimes with water or other means—until she climaxed.
This practice continued right up until the popularization of the vibrator
in the late nineteenth century in Europe.

But naturally, Europe was not the only place given to an appreciation
of phallic novelties: The dildo has a long and noble history in China, too,
where great men were known to keep wives, mistresses, and virtual
armies of concubines, all of whom were expected to stay faithful to the
one man in charge. Left with a lot of free time between conjugal visits,
these women were often gifted with dildos made of bronze and other precious materials to keep themselves company until the man of the house
could pay his next visit. In India, ivory and gold were employed for cer-
emonial defloflowering ceremonies in which a holy man would sometimes
penetrate a virgin on her wedding night to avoid besmirching her new
husband's penis with hymen blood.

A charming story from the last years of the BC era tells that the
forward-thinking Cleopatra filled a gourd with a swarm of bees, then
shook it. The buzzing of the angry insects inside provided a pleasant sensation that the queen quite enjoyed on her nether regions, and thus the
vibrator was born. Whether this story is true or not (and it's very likely

not), vibrations have long been known to titillate the sensitive organs between our legs. But it wasn't until 1734 in France that a mechanical apparatus for buzzing one's bits was invented—the Tremmoussoir was a handheld device that had to be wound up with a key, and which actually was quite a nice model. It never took off, however, and wasn't replaced until Victorian times, when hysteria became a prevalent medical condition in England and America. Doctors' hands were getting tired from delivering so many pelvic manipulations, so, in 1869, American doctor George Taylor patented the steam-powered "Manipulator," which reportedly took up an entire room but nevertheless got the job done. In 1880, Dr. Joseph Granville of London developed a smaller electric vibrator, and the field of sex toy development took off at a gallop from there.

When I hit Vegas in 2010, I was witnessing a groundswell that has since become a tidal wave of sex toy innovation and popularity. With the advent of easy online browsing, research, and purchasing, sex toy customers were now able to discreetly purchase—without the black-plastic-bag walk of shame from the sex shop—any sex toy they wanted. From the adult industry's perspective, consumer preferences were being illuminated by way of easily countable, trackable, and follow-up-able dollars being spent online. Sex toy customers, it became clear, wanted a variety of sex toys as diverse as their bodies and desires, and they wanted quality. And, now that buyers were at last able to contact manufacturers easily and privately via e-mail, discuss their purchases in online forums, review them, rate them, and demand more from them, something amazing happened: Consumers, especially women, became an active, vociferous, and lucrative demographic for the adult industry's novelty division.

Of course, women have always been on the lookout for sex aids, as my first incredulous experience with "Boner Beach" had so graphically shown me, and as the unflagging popularity of the Magic Wand "personal massager" has proven since the early 1960s. And once the sex toy industry learned how to market its wares to women in more palatable ways, women responded.

First of all, the landslide of opinion favored better design. Jelly dongs and lifelike phalluses had their place, of course, but it turned out that most consumers preferred something a bit less obvious. Something they could take on vacation without fear of embarrassment should their luggage be searched. Something they could show to their lover. Something, well, *pretty*.

Ergonomics, too, are a big draw for modern sex toy consumers. Devices that don't take a lot of explaining, are easy to use even in the throes of passion, and which won't make your hand or other body parts cramp up mid-session are attractive to the average consumer. Toys that can hit the G-spot or P-spot (the prostate) without contortions, or which can be removed easily from a butt without fanfare, are big winners. There's also a growing market of toys designed for disabled folks, sufferers of carpal tunnel syndrome, and people with larger bodies for whom some older designs were difficult—sexual pleasure for everyone! Hooray!

The democratization of 3D printing has vaulted the sex toy design field forward. Now that designs can be dreamed up and then made real in a short time by any company with a 3D printer, molds can be developed at low cost and new toys created in small or large batches faster than manufacturers a decade ago dreamed possible. Catering to even a small segment of the population that's looking for exactly what they're selling, small companies making everything from silicone dragon dongs to multi-sized ball gags on relatively miniscule scales are able to succeed because of the ease of manufacturing they can now command.

Today's sex toy shopper is also looking for the finest materials. The days of the cheap plastic dildo are long gone, as is the reign of the carcinogenic, phthalate-ridden butt plug. (As an interesting side note, I recently learned from Sarah Forbes's lovely memoir, *Sex in the Museum*, that the "adult novelty" title so often applied to sex toys came about because sex toy companies could "get away with selling . . . toxic items by simply attaching the word 'novelty,' implying that it shouldn't actually be used." Gross, right?) These days, the savvy consumer can find toys of medical-grade silicone, annealed glass, stainless steel, and other nonporous, nontoxic, body-safe substances. Many of these are on offer from manufacturers that take care to reveal as much about their production process as possible, some of whom go so far as to source their materials sustainably and power their production renewably.

And, of course, no matter how well a company has a specific customer pinned down ethics-wise, sex toy purchasers have bodies, desires, and sexual needs more diverse than anyone could expect. Variety is key to success in the sex toy industry, which means that as companies find their target demographic and work hard to supply it with what it needs, there is virtually always another demographic waiting for its turn. The diversity of human sexuality translates into an almost inexhaustible marketplace in which the only limit seems to be imagination. And as the means of production continue to democratize themselves with better technology and faster production, imaginations are running wild.

The latest development for many toys is a growing capacity for "smartness." That is, many adult novelties are now programmable or tech-responsive. Some have memories of their own that can record and play back your favorite vibration patterns. Others can be linked to an app that tunes the device into music. A few can be controlled remotely, enabling couples in far-flung corners of the world to maintain long-distance relationships with very real sexual intimacy. And there's an advancing arm of the industry specializing in pairing interactive webcam technology with sex toys that users on both ends can experience—some of which can be paired with virtual reality technology for a fully immersive experience. Every new advance in consumer electronics is up for grabs in the sex toy world, and sex-tech start-ups are taking off everywhere you look.

And then, of course, there are the porn tie-ins. Most sizable production companies now offer their own branded lines of sex toys, and porn stars sometimes have branded signature novelties under their name. Naturally, male porn stars like John Holmes and Lexington Steele have had their most famous body parts immortalized in rubber and silicone for years, but the big money in porn star genitalia reproduction these days has shifted to the ladies. The Fleshlight company got its start in 1998 with a simple masturbation sleeve cased in an oversized container that posed as a flashlight. The brand, however, rose to a stratosphere of stardom rarely experienced in the jerk-off-sleeve biz by contracting female porn stars to have their mouths, vulvas, and anuses molded, then re-created in Fleshlight's patented (phthalate-free!) secret material (using a proprietary molding goop that none of the models I've asked have been willing to divulge—I've heard a rumor that it employs seaweed or maybe algae, however). These Fleshlights are then made available for purchase by lusty fans worldwide. The Fleshlight Girls, as they're called (and now the Fleshjack Boys), are basically a roster of porn's hottest stars. Discerning fans can purchase their favorite model's most delicious orifice and pair it with one of a wide variety of inner textures, making for a virtually endless set of masturbatory possibilities. The Fleshlight is far and away the most popular sex toy line ever marketed exclusively to people with penises, and its easy tie-in to pornography's biggest names has made it an industry favorite. And, since the company is rumored to offer a fantastic royalty rate to models whose naughty bits are made into toys, everyone seems to win.

But the Fleshlight isn't the only rodeo in town for fans looking for up-close-and-personal experiences with their favorite performers: The RealDoll takes the concept to a completely new level. While blow-up dolls with porn star faces are nothing new, RealDolls are fully articulated, life-sized, silicone recreations of human sex partners. In addition to its fully customizable line of standard sex dolls, the RealDoll's manufacturer, Abyss Creations, has partnered with high-end porn producer Wicked Pictures to offer realistic recreations of its contracted models. That's right: For a mere seven to ten thousand dollars, Asa Akira—or at least a startling facsimile thereof—can really, truly be yours.

There are plenty of other toys for the be-penised individuals among us, many of which have nothing to do with porn stars, and that segment of the industry is really just getting started. The unprecedented growth of the industry in female- and gay-male-oriented toys has normalized the idea of sex toys in the average American bedroom, leaving many men more willing to experiment with sexual aids than they may have been in the past. Vibrators and dildos are increasingly designed for use by both sexes and all orientations. Strap-ons are getting more popular with people of all body types as "pegging" (penetration of a male-bodied partner with a strap-on) is becoming more mainstream. Masturbation sleeves not produced by Fleshlight are entering a new renaissance with the advent of smart technology that can turn an MP3 player or phone app or webcam session into an interactive experience. Many of these sleeves contain internal mechanisms that vibrate, squeeze, and pulse like the inner workings of a human orifice, and they're surprisingly sexy. (I know. I stuck my finger in a few at ANE in 2016.)

In short, the sex toy industry is booming, and it seems that everyone is benefiting. As of late 2015, the global sex toy market was estimated to generate $15 billion in revenue yearly, with projections neatly into the $20 billion range by 2020. Sex toys have become more accessible with online shopping and friendly, sex-positive brick-and-mortar stores, but they have also exploded as luxury items, with high-end brands like Lelo and Jimmyjane offering beautifully designed, ergonomic, body-safe "pleasure objects" at the top end of the market. Meanwhile, populist players like Trojan and Durex have been given shelf space in the "sexual wellness" aisles of CVS and Wal-Mart stores, next to the condoms.

Sex toys are more acceptable socially than they have ever been, with sex toy review columns hugely popular online, customer reviews proliferating on sales websites, and the so-called "passion party"—a sex-toy-selling party often held in private living rooms—taking off in suburban homes worldwide. Sex subscription boxes, like Unbound Box, The Pleasure Pantry, and The Nooky Box are cashing in on the subscription box craze and sending sexy goodies to subscribers in discreet packages on a rolling basis. Sex toy review blogs continue to proliferate, as more people of all ages and creeds catch on to the idea that writing openly about one's sex life can result in an embarrassment of sex toy goodies, much as I did back in 2010.

I WALKED OUT OF THE Adult Novelty Expo that day with bags full of hundreds of dollars' worth of sex toys. I'd exchanged information with numerous booth mavens and promised to be in touch about butt plugs, couples' vibrators, and a few complicated-sounding wireless devices. In short, I was in sex blogger heaven.

Today, I have an entire dresser filled to the brink with sex toys in my bedroom. It's become something of a conundrum during moves—it doesn't make sense to keep them all, but selling "lightly used" sex toys on the Internet seems like a rough path to travel, and offering them to friends puts me right into Creepazoid Territory.

Back in Vegas in 2010, I was just learning where the borders of that fabled land fell.

With Jenna Haze the first time we ever met, at Exxxotica New Jersey in 2009.
I was trying SO hard not to be a dork! Did it work? (PHOTO COURTESY J. VEGAS)

CHAPTER 11

Creepazoid Territory

I SHOULDN'T SAY THAT the borders of Creepazoid Territory are clearly defined. And far be it from me to judge books by their covers. But let me tell you that if one were to seek the fuzzy line between the creep and the non-creep, one might do well to look in a vague circle around the Adult Entertainment Expo in Las Vegas in mid-January.

I don't say this to be mean. In fact, I'm probably not even referring to the people you think I am. Sure, there *were* fans that fit the stereotypes: basement dwellers, oversexed couples trying to nail a porn star, guys who spent enormous sums on gigantic zoom lenses, and so on. But these folks were all at the convention for the same reasons I was—to rub elbows with porn stars—and I'm not here to denigrate them. After all, whatever is left of their paychecks after investing in Canon's latest ultra HD hooziewhatsit (I'm not much of a camera wiz) is poured into the porn industry's coffers at AEE. Without them the industry would be brought to its knees (I know, I know). Almost every porn star I've interviewed has declared their love for fans. In 2012 at AVN, Capri Anderson and I tried to film an on-the-spot interview ourselves, helped out by fans who stopped to hold up lights for us, unasked. "I feel a profound sense of gratitude for the following that I have," Capri told me, "and the support that I get from these people." Her devotion was heartwarming, but many among the porn fan flock are odd ducks, indeed.

An anecdote to illustrate my point: The Sands Expo Center didn't allow drinks on the show floor, so in the accommodating way of Sin City, the Venetian provided small bars just outside almost every entrance, in order that we might nurse our hangovers with overpriced and convenient Bloody Marys. On my third afternoon in Vegas, I stood in line at one of these pop-up bars marveling at the fans walking by. They were stupendous.

I took a break from my musings to gauge how long it would be until I could re-up on my vodka and tomato juice reserves, and realized that the man in front of me was perhaps the finest example of *Pornus conventionus sapiens* I'd ever spied: Resplendent in white sneakers, camouflage cargo pants, a flowing white poet's shirt, and shoulder-length, thinning, bleached-blond hair, he turned from the bar toward me and held his drink up with a smile. I beamed back, tickled to the bone that I'd encountered such a specimen, and imagined him that morning, regarding himself in his hotel mirror. He might have looked himself up and down, then nodded with gravity. "Yes," he may have told his reflection. "*This* is the outfit."

I shouldn't poke fun, though. If there's anything I've learned from porn, it's that this world truly is made up of *all* types, and they're all as necessary as they are different. Poet Shirt Guy may have raised eyebrows in almost any environment, but at AEE, he was an honored guest.

I have always been impressed at the respect that the porn community shows its fans. After all, many of the unknown quantities that keep people from feeling comfortable with one another are already cast aside when a porn fan meets a porn model: Active interest in sex? Confirmed. Accepting of various expressions of sexuality, particularly the kinky? Most likely. Willing to spend money on pornography? Let's find out.

With all the awkward stuff out of the way, the porn industry feels little need to spend time or energy judging those who support it. Perverts of all sizes, shapes, colors, creeds, and levels of ability are welcomed. In fact, I cannot think of any place I have ever been that is as welcoming to disabled people as a porn convention. Our dominant culture too often handles the visibly disabled with kid gloves, as if they don't experience the same emotions and desires as the rest of us. But the porn industry welcomes their patronage and is happy to treat disabled convention-goers as just more wonderful, money-spending, horny fans. Which they of course *are*. Why else would they be there?

There's one man in particular whom I have seen at numerous conventions. I don't know him personally, and I've had no luck tracking him down via expo contacts or Internet searches, but he's basically an expo celebrity. He has one of those ultra-high-tech, super-versatile wheelchairs, which he has tricked out like a Bond car. This guy rolls up to his favorite porn stars like a boss, inviting them onto his chair with him, and then performing feats of wheelchair acrobatics that draw a crowd, all with said porn star balanced on his lap. I've seen him perched many feet up in the air, executing all sorts of turns and tricks, while the model of his choice squeals and poses for the cameras, at every convention he attends. I'd imagine a man with that kind of charisma is likely a big deal wherever he goes, but I also imagine he gets quite a bit less recognition in his daily life.

As I said, humans of every type are welcomed in the world of porn, where the social contract that keeps most of us from taking off our clothes, or staring at those who do, has already been broken. It's freeing to be in a crowd of others who are self-proclaimed perverts, freaks, and weirdos, and I count myself happily among them. But the *nefarious* weirdos are rarely the fans.

I think it's worthwhile to point out these folks in their own segment because I want to establish that only a minority of my experience with pornographers has brought me into contact with people I'd consider creepers. They exist, and tend to cluster in certain parts of the adult entertainment field, but they are rarer than you might expect. I prefer to isolate them in this chapter rather than let them run amok throughout this book and give the impression that they have more influence than they really do.

The denizens of Creepazoid Territory are usually the hangers-on. There is a certain demographic that is drawn to porn by the allure of "sinful" activity, the illusion of easy money, and porn's often vague boundaries between the legal and the illegal. While none of these attractions are based entirely on false information, and while I suppose all of us who gravitate toward porn share one or two of them, some people are more driven by the idea that pornography is "bad" than others. Those who want to get away with "bad" things make up a not insignificant portion of the crowd at any porn convention. For instance, the would-be "agents" and "managers" who arrive accompanied by a bevy of heavily made-up women in tight dresses and high heels. These "agents" parade women around as if hawking wares at a flea market, no doubt hoping to attract the attention of porn directors on the lookout for new talent, but also invariably attracting the notice of private individuals on the lookout for company for the evening.

Now, I want to be clear that I am *not* opposed to escort work. The sale of sexual services among private individuals, in my mind, fills a real need that's been with us for as long as we've had a rudimentary barter system. It will never go away, no matter how much those in charge may be opposed to it, and as such it should be considered part of our economy. I think that sex workers of all kinds should be entitled to the same rights and legal recourse as everybody else in pursuit of making a living. The criminalization of prostitution in most of America leaves an already vulnerable population all the more open to persecution, prejudice, violence, and victimization. If it were legalized, I believe that much of the shadiness, exploitation, and fear that surrounds prostitution would eventually dissipate as sex workers felt safe enough to come out of the shadows that currently shroud them. If sex workers were able to speak up for themselves without fear of legal repercussions, they could advocate better for health and safety standards that they need and deserve.

That being said, the "agents" parading their female wares around at porn expos make me uncomfortable at best. Make no mistake: These "agents," here in Creepazoid Territory, are not the same as the agents that work above the board in the San Fernando Valley. The Licensed Adult Talent Agency Trade Association (LATATA) is a non-profit trade organization comprised of talent agents licensed by the state of California, with the goal of "assuring the longevity and well-being of the adult entertainment industry as a whole, while promoting the interests of the Artists and Agencies so working within it." Its nine members meet periodically and, to the best of my knowledge, represent the interests of their clients in a professional, legal, and legitimate way. (This isn't to say that their clients *don't* also do escort work, but that's a discussion for another time—like Chapter Nineteen.)

Perhaps their most well-known member, Mark Spiegler's agency, Spiegler Girls, is considered the best in the industry. His clients routinely book the best-paid gigs and go home with the biggest awards the industry has to offer. While many of his compatriots at LATATA represent hundreds of clients at a time, Spiegler is the tireless advocate of just twenty to twenty-five performers at once. He estimates that he turns down about two hundred hopeful clients a year in order to focus on acting as a mentor, counselor, and sometimes family member while fiercely representing the professional interests of his clientele. Companies know that a call to

Spiegler will pay off in the form of a sober, relatively on-time, experienced, and professional performer, and so they contact him instead of one of the skeevier so-called agents I'm calling out here.

Another LATATA member, Ideal Image Models, is headed by performer-and-producer-turned-agent Tee Reel. Reel prides himself on his professionalism and staying power. "In the adult industry, there are really only eight or nine reputable or bonded agencies," he told me in 2016. "Not everybody who's an agent or manager is really as reputable as they should be." He's proud to be among the few who have done the work of making a successful business as a talent agent in porn.

So when I talk about Creepazoid Territory, I'm not talking about the Mark Spieglers or Tee Reels of the world. These agents aren't licensed. They don't go to LATATA meetings. They operate with basically a pimp-and-prostitute mentality, and their clients can often be seen clinging to their arms in skimpy clothing while they're being looked over by convention-goers. They are often spotted having confidential conversations with men on the show floor or at nearby bars, and it takes very little in the way of imagination to understand the transaction that's going down. Many of these deals are made with the goal of producing pornography, but a lot of the porn that gets made on these skeevy deals is the kind that turns many viewers off of porn in the first place. The kind in which an inexperienced young woman signs paperwork before realizing that she was going to be put in a position she didn't want to be in.

There's one guy who sticks out in my mind when I contemplate Creepazoid Territory. He kept popping up over the course of Exxxotica weekend in New Jersey—at the convention, at the bar, in our hotel room. He dropped names at every opportunity, but never seemed to be interacting directly with the people he said he knew. He lingered on the outskirts of large gatherings of people, rarely entering the conversations, but watching them instead. At some point I saw him leer at one of the skeeze-ball "agents" walking by with a group of attractive women, then approach and speak directly to the man in the midst of the group. Later that night he mentioned to my colleague that he'd been booking some new talent. Turns out he was a "casting director" for a site whose name I won't give here, but which involved the mention of violent actions being enacted upon a specific body part of the females they employed for their scenes. It's perfectly okay to enjoy rough sex and participate in it on camera, but

I got the distinct impression that these women were being lured into something they would not enjoy doing, for far less money than they deserved, at the behest of their "agent," who would likely pocket more than the standard fifteen percent.

I'm calling out this kind of behavior not because I want to play into anybody's ideas of how nasty the porn industry can be, but because it's important that I not overlook those nasty corners that do exist. A lot of the rumors and scary stories you hear about pornography *are* true. I can't deny that exploitation, coercion, and gross behavior of many kinds does occur on porn sets and in porn industry interactions.

But the truth is that a very high proportion of these unpleasant realities exist far more on the fringes of the industry, off the beaten path of good lighting, fair pay, and great working conditions. Most in the industry abhor people who take advantage of models. Like director Ivan told me once, "Who are we to mistreat anyone? . . . I can't stand directors who mistreat the girls and better yet ask for special services [by] making girls feel that their job is on the line. Fuck those guys."

Anyway, it's not just the agents and casting directors that populate the Creepazoid Territory at the periphery of industry gatherings like Exxxotica and AEE. There are also the "managers." When we're in this dimly lit zone in which ethics are slippery, the difference between "agent" and "manager" can be nebulous, but in theory, there is a delineation of tasks for each role. Tee Reel explained to me: "By California law, which is where ninety percent of the agencies work, there's a legal difference . . . Legally, agencies are allowed to negotiate and procure work, and they can't charge more than twenty percent in California. Managers can charge whatever the fuck they want, but they can't book work and they can't charge a commission on that booking."

So, while the agent has at least a clear legal purpose in a performer's career—booking work—the manager's role is not so clear, and this can make for a lot of skeezy setups. There are plenty of real, legitimate managers in the porn industry, but there are just as many who are glorified boyfriends or hangers-on.

These guys (and they are almost always guys) are nicknamed "suitcase pimps" because they wheel the overstuffed luggage that female performers bring to sets and conventions (filled with sexy clothing for shoots, toys and lube, makeup, and so on), and because they collect the money those stars earn—just like a pimp. Of course, they're often just nice guys who want to help their girlfriends get to and from career engagements without breaking an ankle in those skyscraping heels. But a hefty proportion of "managers" are, instead, jealous types who try to cover their discomfort with their girlfriends' careers by making a living off them, and by forcing their louche presence into as many facets of those livelihoods as possible.

At conventions, they spend a lot of time standing directly behind the performers they work with, glowering at fans who approach, handling all the money that changes hands, and making everybody feel uncomfortable. In my experience, they are often large and muscle-bound, tend toward Ed Hardy couture, and sport a lot of neck tattoos. They don't talk much, and I suspect that many have worked as bouncers.

They're a staple of the industry, and they're largely innocuous, but there have been stories about "suitcase pimps" losing it and acting out their jealousy and insecurity on the bodies of the women they'd once protected. The most heinous example of this phenomenon was the brutal beating that porn star Christy Mack—a gorgeous, busty, tattooed powerhouse performer—endured at the hands of her ex-boyfriend and "suitcase pimp," the former MMA fighter War Machine. Months after they broke up, he arrived at her house in the middle of the night "to talk," became enraged when there was another man there, and spun out of control. The encounter left her with a blowout fracture of her left eye, several other broken bones in her face, two missing teeth, a lacerated liver, broken ribs, and serious bruising. (In early 2017, he was found guilty on twenty-nine of thirty-four charges in relation to the incident, and as of the time I'm writing this, he faces life in prison.)

Ex-porn actress Aurora Snow wrote in an article for *The Daily Beast* in the wake of the horrific Christy Mack incident that, "Yes, most of us in the adult industry have experienced the stereotypical porno dude who becomes the 'manager.' He books your work, drives you to set, wheels your suitcase in, helps you collect your check and, of course, spends it. Along with all this comes a certain possessiveness; these manager-boyfriends begin referring to you as their property, and a sense of ownership is created."

I don't mean to imply that all adult industry managers are ticking time bombs of horrific viciousness just waiting to go off, of course. Far from it—

most performers who work closely with their boyfriend/managers never experience anything remotely akin to what Christy Mack did, thank goodness. But, at conventions, I try to give men with neck tattoos a wide berth.

A good chunk of the guys who position themselves as amateur agents or managers for inexperienced women have an ulterior motive besides skimming from their clients' profits and controlling their bodies: They want to perform, themselves. Because it's so difficult for men to break into straight porn, many aspiring guys will hitch their carriage to women who could do well, then talk those women into requesting to work with them on camera. If it goes well, they may be able to stick around as woodsmen. Many a fixture in the porn industry got his start this way, which is to say that not all men who attach themselves to female talent are necessarily scummy. But still, ulterior motives are ulterior motives. (Perhaps incidentally, War Machine appeared in twelve adult films during the course of his relationship with Christy Mack.)

Rounding out the population of the porn expo Creepazoid Zone, I must be careful not to forget the industry groupies. This is a motley crowd comprised of miscellaneous hangers-on: party promoters, low-level rappers and rockers who want to up their "cool" cred, models from other industries sizing up their chances as porn stars, drug dealers, pro- and anti-porn activists, and, of course, journalists.

Like me and the *WHACK!* crew.

I'd be negligent not to count myself as one of the spongers. After all, here I am, an outsider with stars in her eyes, showing up at industry events with a microphone in hand and trying to get Internet famous. It's been pointed out to me by at least one prominent porn star that I'm basically standing on the bare backs of adult actors to make a living, and I can't deny there's truth in that. But I will defend myself by mentioning that I've never made anything close to a "living" on writing and reporting on pornography—I have always worked full-time at other jobs, occasionally eking extra cash out of my porn reporting career, but more often using the money I made at my full-time gigs to support my porn-reporting habit.

But that's not the point. I won't deny that I'm too afraid to take off my own clothes on camera, yet I'm happy to stick a camera in the face of someone who *does* and ask them about their life. I've always told myself that the work I do seeks to humanize the people of the porn industry, normalize the work they do, and give them some positive PR in a world that enjoys scorning them. But I also want to get into the after-parties. And so did my cohorts at *WHACK!*

The groupie mentality of the *WHACK!* pack was displayed for all the world to see at the 2010 AVN Awards, the culmination of the previous year in porn. *WHACK!* had been unable to get press passes to the event itself, or even to officially cover the red carpet extravaganza preceding it, so we all trucked over to the Palms, where the awards ceremony was then held, and found a spot on the wrong side of the velvet ropes. We were surrounded by rabid fans, drunk frat boys who'd wandered over from the strip, cameras of every shape and size. But, sadly, we were not surrounded by other reporters, because the legitimate ones had mostly gotten onto the red carpet itself, where rock stars and porn luminaries conducted video interviews with the porn glitterati as they swept up the carpet in their gorgeous duds. We got a few quick poses from some of our favorite stars: Jenna Haze and her then-boyfriend Jules Jordan, Joanna Angel and her crew of alt models, sweetie pie supreme Teagan Presley, a few of the new acquaintances we'd made over the weekend, and gonzo director Ivan in his finest hockey jersey, furry hat, and matching kicks. But for the most part we were overlooked like the insignificant hangers-on we really were.

That sucked. After the hubbub died down and the AVN Awards got under way, we wandered off toward the strip and decided to console ourselves with a few drinks at the Circus Circus Casino, the location of one of the most memorable passages from Hunter S. Thompson's *Fear and Loathing in Las Vegas*, during which Doctor Gonzo and Raoul Duke take ether and attempt to board and then disembark the casino's famous rotating Carousel Bar. Matthew, vegas, and I found the bar, which was surrounded by confusingly family-friendly carnival games, where kids with cotton candy puffs in hand squealed over their chances to win oversized stuffed animals. Freaked out by the unexpected family dynamic, we boarded the Carousel Bar without much trouble, and set about sipping watered-down drinks while a trapeze act took place far over our heads. It was delightfully weird, but as it turned out, the bar didn't spin very fast, the drinks were too expensive, and we were all too exhausted to enjoy ourselves after our unsatisfying go at the AVN red carpet. We felt like the groupies we were as we sat at the disappointingly real bar, spinning slowly in a vestige of Vegas's golden age.

The AEE convention and the AVN Awards are much like the Circus Circus, really: glittering homages to a bygone age. Every year, AVN week in Vegas gets smaller and more sparsely attended, as the industry reinvents itself in the Internet age—smaller, sleeker, more spread out, and less tied to the same old places it used to hang out at. In 2016, Tee Reel told me about the good old days: "I remember going to my first AVN Awards at the Sands and staying at the Bellagio, and companies having black cars and renting, not even rooms, but whole *floors*."

It's always sad to watch an institution of debauchery like AVN Week—and, similarly, old Vegas standards like the once wild Circus Circus—lose face and luster as times change. And yet nowhere is this fading more fitting than in the porn industry, where meteoric rises and falls of boners and careers and companies and trends are standard. Times change faster than any industry—pornography or casino gaming—can predict, and anyone who's not fully prepared to cash in on the next big thing is bound to miss a winning shot. The Internet has altered the porn landscape more drastically than anyone could have predicted back in the nineties, when adult entertainment reached its apex and AVN week in Vegas reached maximum glamor.

Things change fast these days, and irrevocably. Case in point: Four months after our visit to the Carousel Bar at the Circus Circus, it was turned into a snack bar. In keeping with the family-friendly feel of the casino, the redubbed Horse-A-Round Snack Bar now serves gelato, popcorn, and lemonade rather than the whiskey the *WHACK!* staff downed that night, quiet and tired, until the bar closed around 11:00 p.m.

CHAPTER 12

The New Girl

BACK IN NEW YORK in early 2010, my life had taken on a surreal quality. For the book I was trying to ghostwrite, I was still attending swinger parties—sometimes alone and sometimes with Matthew or friends from the swinging community. I didn't participate in the action beyond a few make-out sessions, but I watched a *lot* of live sex. It was an odd parallel to my porn reviewing career, which was continuing apace at the print magazine for which I watched a lot of hardcore gonzo porn, and at *WHACK!* for which I was tending more toward feature films and parodies.

It confused and disturbed me that, although I was frequently surrounded by sex and by prospective sex partners, my interest wasn't piqued by much. It had, however, been *quite* piqued by a good friend, who we'll call Jenn. She and her fiancé, who we'll call Adam, had moved in downstairs from Matthew and me in Harlem, and now the four of us got together once a week or so for video games, movies, food, weed, and booze. Jenn and I had been growing closer, and when she and Adam showed interest in the swinger parties I was attending, Matthew and I decided to invite them to one. Things got intense at the party, and I walked away from the encounter with the rather surprising understanding that I had a massive crush on Jenn.

As my understanding of non-monogamous relationships and my own sexuality deepened, I began to consider that my long-term relationship with Matthew might not be the only one I could maintain. So, after some very long conversations with Matthew, Jenn, and Adam, as well as some more fooling around, Jenn and I started formally dating. It was an interesting dynamic between the four of us. Matthew and Adam were in no way interested in each other, and Matthew wasn't interested in Jenn, either.

But he wasn't opposed, he said, to *my* relationship with her. Soon, Jenn and I were going on dates and spending nights together.

And so, I became polyamorous. And I felt really good about it. I also felt good about really exploring my sexuality. Now that I was getting a look at the wide world of sex on film and at sex parties, I realized that gender wasn't really an issue for me at all. If Jenn had been a man, or a transgender woman, or any other gender at all, I would have been magnetized just the same. When I interviewed Sophia St. James, a gorgeous, buxom queer porn star, she told me, "for me, being queer means that I'm an equal opportunity lover. I enjoy many different sexualities and many different genders . . . Queer can also, for me, mean that you've taken your sexual realm and identity outside of the societal, heteronormative views of what sex should be." These ideas were directly in line with my evolving understanding of myself, and when I began dating Jenn seriously, it occurred to me that I wasn't really bisexual—attracted to two specific genders as I'd considered myself for years. I am queer—attracted to whatever gender a person who interested me happens to be.

ON THE PORN-REPORTING front, I was trying to keep up with a seemingly endless roster of "new girls" in adult entertainment. Publicists had gotten wind of *WHACK!* and wanted their clients interviewed, but no matter how many Q&As we conducted, there was always a brand-new actor to talk to. That night at the Circus Circus kept popping up in my head. In just a few short years I'd seen several merry-go-rounds of adult talent whiz by, each new wave of up-and-comers ready to reinvent the carousel.

I doubt that any industry, except maybe food service, has a quicker turnover rate than porn. And I'd be willing to bet that porn has the most spectacularly meteoric career trajectory, with new talent rising through the ranks in the blink of an eye, spending a few months at the glamorous top, then opting out—often in a crash-and-burn fashion. When I started writing about the industry in 2007, the estimate for the average female porn performer's career was an eighteen-month blitz. But by the time I attended the XBIZ industry conference in Los Angeles in early 2016, panelists were saying that most new female talent only lasted three or four months.

This incredible career brevity is due to a number of variables: Many young people use the sex industry as a way to make quick cash, moving on when their debt is satisfied, school finished, or purchase made. Others try it to sow their wild oats—they get some kicks, but never plan on staying. Plenty have their sights set on fame and fortune, but then realize that porn is more difficult than they'd imagined and abandon the idea.

And of course, some actors are quickly disillusioned by bad experiences with unscrupulous producers, agents, or costars. Performer Mickey Mod told me once, "It's really a misconception that everyone in this industry is exploited. But it is true that sometimes people can get taken advantage of," particularly when they are being pressured by "someone who may have a financial interest in their performance or their career path." For many who experience manipulation or coercion of this kind, careers in porn don't last long.

And it's important to realize that, pop culture's fascination with successful porn stars' glamorous lives aside, it's not easy to achieve success in smut. Performer Mandy Morbid told me once, "It's hard to support yourself in porn unless you're willing to take almost every job that comes along," and not every job is worth a performer's time. Careers are difficult to sustain, after the initial burst of work during which many female performers find money practically falling into their laps. New girls in porn are human commodities the likes of which simply do not exist in other industries. In an interview for *WHACK!*, performer Sheena Ryder told me, "They're just letting girls get off the bus and putting them through [the industry] on like conveyor belts"—and those conveyor belts serve as the industry's main artery to relevance. Both novelty and youth are hugely popular in terms of human arousal worldwide, and new girls usually possess both of these attributes; as a result, they are coveted by pornographers and consumers alike.

There's a standardized trajectory for a new porn model to follow with regards to the sex acts she performs on camera, with pay rates escalating along with the level of "hardcore" acts she's willing to engage in. This trajectory isn't one-size-fits-all, and it's falling out of fashion as the industry shrinks and new performers enter the biz already savvy about choosing their own career paths. But the step-ladder ascent of yesteryear was quite structured, as Tee Reel explained in a 2016 interview: "Ten years ago, there were dozens of solo companies, and anal companies, and interracial companies," he said. "The list goes on and on and on. At that time, the attitude of agents, from a business perspective was, 'I can bring a girl in in January and have her do solos or girl/girl work for an entire year.'"

(An important note: Although many of these girl/girl scenes are marketed as "lesbian" scenes, they are called "girl/girl" within the industry because female performers are expected to be "gay for pay." A higher percentage of porn performers self-report as bisexual than in the rest of the population, so rarely do girl/girl scenes involve partners who are truly repulsed by vulvas, but these scenes are nevertheless not considered "gay." Also worth noting: Scenes between clearly not-gay women in mainstream porn aren't hard to find, and they are just as disappointing as you would expect.)

Tee Reel continued in his hypothetical porn star progression: "'When she's shot out with those [girl/girl] companies, the next year she can do boy/girl. And I can probably up the price and get more money out of a production company for her first boy/girl. So she's shooting boy/girl for the next year. And then maybe I can stretch it out for another year for her first anal in year three. And then in year four, maybe I can stretch it out for interracial.' It was a business decision."

This master list of on-camera firsts, and the order in which they happened, is becoming outmoded. Now, there are only a fraction of the number of companies shooting any of the above types of content, so Tee Reel told me that a model entering the industry in January would be able to work with every girl/girl, boy/girl, anal, *and* interracial company by March—three months after she started. There's not much of a point putting off boy/girl scenes for all of the two weeks it would take to work with every girl/girl company.

Moreover, the new millennium has brought with it a bit more candor around sex in America (linked arm-in-arm, of course, with easy access to its visual depictions vis-à-vis the Internet) than existed when a first-time anal scene was a game-changer for a new performer's career. Fewer hang-ups around sexual taboos have liberated many porn actors from compunction about jumping into double-penetration scenes right out of the gate, if they want to try them.

No matter the placement of sexual landmarks in a performer's career —whether she climbs the new-girl ladder rung by rung or plunges right into the deep end of the pool—the pay remains scalable: She will be paid more for a hardcore gangbang than a girl/girl spanking scene, no matter how many times she's done either in her private life. But it's important to point out that pay rates are by no means standard across the industry. Pay is governed by supply and demand, the depth of a producer's pockets, the star power of the performer in question, and the difficulty of the shoot. Naturally, more established companies with bigger budgets can afford to pay more. But also naturally, that doesn't mean that they *will* pay more. Smaller companies with more to prove might be willing to offer more to get the model they want doing the scene they're looking to capture.

But pay does average out across the industry, as agents and producers need to work together to meet their bottom lines. Sadly, rates have fallen precipitously as online piracy has devoured the fat around the middle of the industry. Mark Spiegler told *The Hollywood Reporter* that the average porn star had made around a hundred grand a year in 2002, but that by 2012 he estimated that average had been cut in half. Of course, his clients generally command higher rates and pull in more than the average performer. Spiegler Girls can earn two thousand dollars or more for their scenes, while rates for boy/girl scenes pay most female models between seven and fifteen hundred dollars.

Another detail worth noting when it comes to performer pay is that it's very different for male talent. In a country where women in other industries make seventy-nine cents (or less, depending on race, age, and ability level) per male dollar for the same work, this discrepancy is worth pointing out with an extra-pointy finger. Guys in straight porn earn only about five hundred dollars per scene, on average, with newbies getting blowjobs making as little as fifty bucks and bigger names pulling in up to five *thousand* dollars for a scene. But those at the top tier may find themselves doing a limited amount of work, since most studios either can't or won't pay their rates.

But let's get back to the new *girl*, and what happens once she ceases to *be* a new girl. Once all interested companies have filmed what they wanted and she's checked off all of the boxes on her to-do list of sex acts, she will find that work slows down. She's got fewer "firsts" to offer producers, she's worked with most of the people she wanted to, she's figured out whom and what she enjoys on camera, but now there's another brand-spanking-new crop of fresh faces arriving in the Valley, ready to climb the ladder she just traversed.

Kelly Shibari summed it up neatly for me in an interview: "In the be-

ginning, when you get in, you're the new girl, and so you're friendly with
everybody, and you go to all the events, and you go to all the night clubs,
and you go to all the signings. That whole first year, everything's amazing. It's perfect. Then the second year happens, when you don't get as
much work . . . By the third year, a lot of girls have either decided if
they're going to stick it out or if they're just done."

When a new face is no longer new enough to ensure constant work,
it's time to make a decision: Take a stab at a career by building one's
brand and really going for it? Or bow out, take whatever money is in the
bank, and get a different job? Many pick one of these options, but there
is also a contingent of models working in porn today who have chosen a
mix of the two. They've found that porn can pay some of the bills, but
often not all of them. Some performers have other jobs to supplement
their income, or see porn itself as the supplement.

FIVE DAYS AFTER MY twenty-seventh birthday, on which I had been able
to enjoy some of the sexual excess that my polyamorous, swinger-party
attending, porn-reviewing lifestyle might suggest, I received an e-mail
from someone named Lindsay who worked in development for a television production company in Los Angeles. She had become a fan of my
column at *McSweeney's*, she said, and was interested in setting up a meeting. Five days later, I left a night class early (growing tired of being a receptionist, I was pursuing a certificate in publishing) and hid out in an
adjunct professor's office while I took the scariest, most exciting phone
call of my life. I told myself to be calm, take the call, and try not to pee
my pants.

Unfortunately, I *really* had to pee when the phone rang. I didn't know
where the bathroom in that part of the building was, and I didn't want to
miss the call or be forced to answer the phone in mid-stream, so I had to
hold it. Have you ever had to urinate so badly that your brain can no longer
process information? Combine that sensation with an elevated breathing
rate, quickened pulse, dilated pupils, and overexcited shivers, and then
pair all of that physical inundation with the scattered brain of someone
who's been anticipating a possibly life-changing phone call for days.

All things considered, it makes sense that I barely remember the phone
call. It was me on one end, with the President of Television for the com-

pany, the woman who had initially contacted me, and someone else whose title now escapes me conferenced in. All three of them were friendly but to the point: They were *extremely* interested in turning "The Conflicted Existence of the Female Porn Writer" into a television pilot based on my life. They wanted to fly me to LA to meet their team, and, seeing as I didn't have proper representation for an offer as serious as this, they wanted to introduce me to agents while I was visiting, so that they could get to work on a contract *immediately*.

I said yes. To everything.

Then I got off the phone and found a bathroom.

A FEW WEEKS LATER, I arrived in LA. I'd been to northern California before, but never LA. I'd never seen the rows of tall, spindly Pacific palm trees lining the boulevards or experienced the balmy March weather or been able to see the Hollywood sign from a luxurious—paid for—hotel room. I felt like I was in the kind of dream that's so fantastic it's dogged by the certainty that at any moment one might wake up, bereft.

For three days I was the center of a whirlwind of cab rides, coffee, and meetings with television developers and producers, literary and television agents, lawyers, other writers. I was complimented more times in the span of seventy-two hours than I had been in the five years previous, and I got the not-unpleasant impression that rainbows were being beamed up my ass. The agents I met with were fast-talking and driven: They wanted me to be the next Carrie Bradshaw, writing whimsical columns in much more expensive apartments wearing much more expensive shoes than I currently did. I got the taste of magenta glitter in my mouth.

As really nothing more than a literary dork with a more interesting part-time job than most, I was bewildered. I saw my TV doppelgänger as a blundering, sarcastic type who wore old funky sweaters, watched sci-fi, and shopped at the discount store on her block, but these people were envisioning a club girl in stilettos who shopped at stores whose names I didn't know how to pronounce. I wasn't opposed, necessarily, to a marriage of the two, particularly if it meant that I *got* a TV doppelgänger, but neither did I want to be treated like something I was not.

The thing about LA, I discovered, was that it moves just as fast as New York, but the people are more concerned with fluffing each other's egos than talking business. After only a few short days, I had a head the size of a Volkswagen. I had an entertainment lawyer. I had the private numbers of some of the hottest agents in town. Everyone had wanted a piece of the shiny new penny—I think one of the agents actually called me that during our meeting. If I could keep up this momentum, I told myself, I could be *rich*. (Or at least richer than my receptionist-and-writer life had thus far made me.) And if a TV show were made based on my life, I could be *famous*.

It was so *easy*.

In my New Yorker's heart of hearts, though, I knew that it was *too* easy. I could hope for all these dreams to come true based on the strength of the columns I had written for *McSweeney's*, but I'd better not count on any of it. None of the people I talked to in LA admitted to having read my reviews or seen any of my interviews. I had no experience handling people who made million-dollar deals; I worked *for* those people as a receptionist. I knew how to be subservient to their whims, but I had no idea how to have my *own* whims, much less enforce them. The only people I knew who had any kind of experience with this particular breed of madness were porn stars.

I imagined myself navigating LA via the porn industry instead of Hollywood as a new girl. I'd been told by agents and producers alike that I was attractive—now I imagined being told that by people who were paying me for it. Even now, squarely in my mid-thirties and having spent a solid decade writing about feminist thought, action, and community, it's impossible for me to overstate the impact of being told that I'm pretty. For whatever reason—societal or biological or something else—there are very few women I know who will *ever* get tired of physical compliments. And I'm in no way exempt from this phenomenon. A few Hollywood types commenting on my attractiveness was enough to have me envisioning myself living a bicoastal lifestyle with large, sunny apartments in New York and LA. I couldn't fathom how I'd be feeling if those people were instead complimenting me on the way my ass looked in boy shorts or how enticing they found my smile. In the porn industry, I realized, I'd have followed the same trajectory as any other model until that new-penny sheen wore off. As far as I could see from my first interactions with Hollywood, show business was show business—compliments, coffee, and the whiff of easy money—no matter which LA industry you were working in.

The agents also told me that they were excited by my connections in porn. They wanted to know if actual pornographers would be interested in doing television appearances. Would porn stars talk to me for the book I was clearly going to write—a memoir, perhaps, with a glittery magenta cover? Not wanting to show all my cards, I told the agents that I could likely pull some strings and get porn stars on my TV show and in my book. I tried to make it sound as if this would be an insider's job that only I could pull off. They looked pleased and jotted notes.

But inside I was appalled. Some part of me had been holding out hope that the divide I'd perceived between the "us" of the mainstream world and the "them" of the porn community wasn't as wide or as deep as I feared. Surely, I'd let myself think, in Los Angeles, where the Hollywood elite live and work and shop and eat right next to porn workers, there's more overlap than I'd seen. Less division. More acceptance.

But at the talent agencies and the production company, the chasm between the industries yawned wider than it did from my far-flung perch in New York, where the sheer density of human beings forces divides to narrow. The porn industry exists in literally *the same city* as Hollywood. There is porn being filmed all over Los Angeles all the time, especially in 2010. There was no actual geographical divide between the daily lives of most Angelenos and their porn-making brethren. The divide existed only in the human mind, but the Hollywood folks believed it was real.

What made this divide even more curious was the fact that in 2010, the perpetual itch of both industries to cross the gap was at a particularly feverish pitch. The height of the celebrity sex tape phenomenon coincided almost perfectly with the peak of the porn industry's analogous crossover madness. And the intermingling of mainstream and adult entertainment is sometimes even more literal than "leaked" sex tapes. Reality TV shows are no stranger to porn stars, and neither are many major networks' on-line series. Late-night cable TV has long shared cast lists with adult films. I had heard lots of whispers about A-listers crossing the divide to spend their Hollywood cash with porn stars at clubs and private parties. In fact, in an interview with *WHACK! Magazine*, rock star Dave Navarro told me in no uncertain terms that he'd been intimate with a few porn stars. And yet, in the same city in which he lives, I'd watched agents' eyes light up at the prospect of getting a real, live porn star on their contact lists. It was bizarre.

At that same time, maybe unbeknownst to the agents and producers I met with, mainstream entertainment and other industries were already opening up significantly to crossover talent coming from the porn industry. Nikki Benz, who I interviewed for *WHACK!* in 2011, was that year's Penthouse Pet of the Year—the first porn star to earn the distinction—and, when I spoke to her, she had just signed a contract for her third year on the show *Cubed* on Fox Sports Network. She told me that she didn't see her crossover work as an outlier: "I feel that porn, and the whole adult industry, is a part of pop culture right now," she said. "It's very popular, and it's not taboo anymore."

When I met with agents in LA in March of 2010, porn star Sasha Grey had just starred in acclaimed director Steven Soderbergh's film *The Girlfriend Experience*. Although critics weren't sure what to make of her performance, the porn industry was beside itself with excitement at seeing one of its own making such a splash in the mainstream. Grey was one of the youngest, brightest, and most bankable actors in the adult film industry, having forgone the standard "new girl" ascent up the ladder of sex acts by performing in a gangbang in her first-ever sex scene at age eighteen. She then astonished fans with her intelligence in interviews, continued to turn in scenes with blazing sexual intensity, and won the coveted AVN "Performer of the Year" award in 2008 as the youngest woman ever to receive the accolade. A few months after my trip to LA, still high on her *Girlfriend Experience* success, she started an ongoing role on the successful TV series *Entourage* and summarily retired from porn about a year later. Since then, she has continued to work in mainstream entertainment as a successful—if no as longer wildly hyped—actor, voice actor, artist, musician, and author.

Grey's crossover success was notable for many reasons, including the relatively high profile she earned on the other side of the porn/mainstream divide. Many who attempt to make the same leap find themselves strapped to far-less-notable vehicles, like B horror movies, badly-edited memoirs, and music videos. Jenna Jameson, perhaps the most famous crossover star of all, arguably never crossed much of a divide, at least as far as her industry affiliation was concerned. She became world famous entirely on the merits of her porn career. There's nothing wrong with that, especially because she paved a path for others to follow. As adult director Ivan said in an interview, "Some porn people become novelties that are thrown into mainstream world just for being a 'porn star.'"

But Sasha Grey broke that mold by being regarded by many as not a porn star who could act, but as an *actor* who had done porn. While she may not have landed blanket approval from the big guns in Hollywood, she was perhaps the first porn star to be taken moderately seriously by the *other* film industry in LA. But she was not the last.

James Deen actually started in porn earlier than Sasha Grey, but as a man working in the straight industry, his star was not as quick to rise. There is no "new guy" phenomenon analogous to the "new girl" trajectory in straight porn. Men are the workhorses, expected to be experienced from the get-go, with little added stigma attached to the sex acts they film (unless they're perceived as "too gay"—but we'll talk about that later). Deen got started in 2004 and worked steadily in the industry for years before he gained widespread attention. He had, in fact, appeared in an issue of the first magazine I wrote for back in 2008. There was no fanfare over the set of double-penetration photographs he posed for, and though I'm sure he crossed my radar in some of the films I reviewed, he didn't interest me until he won his first "Male Performer of the Year" AVN award in 2009.

Around that time, a peculiar thing had begun to happen: Women watching porn started to take note of his average physique, his guy-next-door charm, and his chemistry with his costars. They started to talk about him. To tell their friends. To create fan pages. I noted the stir he was creating and sought him out for an interview in mid-2010, looking to cash in on his budding reputation as the thinking woman's male porn star. We exchanged e-mails, and the responses he gave were friendly, sort of funny, but not clever or interesting. When I asked him how he'd gotten so successful, he just said, "I'm the luckiest boy alive."

Despite his retiring nature, women all over the world started to seek out his work. And, significantly, they started *paying* for it. If I've said it once, I've said it a million times: Porn producers will do what makes them money. When they started to realize that not only was the cute, personable Deen a reliable performer, but also a guarantee of financial success, a singular phenomenon began to occur: He got *really* famous. Not just male-porn-star, Ron-Jeremy famous. I mean legit *famous*. I mean costarring-with-Lindsay-freaking-Lohan-in-*The-Canyons*-written-by-Bret-Easton-Ellis, mainstream, Hollywood famous.

And it was all because *women liked him.*

The importance of this distinction cannot be overstated. Not only was Deen breaking down barriers between pornography and mainstream entertainment, he was doing it on the good graces of women who enjoyed depictions of enthusiastic consent in their porn. There was no icky ambiguity—even in the kink and hardcore scenes he was known for—about whether his costars were enjoying what they were doing. He told me in our interview, "When it comes to sex I think it is all about communication and connection." This line of thinking made feminist porn consumers feel safe watching him perform and, more importantly, paying for the privilege.

I also watched his rise to fame with curiosity because, as early as 2011, I had begun to hear vague and unpleasant rumors about him. Nobody said exactly why, but there were some in the industry who gave him a wide berth. Those who knew him well clammed up when his name was mentioned. There were a few terse utterances of "I don't want to talk about James Deen" and "that guy gives me the creeps" and even, once, "he has dead eyes." A friend of mine, who had become close with numerous performers, including Deen's then-girlfriend and industry legend Joanna Angel, mentioned several times how horrendous their breakup in 2011 was, but didn't elaborate.

On the merits of these foggy rumors, I avoided Deen. While I sensed a dark story beneath the golden-boy reputation, I wanted just as much as anyone else to believe that he was as good as he seemed, which, it turns out, he was not.

ON NOVEMBER 28, 2015, porn star, writer, and performance artist Stoya wrote two tweets that broke the Internet: "James Deen held me down and fucked me while I said no, stop, used my safe word. I just can't nod and smile when people bring him up anymore."

Porn's biggest "power couple" in 2013 and 2014, Stoya and Deen had broken up quietly and gone their separate ways, occasionally working together for their own fledgling production companies after their break. So, more than a year after their split, the social media bomb went off unexpectedly and set off an avalanche. Joanna Angel sided with Stoya almost immediately, then went on to tell the story of her six-year relationship with him as one of perpetual abuse, both physical and emotional. And the flood gates burst.

Those vague rumors I'd been catching whiffs of for years came spilling out in horrific detail as twelve other women in and around the adult industry came forward with their own harrowing accounts of sexual misconduct, abuse, and assault at the hands of Deen. The stories ranged from off-set assault to on-camera brutality to flat-out rape. His dark reputation, it seemed, was a not-very-well-kept secret in the industry. But he was a powerful man with a sterling image in the outside world. He was profitable, reliable, and wildly popular. And so the women he assaulted kept mostly quiet, sometimes appealing to directors and studio heads for recourse, sometimes simply trying to forget about it.

But in the aftermath of these horrendous accusations and blossoming sickness in the pits of stomachs both in the adult industry and without, something just as amazing as Deen's initial rise to fame happened. Instead of a too-familiar Bill Cosby scenario, in which the motivations of the women alleging abuse were questioned and discredited, pornographers quickly (though by no means unanimously) sided with Deen's alleged victims. Companies and performers canceled shoots and contracts with him. The press interviewed the women speaking out against him and published their words, rather than twisting them into unreliable-sounding bits of copy. Discussions of consent in pornography ricocheted around the Internet, and many in the industry vowed to rethink their policies around consent on- and off-set.

The fallout continues to rain down on the industry as of me writing this, but no legal actions have yet been taken against Deen. And sadly, though the industry seemed to have abandoned the popular actor, "the well-hung boy next door" is still working steadily in porn. He's been producing more of his own films and working less with other companies, as fewer are willing to hire him, and fewer women are willing to work with him. But while his name appears to have been tarnished, especially amongst the feminist community, his sexual skills have not. In an industry that prizes the rare men who can handle the rigors of the job, his abilities seem to have spoken louder than his alleged transgressions.

With Asa Akira in the VIP booth at a strip club in New York City

(PHOTO COURTESY J. VEGAS)

With one of my biggest porn crushes, James Darling, at the Feminist Porn Awards in 2014, with Carlyle Jansen photobombing

(PHOTO COURTESY OF THE AUTHOR)

CHAPTER 13

Editor in Chief

IN SHORT ORDER, I SIGNED with William Morris Endeavor and began contract negotiations—through my newly acquired TV agents (one in New
York and one in LA), literary agent, and entertainment lawyer—to write
a television pilot based on my experiences in and around the porn industry. The production company was keen to find me a co-writer with more
experience writing scripts than I had, which is to say *any* experience.
They wanted the writing and production staff to be entirely female, and
I eagerly agreed, but that slowed the process down. As it turns out, finding a female television writer is difficult enough. Landing one who wants
to work with a newbie on a show about pornography? Even tougher.

The "new girl" glamor I'd briefly enjoyed died off quickly when I
turned down the other agents; I felt the goodwill dry up, and I hoped to
lean on the agents I'd signed with to bolster my self-esteem. But after one
quick meeting for coffee near the art gallery, both of my New York agents
retreated into e-mails and phone calls to keep me posted on contract negotiations. I didn't get so much as a fancy lunch.

I started talking with my literary agent about what I was willing to
put into a book. The magenta-glitter feeling came roaring back; I was
encouraged to write a fictionalized memoir, ostensibly to avoid exposing
people's identities. But I suspect that she was really hoping I would
embellish and multiply my few stories about partying with porn stars,
up my flirtations with Sean Michaels and Mr. Marcus into more intimate
encounters, that kind of thing. I didn't blame her, necessarily; my life was
not very exciting, so she thought my "character" could live in a hipper
neighborhood and spend a lot more time rubbing elbows and other body
parts with the porn elite in more screen-worthy places than expo show
floors.

Hollywood and often pornography may revolve on the act of faking it, but I didn't jump on the bandwagon for my book. The truth of the matter, I found myself reiterating, was that my interactions with the industry were limited because there wasn't much activity for me to participate in where I lived. There were a few porn stars with big names in New York, and there were some companies that shot content in the city, but for the most part, the hub of the straight industry was—and is still—in Los Angeles.

Most porn is filmed in California because, while pornography that doesn't qualify as obscene is protected by the First Amendment everywhere in the United States, it's not strictly *legal* in most places. In the late 1980s, pornographer Harold Freeman was dragged to court by the state of California and charged with pandering—procuring people for prostitution—for hiring actors to perform in his films. Freeman was convicted and sentenced to probation, but he appealed his case to the California Supreme Court, which ruled that not only does hiring actors for pornography *not* satisfy the state's definition of prostitution, but even if it *did*, the First Amendment would need to be amended to cover pornography: The potential deletion of an entire genre of free expression would run flagrantly counter to the Constitutional right to freedom of expression to be allowed.

The State of California turned to the United States Supreme Court, hoping that it would side against smut, but Sandra Day O'Connor put the kibosh on that notion, denying a stay and finding the lower court's ruling appropriate. This effectively gave a Federal nod of approval to the filming of pornography in California—the only state in the nation to expressly allow porn. (That is, until 2008, when New Hampshire followed suit in a similar case. Oddly enough, however, the industry has yet to flock to the Granite State to take advantage of its legal bounty.) The American porn industry, accordingly, moved to California and set up shop as a legitimate industry, primarily in and around Los Angeles.

So, whereas it's not *illegal* to shoot porn in New York, like many did in the seventies, it's not strictly *legal*, either. Folks shooting explicit content in my fair city, accordingly, tended to do so quietly. Whereas porn companies in California can and often do shoot with film licenses, in complete compliance with the law, New York pornographers have less legal protection and could easily find themselves brought up on incidental charges.

Although I knew some performers who split their time between New York and LA, there wasn't much of a local industry scene for me to take part in. The yearly Exxxotica convention in New Jersey and a rotating schedule of porn folks visiting New York for strip club gigs, public appearances, or surreptitious shooting or escorting jobs provided me with an oft-interrupted flow of interviews, but as far as spending quality time with porn people, my repertoire of stories to sensationalize for a "fictional memoir" was pretty lame.

Much as I love glitter, magenta has never been my color, and I dug in my heels about making things up just to appease my literary agent's ideas about what it means to work with pornography. Porn stars are just people whose day jobs look markedly different from what most of us are used to. (As Kaylani Lei put it in an interview, "Although yes, it is sex, and I get to sit and cum all over somebody, I still have to wake up to an alarm clock and drag my feet in the morning to get to work on time.") But this doesn't mean that spending time with them—in a formal interview setting or at a private after-party—implies wild exploits. Sure, it *can*. Sometimes it does, especially during conventions. But the same might be said for bankers or restaurant industry workers.

Nevertheless, buoyed by the fact that I had agents and lawyers screaming on my behalf (or so I was told) at television producers in Los Angeles, that I was getting increasingly positive feedback on my writing for *McSweeney's*, that *WHACK!* was gaining more readers every week, that invitations to attend strip clubs as a VIP for porn star feature-dancing gigs were piling up, and that I could no longer stand the stuffiness of the art world, I quit my job at the gallery in the summer of 2010. This was a classically terrible move, but I'd had enough of laboring endlessly as a receptionist for little acclaim and even less money.

Around this time, I was appointed editor in chief of *WHACK!* I would be responsible for managing all the content on the site, where we had recently taken on several new writers. I would be assigning stories, scheduling articles, reviewing and editing content, and basically taking the reins of daily operations. By this time we had more or less given up on *pornocracy*. We'd done what we could, but despite the great footage we'd already gotten and our hard work at *WHACK!*, there simply was no money coming in for the web series. We'd gotten so busy at *WHACK!* that, furthermore, we had no time left over to focus on much else.

Excited about my new title, I decided to look for review material that would make me think harder. I'd already begun to branch out from the gonzo content I'd been reviewing for the print magazine, instead taking in higher-end fare from big companies like Wicked, Vivid, and New Sensations. Feature films had been taking off as the gonzo era played itself out, and they were doing well in the pirate-strewn landscape. As Tracy Clark-Flory wrote for *Salon*, "If the sex scenes are made sexy by the larger, complex narrative at hand—rather than the shorthand of X-rated clichés . . . they won't end up as free jerk-off material."

These were *movies*: They had plots that were mostly coherent; they took the time to explain who the characters were and why they were going at it; they featured professional lighting, camera work, sound, and editing. They weren't all masterpieces of philosophical exploration, and many of them played into stereotypes about gender roles and sexuality that I found patently offensive, but after years of compilations like *Elastic Assholes #6*, I was ready for something a tad more mentally stimulating.

But, when I got honest with myself about it, the feature films often left me wanting, too. The plots, though mercifully existent, were often worn-out tropes clearly aimed at women transitioning from romance novels into pornography with their partners. There were exceptions, but in many of these films, the sex felt over-produced and restrained, as if it were trying not to scare anybody. And the performers tended toward the notorious pornland Barbie-and-Ken look, which did nothing for me. Watching their clean-shaven white bodies gyrating in perfectly choreographed, softly lit rhythm gave me none of the illicit charge that gonzo packed, not to mention any variety in sex acts or body types. I also found the writing dull, as if it were trying to emulate romantic comedy scripts. Both genres frustrated me in the naïve and damaging ways they portrayed men and women, and particularly in the ways they related to one another —wild generalizations and the application of gender norms that had no basis in my reality flew all over the place, presented as "facts of life" that I found ridiculous. Ugh. I was ready to look elsewhere.

Parody porn offered an alternative to typical feature films, so one of my first moves as editor in chief was to seek them out. The porn parody genre was nothing new—it goes back almost as far as porn itself and has been consistently popular due to hilarious titles (*Hung Wankenstein* in place of *Young Frankenstein*, or its later cousin, *Fuckenstein*, anyone?).

But in the mid- to late 2000s, they hit a real stride with the porn-viewing public and became big business. Now that consumers could purchase films easily online, one hardly had to go out of one's way to nab a copy of *Whore of the Rings* (or its sequel, *Whore of the Rings 2*, which I feel really could have capitalized on the imagery in *The Two Towers* more effectively, don't you?). And with the couples' porn market growing as more women showed more interest, parody porn offered the perfect middle ground between dirty and funny, exciting and safe. Director Will Ryder told me that parodies were a sure thing: "We don't have to sell the characters . . . They're already sold. We just have to re-create them in a way that's believable and introduce vaginas into the picture. And we've won."

I screened several parodies with a mixture of excitement and trepidation. *Not Jersey Shore: Jersey Whores* touched on the reality TV milestone, but let's be honest: does anyone *really* want to see those people get busy? But I was eager to try *Sex and the City: The Original XXX Parody*—I'd been a fan in college, where my roommates and I would watch the show on Sundays until our hangovers dissipated, and the chance to see my old favorites engaged in a four-way orgy drew me in. Said orgy was sadly disappointing, though, as that movie fell into the trap of trying not to offend its lady viewers with "weird" sex. Boooooring.

But, in a few notable cases, parodies were able to transcend the couples-friendly dead end. Sometimes the strength of the script was notable. (*The Big Lebowski XXX* is, to date, the best porn parody I've seen, followed closely by *The Graduate XXX*, largely due to the writing.) And in others, the silliness of the setting (for instance, a bonanza of boning between virtually every character in the Batman universe in *Batfxxx*, and a similar sexual spree in *Bonny & Clide*) translated into fun scenes where spontaneity and chemistry were allowed to shine.

But as editor in chief of *WHACK!* I felt compelled to keep looking for the porn that I knew had to exist out there, somewhere. The porn that wouldn't just suffice, but exceed my expectations. I sent out feelers to a variety of studios and distributors looking for something new. I'd been aware of indie porn for a while, but I had never pursued it because in my estimation, if the gonzo gag-and-spit-fests I was familiar with were any indication of the quality I could expect from studios with low budgets, I didn't want to go there. I had let my squicky feelings about the questionable ethics of low-rent gonzo porn seep into my understanding of film production. The wires between "this looks cheap" and "this looks painful and sort of violent" had gotten crossed, and I'd written indie porn off without thinking about how it's the ethos behind the production, not the money, that informs the content.

In my quest for the perfect adult film, I came across the term "queer porn" (not to be confused with gay male porn, which is its own distinct industry), and something clicked. The images on the websites were of gorgeous, often androgynous humans with tattoos and piercings and cool haircuts whose bodies were different from the ones I'd grown accustomed to in my reviewing fare. They looked sexy, and *interesting*. Like the people I was personally attracted to. And most of it was marketed as *feminist*. I needed to get my hands on some of this.

Most of the porn companies that fit under the umbrella term "feminist porn," many of which also identified as queer, were bootstrap indie outfits with relatively tiny distribution chains, but I managed to nab a review copy of Pink & White Productions's first DVD, *The Crash Pad*, for review. It was a collection of scenes from a series that has now been filming for over a decade, and the DVD—now just one of a large collection—was an iconic moment in barrier-breaking, alt-lifestyle-depicting, incredibly *hot* sexual entertainment in 2005.

Although I was a few years late to the party, when I reviewed *The Crash Pad* in 2010, I thought I'd left naivety behind years earlier. But as soon as the action started, I realized how wrong I had been. How much I had yet to learn.

There was something different going on here, something powerful and refreshingly *real* that I didn't have a name for at the time, but which left me sitting slack-jawed, uncertain whether my brain or my nether regions were more excited. I was witnessing queer sex in a subversive, individualistic, raw way that set me on fire. It felt like the actors were hardly aware that they were being watched, not because they were told to forget about the camera but because they were *so* into each other. I'd witnessed scenes like this in the porn I'd already watched, of course: stand-out sex scenes in which the actors were deeply involved in what they were doing and loving every minute of it. Those scenes were capable of transporting the viewer, and I'd been transported before. But never by performers who looked or behaved like these. Their bodies were less manicured, more hairy, less toned. And they were grinning, laughing,

wrestling, connecting with each other. And they were fucking with fero-
cious, joyful abandon in ways that I had never seen before. Sure, I'd seen
strap-ons and cunnilingus and so on, but let's just say that queer sex has
its own designation for a reason.

The vast treasure chest of sex acts that are considered queer allows
for things that heterosexual people just don't often *think* about. We've
all been told that "male" people like things one way and "female" people like things another way, and when they get together sexually, they
do things that conform to those preferences. And the majority of mainstream porn portrays these ideas in a variety of unsurprising ways that
reestablish masculinity and femininity within the prescribed roles that
society has placed upon them: dominant/submissive, active/passive,
pleasure seeker/pleasure giver. You know the drill. (Har, har.) But in
queer porn, these standardized roles are tossed out the window in favor
of whatever works for the people in the scene. The "script" often used
in straight porn (tease, blowjob, maybe cunnilingus, penetration,
switching positions, maybe anal, cum shot, done) doesn't exist. Orgasms might be multiple, or nonexistent. Play is encouraged. Cum shots
are rare. Self-expression is encouraged. And that expression, in turn,
encourages people like myself to explore and express themselves in new
ways. As Joanne Spataro wrote in *Tonic*, queer porn helps its audience
by "giving queer people a voice not only by showing actual queer folks
making love, but empowering them to have more control over how they
are viewed."

In other words, *The Crash Pad* blew away everything I thought
I knew. New questions emerged, centered mostly around three questions:
Who are these people? How could I get to know them? Where could
I find more of their porn?

WHEN I READ IT NOW, the review I wrote in 2010 feels adorably adoles-
cent. It has the breathlessness of new discovery without any depth of understanding. Not only had I been unprepared for the hotness of *The
Crash Pad*, I didn't even have the language to translate my experience
properly. I cringe to admit that called the performers, all of whom had
vaginas but few of whom identified as women, "ladies" and "chicks." I
was unaware at the time that many of these people were genderqueer—

meaning that they don't identify exclusively with the labels "male" or "female," much less with terms like "chick" that can be perceived as condescending. There's nothing *wrong* with what I wrote, necessarily, but it feels juvenile from the distance of a few years.

I mean, I actually wrote the following sentence: "These ladies are so dedicated to getting each other off that some of them are covered in sweat by the time they're finished." What I either didn't say specifically or, more likely, didn't understand was that the "sweat" was female ejaculate in prodigious quantities, which had been obtained via vaginal fisting between two genderqueer partners, neither of whom identified as ladies. Color me embarrassed.

In my defense, the DVD version of the scene in question had been edited to obscure the fisting and the squirting. This DVD was the first produced by Pink & White for distribution to a wide audience, and it could have ended up on the wrong side of the Atlantic or in an obscenity trial if it went too far in what it showed. (The online versions of these scenes show the—really hot—nitty gritty, because materials distributed online are much more difficult to subject to "community standards" of obscenity—more on that in later chapters.) But still, as someone who had taken in hundreds of hours of pornography and written about it at length, the tone deafness I displayed in my first-ever queer porn review is embarrassing.

Terminology in the queer community, particularly the queer sex work community, is a complex and ever-evolving tangle of ideologies and expression. Explaining it is a task I can't properly undertake here; as a writer and a lover of language, as well as a queer woman with a lot of opinions, that's a rabbit hole I should probably steer clear of. Still, it's important to touch on some of these ideas.

For many queer people, who have for most of their lives dealt with oppression, repression, ignorance, and the outright denial of their existence and experience, naming is important. It is a way of fighting back against a world that has tried to silence and erase us. Words like "queer," "trans," "squirting," and "fisting" aren't just accurate; they're important. They establish the speaker's recognition of these identities and acts as real, legitimate, and active in the world. As performer, activist, and educator (and super-hot human) Jiz Lee wrote in their essay about fisting in *Best Sex Writing of the Year, 2015*, in naming and recording queer sex, "We're representing marginalized communities, taking power through creating our own images of desire." For people who have never had access to media that represented people like them as sexual entities, pornography can be of great importance—a gift that can show them that they are sexy, too. Buck Angel, a trans man who has lived his sexual life openly as an example to others, once told me, "[Porn] is a big support in helping other people to become their true selves. When you embrace your body and your sexuality it can really make a big difference in your quality of life."

Much has been made in recent years about the rising tide of "political correctness" in language, by those who feel uncomfortable substituting "transgender woman" for "shemale," or "person of color" for any number of terms that have long been used by people in power to humiliate people who don't look, talk, think, or live like them. But the point in these corrections is not to make everyone "PC" or to water down a once-colorful language. The point is to treat other human beings with respect, and when those human beings have legitimate reasons for detesting terminology that has been used for centuries to oppress them, it's a sign of respect to use the terminology they choose.

When I wrote my review for *The Crash Pad*, I didn't know who these performers were or how they identified. And frankly, if I had, I would have been confused because at that time I was only vaguely aware of the many identities that existed in the queer community. I knew about trans people and lesbians, but I wasn't hip to words like cisgender, genderqueer. Nor did I understand the importance of recording and naming queer sex acts like fisting. I just threw around the words that I thought applied to acts and identities and left it at that. But it was the beginning of a long journey that I'm still on, and I'm really thankful that, though the review probably resulted in its share of rolled eyes, the people who were involved in making *The Crash Pad*, and the rest of the queer, feminist porn world, didn't write me off as a lost cause. In the years since, I've interviewed and befriended many of them and their protégés. They're marvelous humans, and they make outstanding porn.

In an interview in 2013, queer porn star James Darling echoed a sentiment that queer and feminist porn, and my own way of thinking, reflected: "I think porn is a really important part of our culture . . . Authenticity in my performances and the porn that I produce [is] very important to me." Many others agree. And so, in an effort to subvert the mainstream porn script, many queer, feminist pornographers focus on authenticity in their content. Authentic representations of performers' personal identities and desires.

But the word "authentic" is a slippery one. Authenticity has become a sought-after attribute in everything from cuisine to art to porn in recent years, a buzzword that makes people like me feel hip when it's applied to their dinner or their latest Etsy purchase. But defining it is another matter, particularly when it comes to performative sex on camera. After all, any constructed situation, no matter how real it feels, is still constructed, right? Particularly in porn, even if artifice has been removed as much as possible to allow for an "authentic" sex scene, the action is usually happening in a prepared location. The toys and lube and water and snacks are all set up nearby. There are lights and at least one camera. And, as particle physicists will attest, the act of observation is not as passive as we once thought.

Does this mean that all porn is by definition *inauthentic*? Are the moans from the actors suspect because they might be quieter if this sex had happened privately? Does someone's writhing in pleasure not count because it might be exaggerated for the camera's benefit? Should we discount the very real excitement that exhibitionists derive from mugging for the camera, just because there's a camera there in the first place? Well, no. But there's no clear delineation between authenticity and inauthenticity. It's not so simple.

It would be unfair and inaccurate to say that all mainstream porn is inauthentic, and just as inaccurate to say that all queer or feminist porn is authentic. Most porn performers do what they do because they *like* it, and that means that most of their performances are genuine representations of them having sex that they enjoy, at least to some degree. That doesn't mean that they're always having sex the way they do at home, or the way they feel like doing it at the moment of filming, but by and large the people you're watching in porn films are doing something that makes them feel pretty good. There is usually real pleasure exchanged, but one can feel the presence of the camera and the expectations it brings with it.

On most porn sets, performers are expected to "open up" their positions to the camera, resulting in poses that look great but don't feel so fantastic. Women are reminded to keep their faces turned to the camera even when it's uncomfortable, to curl their toes, to arch their backs. India

Summer, in an interview for *WHACK!*, told me, "Here is a good rule of thumb: The hotter a position looks on your screen, usually the more uncomfortable or athletic it is for the performers to do. Try putting yourself into camera-friendly positions and then going at it hard and fast for extended periods while maintaining balance, poise, and posture . . . Try having the stamina, energy, and intensity it takes to get through a normal or long adult-video sex scene and still photography shoot."

Keeping oneself truly aroused and interested in the goings-on under these circumstances is not easy, and as a result, too many porn scenes end up feeling flat, uninspired, impersonal. In a word, inauthentic. But in *The Crash Pad*, every scene hit a similar level of ecstatic passion that made me giddy. Many featured real-life lovers with established sexual chemistry that glowed, or performers who had been paired up at their own request, guaranteeing that sparks would fly. Even better, the director, Shine Louise Houston, was careful not to actively *direct* the scenes, and to this day she maintains the same style. Nikki Darling, a performer who has since worked on the *Crash Pad* series, had insights into the process: "There is something magical in the technique that Shine uses, which is very voyeuristic . . . The scene is what you and your scene partner negotiate beforehand, and then move forward with doing. And Shine happens to capture those things very well and very beautifully."

The Crash Pad also opened my eyes to the possibility of showing clear, ongoing, and enthusiastic consent during a porn scene. Whereas in most porn I'd seen, consent was merely implied when the woman, for instance, crawled across the floor, drooling, to get to the exposed cock waiting for her on the couch, in this new world of queer and feminist porn, permission was often asked for and verbally given. Seeing this negotiation on camera tickled a part of my brain that I hadn't been entirely aware was starving for attention: I knew without a shadow of a doubt that the people in these scenes were having fun. Their facial expressions, their body movements, and their words all added up to explicit consent. I'd become accustomed to assuming consent was given, knowing as I did that the people I was watching in mainstream films were being paid and had the ability to dictate their own terms on most sets, but in many scenes in which negotiation and consent were edited out, anything less than exuberant, authentic-looking ecstasy could feel a bit icky. How could I be *sure* that everyone was okay? But when the negotiations were included in the film, there was no guesswork, and I felt the PTSD-ridden parts of my brain latch on to this new form of erotic entertainment with glee.

And feminist porn went above and beyond showing consent in explicit terms: In these scenes, rather than editing out every application of lube, the bottle would sometimes stay in the shot for a minutes at a time, along with negotiations between actors as they decided what position to try next, who should be on top, or what toy to use. I was floored. Feminist porn director Jennifer Lyon Bell told me once that in sex, "the tiny awkwardness or confusions along the way actually add to the excitement rather than subtracting from it," and *The Crash Pad* really proved how true that could be.

In short, queer porn changed *everything* for me. Questions that I had been asking already about the morality of the things I was watching deepened—I became more concerned with the ways in which performers were depicted in their films. Was their consent clear and ongoing? Were they aware of the ways in which they were being portrayed? Did they agree with them? Did they care?

Even as I began to grow more critical of issues in mainstream porn, I branched out to write for more magazines, since my receptionist income had ceased and the magazines I was writing for were tilting once again toward bankruptcy. The shadiness of my encounters with Charles, the editor at the first magazine, had become more pointed—we would meet in public parks or on street corners, rather than at his new office in far-off Jersey. He would arrive at the predetermined time in very dark sunglasses and a hat, and he would pass me a black plastic bag full of DVDs, say a few pleasantries, and then walk quickly away, as if we were involved in a drug deal. The weirdness of these interactions spooked me and seemed to cast a darker shadow onto the magazines themselves, which were getting creepier. The one for which I wrote DVD reviews was getting thinner with each issue, with the ads in the back taking over a higher percentage of the pages and fewer sets of raunchy original photos leading up to them. The photos themselves seemed to be of lower quality, even, although I may have just projected my newfound sense of squeamishness onto them.

But at another magazine, for which I'd been writing set copy about young women's "first times" that were then tacked onto "barely legal" photo sets, my uneasiness was definitely warranted. The photos I saw applied to my words had always come as a surprise ("Oh, come on, *that's* not Monica! Monica doesn't have freckles!"), but they had changed in tenor. They models were supposed to be barely legal, but some now appeared to be of actually questionable legality. The sets on which they were photographed were looking cheaper with every issue. When I came across a photo of a cringe-smiling young lady whose figure had yet to fully develop in front of a library scene that was clearly just a large photograph glued to a wall over some natty, stained carpet, I finally contacted my editor to ask where the magazine was getting these photos. The answer I got was a shrugging "Eastern Europe, I guess? They're cheap." And, I thought, much more difficult to trace to their sources.

Things were bad. There was so little money to be made in traditional smutty magazines that in order to avoid bankruptcy, editors were cutting corners in the most important parts of their businesses: the labor they contracted to make the smut. The consent behind these photos was questionable, and that made me extremely unhappy.

This is where independent queer and feminist porn producers were again winning the day: The female and feminist consumer was—unlike many others who were streaming porn from tube sites—willing to pay for rarefied *good porn*. Dollars were willingly shelled out for content that focused on real pleasure and clearly established consent. And although few of the small studios making that kind of material were raking in the cash, they were still able to continue to create high-quality content that their customers appreciated and continued to buy. While the greasy magazines I wrote for were drying up, queer feminist porn was revving its engines.

Women and queers in porn, both on the production and consumption ends, are essential to the continuation of the industry in both feminist and mainstream sectors. In 2010 the market had begun to adjust to the new age of women watching porn with the feature films and parodies that I'd been reviewing, and in the niche queer and feminist markets. Since then it has continued to grow. There are now more studios making porn for women and queers and feminists than I can even begin to mention. Pink & White Productions, which made *The Crash Pad*, has grown and now provides an umbrella distribution organization for smaller producers of indie smut through PinkLabel.tv. Jiz Lee, the online marketing director for the company, told me, "Many queer and indie films have difficulty finding online hosting due to censorship of sex acts, inappropriate language or categorization [or] tagging of performers of color, older performers, transgender [performers], or people with disabilities, or experimental content that doesn't quite fit the typical porn consumer model . . . If we can curate unique and excellent adult films that generate revenue for the artist to continue their craft, we hope to ensure a bright future for our work to thrive."

Porn for women from Europe and Australia by way of filmmakers like Erika Lust, Jennifer Lyon Bell, Morgana Muses, and Ms. Naughty has taken worldwide audiences by storm. Nica Noelle, with her companies Sweetheart Video and Sweet Sinner (among others) has been making award-winning, best-selling movies for women since 2008. Tristan Taormino's feminist and educational series for Adam and Eve has been wildly successful. Sssh.com, founded by AVN Hall of Famer Angie Rowntree, has been operational for two decades and continues to expand.

All of these studios, and many others, focus on consent in their scenarios, on representing multiple kinds of bodies, gender identities, racial backgrounds, and sexual orientations. Rather than lumping performers neatly into categories by body type or race, they tend to adopt an "anything goes" policy, pairing actors who want to work together in the hopes—which are often met—that their chemistry will deliver a blistering-hot sex scene. As filmmaker Marie Madison told me, "Hook people up who are hot for one another and you'll feel the heat without having to even turn the lights on." Viewers the world over tend to agree.

At AVN in 2016, Ryan Driller, an actor who had just won the XBIZ award for "Best Actor of the Year," told me that, "Although [for] almost all porn, even if it's female friendly and female designed, I'd say the primary consumer is men, I think by 2020 . . . it'll be fifty-fifty in a lot of different places. I think you'll have studios that will have a predominantly [female] viewership and female customers. I think it's just catching on with the female psyche and the female population."

With punk porn princess Joanna Angel at an industry event
(PHOTO COURTESY J. VEGAS)

CHAPTER 14

Racism in the Industry

WHEN THE *WHACK!* STAFF went back to Exxxotica New Jersey in November of 2010, we saw familiar faces, went to parties, and interviewed plenty of porn stars. But the most memorable part of the weekend, for me, was sitting at the bar one night, talking with a friend I'd made the previous year. We'll call him Seth. While the after-party raged around us, Seth and I drank whiskey gingers and talked about the industry he'd been working in for nearly twenty years.

At that time, Seth had performed in around fifteen hundred adult films, pseudonymously starred in numerous showcase series from several production companies, directed over two hundred films, won five AVN awards, and been inducted into the AVN, XRCO, and NightMoves halls of fame. Yet, near the close of 2010, he told me that he was contemplating retiring from adult entertainment because he felt undervalued. Sure, five AVN awards sounds impressive, but when I checked them out I discovered that every scene for which he'd won an award had been a group scene. Which is to say that he hadn't yet been recognized by the industry's most prestigious award-giving organization for *his own* performances.

I encouraged him in whatever pursuit he chose and assured him that he had so much to offer that if the porn industry wasn't giving him the respect he deserved, someone else would. But he was already in his early fifties, and although he'd held jobs prior to porn, he felt he was approaching old-dog-new-tricks territory. But his frustration over a lack of appreciation, it seemed, was only part of what was bothering him; He suspected that he was having a hard time collecting on the "legend" status he so richly deserved because of his race.

I'll take a moment here to recognize the fact that I have no idea what Seth's financial background looked like, or what series of events led up to our conversation. But no matter what the details behind the scarcity of financial rewards for his long and distinguished career in adult entertainment, I saw in Seth's laments a microcosm of a larger trend that cannot be ignored. Earlier that day at the convention we had both seen large, expensive booths representing major studios owned by white men. Many of those men had started out as performers, then moved behind the camera before going on to much profit and acclaim. But Seth and I had seen *zero* similar booths owned by black men. Or by black women. Or by Latin or Indian or East Asian men or women. You get the idea. While there had been a good number of actors of color signing autographs, we were both aware that the percentages were off.

Racism in pornography is an extremely tricky subject, as is racism at large. Porn's race issues go just as deep as they do anywhere else in American society, but pornography boasts a combination pressure release valve and complication of the subject. In most forms of entertainment, and in society as a whole, racial differences are commonly downplayed in favor of politically correct cover-ups for the very deep prejudices that still exist. But in mainstream porn, those differences are gleefully and unapologetically put on display. Porn is one place where "politically correct" depictions of race are tossed out the window in favor of blatant stereotypes that are believed to help sell the content.

In a move that was both naïve and cynical, I had double-thought the flagrant displays of prejudice I'd seen in porn into a winking parody of racism in our culture. I gave it the same kind of acknowledgment I'd given to j. vegas's brutal satirical rips on porn stars. This smirking utilization of race is self-aware, I thought. It must be. A critique. Proof that the industry understands how fucked up the stereotypes it re-creates and sells really are. Gangbanging thugs, sexually predatory Mandingos, hugely endowed bulls, promiscuous women putting out for cash, grossly overdone accents—the porn world was filled to bursting with every ready-made label the dominant culture has tailored for black people. A quick look at one African American actor's list of credits is a veritable gold mine of groan-worthy names that turn blackness into a fetish: *Big Black Dicks in Little White Slits*, *Black Cock Addiction*, *Fear of a Black Penis*, *Jungle Beaver*. The people behind these titles seemed to be in on the joke, and to be profiting from it, so I guessed everybody was winning. Right?

Well, I wasn't *all* wrong. Certainly the porn industry is not so backward that it unanimously and seriously believes black men are single-minded monsters who go around despoiling white women and cuckolding their melanin-deficient husbands. The industry as a whole has a dark (for lack of a better word) sense of humor and has long been a hotbed of satirical takes on modern life. The very existence of porn parodies speaks volumes about the genre's ability to take the piss out of our culture. (I refer you to 2008's bestselling *Who's Nailin' Paylin?* in which Lisa Ann portrayed Sarah Palin with panache that rocketed her to the top of the industry and mainstream fame. Over two years after her retirement, she was still one of the most popular porn actors in the world, according to Pornhub's 2016 data.) And yet, for all the laughs its treatment of performers of color may generate behind the scenes, the industry continues to hire black men to play race-related roles. Furthermore, once performers sign their model releases and leave the set, they have no control over the editing and marketing of their work. Thus, even the most progressive of actors may end up in a film like *Big Black Beef Stretches Little Pink Meat #7*. And they often do, much to their dismay. Compounding this already-gross circumstance is the fact that so much modern porn is consumed via free tube sites on which material is often clipped from longer movies, stripped of all context, and relabeled with even more derogatory terminology than the original product.

Although I've had far fewer conversations about the race situation in the gay industry—which is to say, I don't in fact know any black men who work primarily in it—I have heard similar things from secondhand sources. Black men in gay porn are often cast as hyper masculine, physically dominant, sexually predatory thugs in interracial scenes—in which they almost always do the penetrating. Jarrett Neal, in his essay on the subject of interracial gay porn in *Best Sex Writing of the Year, 2015*, wrote that in gay porn he's familiar with, black actors "had no choice but to be marketed in a way that confined them to essential and often stereotypical characterizations of black masculinity."

Given the industry's reductive treatment of black men, and with the market brimming with titles like *Phat Ass Ebony Freakz*, it's not difficult to imagine the kind of climate that African American women face in porn. While a 2013 study of porn demographics revealed that fourteen percent of female porn stars were black—a pretty accurate reflection of

American race demographics at large—the number of those women who work regularly and prominently in mainstream porn is tiny.

Nyomi Banxxx, a friend of *WHACK!* from our very first convention, was very vocal about the situation in an interview with me in 2012. In the the mainstream industry, she told me, "It only can be three of us at a time . . . There are so many more beautiful black women out there that are performers that do not get their due." There was not enough "ethnic" work to keep more than three popular black performers in circulation, she believed.

All-black porn is treated as a "specialty market," relegated to its own category on websites and filmed by specific companies. The line that producers and directors feed media inquiries and call-outs is that the public just doesn't want to see much African American porn. It doesn't make sense to make more of it since nobody would buy it. But this is a chicken-and-egg question that plagues most entertainment industries: Are people just not buying it because it doesn't exist?

Maggie Mayhem, a white performer who left mainstream porn to work with indie companies because she was tired of watching people being demeaned, wrote on her website, Meet the Mayhems: "A lot of things are brushed off with people saying, 'I'm not racist, it just doesn't sell.' I think this has something to do with the fact that people who are white own the content and market it. The industry is essentially what sex looks like from the gaze of the cis[gender], het[erosexual], white male, and those who are the most 'successful' in the mainstream industry are those who create content through that same lens."

Rubbing salt more deeply into the wound is the fact that black actors of all genders are paid less than their white counterparts. Performer Casey Calvert, a white model who has studied pay rates in the industry, revealed to me that if she were to shoot a standard blowbang featuring "random dudes," as opposed to top-tier male performers, "if I do that with all white guys, those random dudes are making four hundred for that scene. If I do it with black guys, they're maybe making one fifty, two hundred."

In 2007, female African American models were making half to three-quarters the rates of their white counterparts, and in a 2013 interview, actor Misty Stone reported that even after she had raised her rates to allow for her massive popularity, she was still making around three hundred dollars less per scene than white models with similar levels of name recognition.

• • •

IT SHOULD COME AS NO surprise that racism doesn't apply only to African American porn performers. There may be a starker delineation between the treatment of blacks and whites in porn, but that isn't to say that adult entertainment is kind to actors of other races, either.

At the end of 2012, Joanna Angel released behind-the-scenes photos from the set of *The Walking Dead: A Hardcore Parody*, which her company, Burning Angel, was producing. The work done by makeup artist Melissa Makeup was on display in these photos, and for good reason: She had transformed attractive young porn actors into rotting zombies from the hit show *The Walking Dead*. She had also, the photos revealed, turned white actor Danny Wylde into the Asian American character Glenn . . . by painting his face yellow, putting him in a wig and baseball cap, and pulling his eyes taught with tape.

Asian-American performer Kelly Shibari called Joanna Angel to task on Twitter in a very public way, and Korean American magazine *KoreAm* published an article on the questionable choice. Feminist website *Jezebel* picked up the story, broadcasting the issue to millions of readers, and soon there was a full-blown Internet frenzy over the issue, with porn insiders and critics taking sides. Danny Wylde, the actor in question, first offered a shrugging pseudo-apology, but later recanted on his blog. "I have spent seven years working a job on which it is okay to be 'kind of racist,'" he wrote. "In fact, being 'overtly racist' has proved for some to be quite lucrative. As a society, we have tolerated racism within pornography to an incredible extent."

And he was one of many who pointed out that, while the yellowface debacle was cringe-worthy, it wasn't the worst of what was going on in porn. In an article for AVN, Peter Warren wrote, "If [critics had] done the briefest Google search, they'd have come up with so many exponentially more demeaning depictions of Asians in porn, it would make this look downright noble. Just have a glimpse at some of the titles that have graced adult retail shelves in the past few months: *Shrimp Fried Pussy* (Wicked Pictures) . . . *Dim Sum Pussy* (Voyeur Media) . . . *Yellow Fever* (Exquisite Multimedia) . . . The list goes on."

I hadn't taken in any of the above jewels myself, but I had witnessed my share of porn in which Asian-descended women used over-the-top accents as they gave out "happy ending" massages with their kimonos hanging open. Almost every Asian-specific adult film in history has relied on stereotypes that simply would not fly in other entertainment.

But other entertainment is not exempt: American culture still labors under the notion that men of Asian descent are less sexually desirable than those of any other race. A Columbia University study published in 2007 found that non-Asian women were thirty-five percent less likely to respond positively to Asian men than men of other races. This may be due in large part to the fact that Asian men are commonly—if not constantly—portrayed in media as nerdy, shy, faltering, and patently unsexy. As any queer pornographer will gladly tell you, representation in sexual media matters, and for Asian men, that representation is rarely positive, if it exists at all.

Of course, none of the above is sufficient explanation or excuse for employing yellowface for *The Walking Dead* parody. And neither is the almost unbelievable truth that, as Peter Warren pointed out, there was at that time exactly *one* feature-film-level, straight, male Asian porn star in the American industry. *One*. His name was Keni Styles, and his mere existence on the adult playing field was so unprecedented that he had become a porn sensation.

Keni Styles's good looks, his muscular body and masculine demeanor, his sexy British accent (he was born in Thailand but grew up mostly in the UK), and his chemistry with women made him the subject of intense scrutiny as well as the longing of thousands of female fans, myself included. And, while there were a few other Asian males in and around the porn industry at the time that the yellowface debacle went down, none had succeeded to the same degree as Mr. Styles. He was, really, the only guy in the industry at the time who might have been considered to step in as Glenn.

It's likely that Keni wasn't available to shoot *The Walking Dead* parody. It's also possible that he was sick of getting called for every single movie that was looking for an Asian actor. And it's entirely probable that, had he been available and willing, Burning Angel may not have been able to afford his rate. Scarcity equals a higher price point in every industry, and porn is no exception.

There are far more female Asian porn models in America than there are men, which is of course not a very high hurdle to clear. But as of a 2013 study of ten thousand porn stars, the percentage of female American porn performers of Asian descent (5.2) was slightly higher than the percentage of Americans of Asian heritage nationally (4.7, in the 2010 census), which means that the porn industry's representation of Asian women isn't too far off numerically. As a matter of fact, some of the top names in adult film are Asian.

Asa Akira, Kaylani Lei, Venus Lux, and others are all big names in the industry, and there are many other women of Asian descent working in porn at varying levels of fame. But the ways in which most of these women are asked to portray themselves and by extension their race is, to say the least, disturbing. The stereotype of submissive, sexually timid Asian females is overtly employed in these films—a titillating prospect for male consumers who enjoy the idea of having their way with a sex partner who's both "exotic" and willing to go along with whatever he wants.

In a recent search for Asian titles on GameLink.com, I came upon the titles *Peking Pussy, Szechuan Snatch*, and *Chocolate Covered Fortune Cookies* (you guessed it—the men here are black). It's a double indictment of the American imagination that so many Asian porn titles center around food: This cuisine-centric titling reveals that Americans are largely ignorant of Asian cultures except for the food, and also that we're more than willing to place racially different bodies on the same level as cuisine—which is to say, available for our consumption.

Sadly but perhaps unsurprisingly, Asian women aren't the only group to be reduced to objects by way of their names. As legendary performer Sinnamon Love wrote in *The Feminist Porn Book*, "Black and Latina women in porn are very often given the names of food, cars, inanimate objects, countries, and spices: Chocolate, Champagne, Mocha, Mercedes, Toy, Persia, Africa, India, and yes, Sinnamon."

For reasons that aren't clear to me, there is a markedly smaller amount of Latin American–focused porn on the American market. Whereas the percentage of most minorities in pornography closely mirrors the overall percentage of those minorities within the general population, Latino performers make up a far smaller proportion of the whole. In the 2010 census, 16.3 percent of Americans reported as Hispanic and Latino, but in Jon Millward's 2013 study of ten thousand porn stars, only 9.3 percent were Latin.

Perhaps the predominantly Catholic demographic is less likely to pursue pornography for religious reasons, but that reasoning feels flimsy to me, since other cultures don't particularly favor pornography as career paths, either. Or maybe it's simply that Latin actors in porn are lumped in more easily with white actors. Missy Martinez, for instance, is a popular actress whose name and complexion hint at her Mexican heritage, but she is rarely cast specifically as a Latina.

The healthy Brazilian porn market may also play into America's paucity of Latin American content. Many American companies shoot in Brazil, where laws are lax and the local talent is lush. A lot of bareback bisexual and trans content is filmed there, with lucrative results for American producers who can hire performers at lower rates on site, then charge a premium for "niche" content featuring "exotic" foreign nationals.

That's not to say that American-made Latino content doesn't exist, however. Or that it's bucking the trend by being particularly flattering. Latino models are often cast as housekeepers and nannies on the one hand, or as landscapers, pool boys, or *cholos* on the other. And recent titles like *Sancho's Horny Hinas #5*, *Maid in Mexico*, and *Madre Make Me Fuck Her Man* turn the stomach *and* indicate a disregard for cultural sensitivity, all in one go.

WHEN MATTHEW AND I—the only *WHACK!* staffers to make it to Vegas in 2011—attended our first (and, to date, only) AVN Awards Show, I steeled myself for uneven representation of race in the industry. But I was still amazed by the four-hour parade of white people with occasional brown folks thrown in for very deliberate-feeling "flavor." Both of the hosts were white. The "trophy girls" who handed out the statuettes (two golden figures embracing atop an "AVN"-emblazoned base) were white. The "Performer of the Year" and "Best Actor and Actress" awards were handed out to white performers onstage, but the entire section of awards for "ethnic" releases—which was further broken down into the categories of Asian, Black, and Latin—*were not even presented during the awards ceremony*. I found this appalling.

I recognize the fact that, if every single AVN Award were to be presented onstage during the ceremony, the event would stretch from a four-hour spectacle into a day-long marathon that would bore attendees to tears. However, the fact that out of the major awards presented that night, only three were given for films or scenes that highlighted the work of non-white actors is telling. As is the fact that there were separate categories for each "type" of "ethnic" release. Granted, these awards provided more opportunities for pornographers of color to win awards, but that night they felt like consolation prizes. The Best Interracial Release is the only award given during the ceremony that rewards the work of black actors, but because "interracial" in the porn industry refers only to a black man with a lighter-skinned woman, the field of play for porn performers of color on the AVN stage is still extremely limited.

INTERRACIAL PORN—ONE OF THE most long-standing, most popular categories of adult entertainment—is its own bizarre world of tired stereotypes, racially motivated fantasies, and outdated economy. Interracial pairings were once at the top of the tall ladder of sex acts that white female performers were encouraged to climb as their careers progressed. As one of the most taboo acts one could perform on camera, it came with one of the highest payouts. That old ladder has been falling apart in recent years, yet it's still common for a white female model to hold out on having sex with black men on camera for longer than she waits to have anal sex or group sex. John Millward's 2013 study showed that only fifty-three percent of white female performers were willing to do interracial scenes. For comparison's sake, eighty-seven percent were willing to take facial cum shots, and sixty-two percent did anal. This, by the way, confuses me from a logistical standpoint: Whereas there is absolutely nothing making sex with a black man unpleasant so long as you're both into each other, anal sex can be quite uncomfortable if it's not undertaken properly. Performer Courtney Cummz told me, of her first-ever anal scene with the extremely well-endowed Peter North, "It hurt like hell! Don't let anyone tell you different. Your first anal experience is not pleasant." And let's not forget the five enemas Madison Young reminded us of back in Chapter 5. So why on earth would anal be lower on the scale of first-time acts than interracial? It's bizarre.

To add another level of weirdness to the mix, when an actress decides to take the leap into interracial scenes, she can often charge hundreds or even thousands more for it. Some studios, I was informed by agent Tee Reel, will offer up to five thousand dollars for a first interracial scene—then prohibit the female star from doing any interracial work for a period of time at their discretion, so that they can capitalize on the breaking of this still-profitable taboo.

It's so common for agents to tell their clients to "hold out" on doing interracial—or even to avoid it entirely because it might "damage" their careers—that when I asked "The Prince of Queer Porn," James Darling, who his heroes in adult entertainment were, he told me, "Any performer who risks their job to say no to racist and transphobic agents. The adult industry is a surprisingly very conservative place and it's hard to stick to your politics and convictions when your job is on the line." I've heard similar sentiments from other performers, sometimes from the other side—those who were talked into toeing the racist line until they realized what they were doing.

An argument that pops up against critiques of racism in porn—aside from the standard, "Oh come on, it's just porn!"—is that the adult industry isn't any more whitewashed than its wealthy cousin, Hollywood. This is true. The AVN awards I attended in 2011 were more diverse than that year's Oscars field by a long shot. But that doesn't change the fact that while Hollywood has a big role to play in perpetuating racial stereotypes, pornography actively re-creates, markets, and plays those stereotypes for laughs, all while creating an environment in which white models can literally refuse to work with black ones. The discrimination here is blatant and unapologetic. As Lexington Steele, one of the most successful male porn stars in history, told *The Root* in 2013, "Quite honestly, adult media is the only major business that allows for the practice of exclusion based upon race."

It boggles the mind to think that interracial sex could be considered taboo enough to earn itself a higher pay rate in the twenty-first century, but the truth is that people who want to see interracial sex are still willing to pay for it, and to ask for it specifically. By name. And in porn, naming is massively important.

Performer Casey Calvert and I spoke about the thorny issue of naming when it comes to interracial porn in 2016. "Interracial as a genre is a purely American construct, based on our country's history. A white girl with a black man is a genuine fetish for many people, especially in the south," she told me. "It's 'taboo,' it's 'wrong,' it's 'dirty.' And I shoot it because I don't want to discriminate against anyone's arousal pattern. If that's what they like, that's what they like. Yes, that sometimes includes derogatory words, but one, all fetishes have their keywords, and two, how many scenes have I shot where I was being called derogatory names? Too many to count. I think real racism is awful, just like real incest, and real rape, but interracial porn is just as much a fantasy as those other genres."

And it's a fantasy that sells. So it's a fantasy that gets turned into porn, again and again. "Mass-market production companies make the porn that they say consumers want; consumers develop viewing habits and a search language based on what is offered and available," Natasha Lennard wrote in *The Nation* in 2016. "The feedback loop produces what we have come to see as natural desires. The 'conservative business model,' as [performer Mickey] Mod describes it, gives the lie to the suggestion that offensive labels perpetuated in mainstream porn could be somehow subversive, turning political correctness on its head to liberate our innate desires." Those desires may not be as natural to us as we've been led to believe, but it's pragmatic to categorize people based on their physical characteristics or sexual proclivities even if it's backward. And, as a consumer, it feels less scary to click on the "BBW interracial anal" link on your favorite site than to go to Google, type in "porn" and hit the "I'm feeling lucky" button. For those who are motivated by fantasies involving racial difference, the "interracial" category provides what they're looking for without fear of getting the wrong content.

"I haven't done the research," said Tee Reel, "but apparently there are a lot of white guys that have that fantasy." And the interracial category makes it easier for them to find and, hopefully, pay for their porn, which keeps the wheels of the industry spinning so that the actors who made it can get paid for more work. Except some of those actors are getting paid less than their colleagues because of their race.

Sigh.

IT'S IMPORTANT TO NOTE that the porn industry isn't unaware of its spotty record regarding performers of color. The industry has begun to take stock of the situation and to make changes. There are numerous awards ceremonies besides the AVNs (XBIZ, XRCO, and others) that work hard to celebrate the contributions of pornographers of color. In 2016, the Adult Performers Advocacy Committee (APAC) released a statement on the matter of racial prejudice in the industry. "Although it is common practice to vary scene rates on performer experience and scene content, it is APAC's position that paying a performer less based on his/her race or charging a higher rate to work with performers of another race is unfair and unethical," they wrote. "Treating a performer's race as a determining factor for pay is a violation of performer rights as well as a violation of federal workplace discrimination laws." And I'm happy to report that AVN no longer gives out awards specifically for each "ethnic" group, as it did in 2011. Though I'm glad to see that performers are being somewhat less pigeon-holed by their racial designation, the change is a double-edged sword: It also *reduces* the number of awards available specifically to people of color.

AVN also took the month of November 2016 to focus on the contributions of black male performers to the industry, conducting interviews with a number of recognized names in the industry. My dear friend Sean Michaels was one of those profiled, and I was thrilled to see that after nearly thirty years in the industry, he had plans to release a book about his experiences—which should be launching at about the same time as this book!

Yet, as I sat at the bar in New Jersey with Seth and knocked back another whiskey ginger, I took in his kind eyes and his snappy suit-and-vest combo and wondered how many times I'd seen his performances on one of the clip sites I frequented, just a disembodied "big black cock" pirated from a movie with an embarrassingly outdated, racially charged title. The chances were very good that I'd seen the part of him that had made him a legend many times, but possibly not recognized him because his face had not been shown. And I pondered how someone with his experience, intelligence, and charm could be struggling to get by when he had brought so much to the industry he chose and worked so hard for. In trying times like these, surely pornography could stand to hear a few new ideas from some untapped minds, but I doubted any of the top brass were going to be tapping Seth for his thoughts on how to move forward anytime soon.

And, recent, small steps toward progress notwithstanding, the fact remains that white actors *are* still routinely paid more than others. Meanwhile, movies with titles and scenes that portray black men as defilers and black women as oversexed urban derelicts still get made. Since Keni Styles retired from porn, there has been no influx of Asian male talent rushing in to fill the void. The porn industry, in short, continues to play into the centuries of overlooking, devaluing, and commodifying bodies of color that plague our culture.

Performer-turned-agent Tee Reel told me that he tries not to let his personal feelings on racism in the industry affect his judgment as a businessperson. He directed me to always, as they say, follow the money to understand where the discrimination comes from. The trail led us back to the presiding power structure in porn, which looks remarkably like most other power structures in America. That is to say, old, white, and male. These men are businesspeople who don't have much time or interest to devote to social justice in the films they produce. They're happy to keep making the same content that has proven lucrative in the past—content that perpetuates what their life experiences have told them people want to see. And their experiences are usually those of older white men who have spent most of their careers surrounded by other white men. When it comes to racial diversity, the results are depressingly predictable. In *The Feminist Porn Book*, performer Sinnamon Love writes, "One of the biggest mistakes mainstream pornographers make is thinking their market is not interested in any other images of black women except these outrageously stereotyped ones . . . [A] lack of market research allows directors and producers to remain uninformed, and to cater only to their own sexual likes and dislikes."

In an interview I conducted with him in 2012, my friend Mr. Marcus and I sat down in his office at his brand-new production studio in Van Nuys and talked about how he hoped to make his company viable. But it was an uphill climb, he told me. "There's not a lot of black men that run their own businesses in this industry. [Producers] want the biggest black dick, because they can make movies around it. But in the executive offices, they're not dealing with blacks at a business level . . . When they go to a meeting, they're sitting around a table with a bunch of white guys. They think, 'Okay, let's make another black movie. What do we know about black people? We know they've got big dicks.'" When thinking of the people you're employing as body parts rather than humans with brains, making the decision to pay people less for equal work becomes all too easy.

Tee Reel broke down the economic picture of a contemporary porn film. "Usually there's a company owner or a corporate owner. They're giving a budget to a director and saying, 'Go make me a movie,' or 'Make me a bunch of scenes.'" Directors often get paid by keeping whatever is left over after production costs have been divvied up among cast, crew, and incidentals. "So," says Tee Reele, "if that director has ten thousand dollars or twenty thousand dollars in his pocket, or usually less nowadays, they're going to try to save a dollar anywhere they can . . . It's economics. If they know an ethnic model—whether it be Latin, black, Asian—is not going to have as many opportunities to shoot, they feel as if they can cut down on that scene rate. If I know the average rate for a boy/girl scene is a thousand dollars, and I need four Latin girls for this project, and there are thirteen Latin girls fighting to be in this project, I can probably throw some numbers around and just get the cheapest girl."

But economic theories about where these outdated prejudices come from can only go so far when it comes to practice. With women of color making an estimated fifty to seventy-five percent of what their white colleagues earn per scene, performer Nikki Darling had some choice words for those in control of the purse strings: "Even if you're talking about the economics of it all, you are economically disenfranchising people within the industry because of their race. And, in my opinion, that is morally and ethically fucked up," she said. "People can make excuses and allow it to happen all they want. But when you go down to the ethics of it, that's disgusting."

It's worth noting here that adult entertainment as a legal, legitimate industry has only really existed since the late eighties. Most of the people who made porn before that time were, literally, outlaws. Jeanne Silver, who became the first American amputee porn star in 1976 under the name Long Jeanne Silver, told me in an interview, "When I did it, it was illegal. I got arrested with Annie Sprinkle [and others]. We all were arrested in Rhode Island for doing a porn publication [called *Love and Hate* magazine]. It was a major sting." Their group was nicknamed "The Jamestown Eight" and made national news. Jeanne had run away from home as teenager. She made her way to New York City and was taken in by a porn magazine maker and his wife. She liked the culture, so she started doing porn in which she used her amputated leg to penetrate partners—subversive, illegal smut that was widely banned.

She and her desperado compatriots were granted all the rights and privileges that working in a legal industry entails when the *Freeman* verdict was overturned, but many of the people who founded the industry were not used to operating according to the rules of law or trade organizations. Social justice was a priority for a few of them, as it is in any demographic, but certainly not all. And, since only thirty years have passed since the industry was granted a clean and above-board slate for operations, many of the people who got into the industry early are *still in charge*. While porn has tried its best, and often succeeded, in keeping up with the pace of technology and rolling with the punches of distribution shifts, its ability to predict consumer trends and to market itself to keep up with the changing demographics of porn consumers' taboo desires may have fallen by the wayside in important ways.

In lieu of coming up with innovative ideas about what consumers in the twenty-first century might want to see, it's often easiest to continue doing what has always worked in the hopes that pornography can shape taste, rather than catch up with it. And to some degree, it's successful. Most of us may not have considered interracial porn, particularly, as a normal fantasy until we saw it on every porn site we visited, and then we summarily normalized in our brains. I know I did.

But that isn't to say that things will stay as racist and uncomfortable for porn consumers who are, as they say, "woke." A 2016 study by Mic.com and Pornhub took a look at the online porn-consuming habits of millennials and were surprised to discover that five of the top twenty most-searched-for performers were not white, that two of the top twelve search terms were for "ebony" and "black," and that young people who watch porn seem to be generally more open-minded about matters of diversity than their predecessors. As Kelsey Lawrence of Mic.com wrote, "What we like doesn't develop in a vacuum. Much like anything else, who we're attracted to is largely shaped by cultural context." As a new generation of porn consumers grows up in an ever-more multiethnic, multiracial world, their tastes will develop along with their experiences. The industry still has some way to go to catch up to them, though.

MakeLoveNotPorn.tv founder Cindy Gallop told me in an interview once that "porn as an industry has gotten so big it's gotten conventional . . . and it's tanking. The economic recession has driven massive fear and insecurity, and therefore even more the tendency to revert to what is familiar and therefore supposedly safe, and just keep doing the same thing you've always been doing." I think this nail-on-the-head assessment of many of the evils that plague adult entertainment is particularly true of race relations: Interracial porn has always been a taboo market, so many producers simply keep making it in the hopes that it will continue to be so, whether consumers agree with the assessment or not. Thus, little headway is made in changing the status quo, with the result that, while porn consumers may be less titillated by interracial scenes than they were forty years ago, the money flowing down from the top of the porn industry continues to treat white women like princesses and black men like predators, and consumers continue to see interracial porn marketed as taboo.

The thing is—it's not difficult to sell it that way.

Being held by the stunning, smart, and very strong Kelly Shibari at Exxxotica New Jersey 2012 (PHOTO COURTESY OF THE AUTHOR)

CHAPTER 15

Other "Isms"

IN AN INDUSTRY WHERE BODIES are on display, it's not just race that differentiates those bodies in the eyes of their beholders, or in the budgets of those who hire them. Virtually every difference is noted, categorized, and given a price tag. Larger bodies. Smaller bodies. Trans bodies. Disabled bodies.

To put it bluntly, pornography is an industry of objectification. It's arguable that in a capitalist society, everyone objectifies him or herself by selling their labor, but there are few places where this is more baldly true than in the adult film industry. And I believe that there is nothing wrong with that. As Nina Hartley told me, "Humans objectify. Actually all mammals objectify . . . So to say that objectification is 'wrong' is just biologically stupid." And, I would argue, it's particularly silly to pretend that it should not be part of the porn industry.

Most of us have been warned of the evils of sexual objectification, particularly the feminists amongst us, but in the selling of sexual entertainment, objectification sort of comes with the territory. In order to price something in the marketplace, that something must be distilled into an object—even if that something is the image of a human body. Like Mandy Morbid put it to me in 2010, "[Porn] is work, and as a performer you are a commodity."

Of course, this can be—and frequently is—a source of negativity in porn, but whether you believe that it's positive or negative, there isn't a way around the fact that there is an element of objectification in the human arousal process. We see the body of another person and get a thrill from the way it looks, just as much as—and sometimes more than—we appreciate the person living inside that body. And in pornography, when the souls of the people whose bodies we are watching are obscured by the distance and technology between us, that process is made simpler. "At the end of the day," Ryan Driller told me, "I'm a penis having sex with most people's crushes . . . the viewer, the people, the fans, don't necessarily want to totally personify the performers because then they feel a little bad objectifying them."

In pornography, each objectified body is placed somewhere within a complicated metric of supply, demand, and operating costs. In order to turn a profit in the age of Internet piracy, pornographers must make difficult choices about how much to spend on performers, and on what types of performers to hire in the first place. Producers tend to err on the side of content that has proven lucrative in the past, since their profits are by no means guaranteed. Very often, this means they shoot content that portrays fantasies that fall in line with what mainstream culture has taught us to value sexually—what feels "safe." Namely, content featuring slender, white, cisgender females with big boobs, juicy butts, and flawless skin. This archetype sells better not because of the objective superiority of those performers, but because they conform to *more* people's sexual fantasies—many of which were formed by mainstream porn in the first place. So many more people are willing to buy this mainstream stuff that performers who fall outside of the aforementioned archetype are marginalized, paid less, and categorized into niches.

And so we come back to the difficult yet necessary gremlin of categorization. Though in so doing it risks fetishizing marginalized groups, the porn industry must label human beings in one way or another. Historically, pornographers have been happy to do so—they've created dozens, probably hundreds, of categories that break down differences between performers' bodies into niches, making it exponentially easier for consumers to locate what they want. This may feel demeaning for consumers, especially considering the wording that gets used. As Natasha Lennard wrote for *The Nation*, "To consume online porn often entails playing a rough and reductive language game. We navigate a discomforting gauntlet of search terms: a jumble of body parts (pussy, cock, ass, tits), body types (tiny, huge, skinny, curvy), sexual and gender identities (gay, bi, lesbian, trans), sex acts (anal, squirting, pissing, gang bang, bukkake, bondage) all woven into a lattice of racist, sexist, transphobic, ageist, and ableist tropes (big black, Asian teen, thug, schoolgirl, MILF, shemale, and so on)." It's pretty icky.

But consider that most human beings scrolling through the list very likely already have a hand down their pants. Their brains are not necessarily operating at one hundred percent. Porn consumers, in most cases, are looking not for a heart-to-heart experience with another person, but for a quick orgasm. Simplistic, politically incorrect terms that highlight deviations from what's considered the norm are the ones that come to mind in such circumstances. And they are the ones that get searched for.

Although, I should probably point out, that this isn't to say that everyone is looking up the weirdest and grossest search terms imaginable during one-handed typing sessions. Lest ye be convinced that everyone you meet goes home to feverishly search for "big-titted amputee granny gangbang" (not that there is anything *wrong* with that predilection, mind you) the nineteen most searched terms on Pornhub in 2016 didn't get a lot further out there than "creampie" (ejaculation inside a performer's body), "gangbang," and "squirt."

Nevertheless, the bluntness of the terminology people turn to when they're looking for their specific cup of pornographic tea leads us to ponder a troubling fact: What turns people on is almost never politically correct. Far from just the terminology applied to it, human sexual fantasy itself is rife with the kinds of things that make social justice activists cringe, or maybe give up altogether. Sure, people are turned on by sex itself, in flavors from vanilla to rocky road, but people are also—and sometimes exclusively—turned on by things like racial difference, disability, age play, and size fetishization (the fastest-growing search term in the year 2015, according to Pornhub, was "giantess"). Our fellow humans are commonly titillated by themes of incest and coercion. If we're being honest, what turns people on is sometimes some of the most disturbing stuff in the world.

We cannot police people's fantasies. We can't tell somebody that his enjoyment of little people dressed up as maids and submitting to the whims of a demented, sadistic employer is *wrong* any more than we can look down our noses on someone who prefers classic rock to R&B. So long as nobody is being hurt and everybody's a consenting adult, it's a matter of personal taste and consumption. Every human mind is its own weird world with its own axes to grind and its own orgasms to procure, even if those orgasms come from things we'd never condone in "the real world." So, given that pornography's job is to create, then market and sell, the fantasies that people want to see, it's difficult to determine where to draw the line between effective advertising and dastardly fetishization. In some cases, they look awfully similar. Language that would get most of us fired gets thrown around routinely during dirty talk both on and off screen, so why should the people putting labels on videos of sex feel any compunction about printing it on box covers or websites?

The explosion of BDSM into the mainstream with the advent of *Fifty Shades of Grey* in 2011, and the exploring that many Americans did after reading it, has brought to light many of these "darker" fantasies that, it turns out, turn on *lots* of people. The biggest kink website in the world, Kink.com, has rocketed to the top of the online porn world as curious newbies seek out content ranging from sex wrestling to electrocution to master/slave relationships. And, although BDSM is most often a safe, consensual, and healthy way for consenting adults to play out their fantasies, those fantasies are usually what most of us would call dark. The words used in many BDSM scenes—meant to humiliate, debase, and objectify the submissive—could come across as derogatory, defamatory, and even abusive. Yet during play, they are the source of deep arousal and a healthy outlet for sexual fantasy.

Another complication to throw onto the pile is the fact that, while pornography sells us fantasies, in adult films the real world *is* the fantasy world. In the act of manufacturing sexy dreamscapes for the consumption of others, real human beings are paid to act out things that consumers want to *watch*, but might never actually *try*. This can include the aforementioned dirty talk and dark, kinky play. It can also include stepping on people's faces or genitals, acting out scenes of incest, or being literally choked with a penis. And while I would never shame someone for enjoying watching any of these practices, so long as I knew that the people who filmed it were all of age, consenting, and being as safe as possible, I recognize the real-world complications that are involved here. I myself have a penchant for group sex scenes—all those bodies all getting off together is so hot!—but I wouldn't feel okay physically or emotionally if I tried to have sex with ten men at once. Thankfully, there are porn actors who are more than willing to act out my fantasy for me, and I certainly hope that they feel safe, secure, and excited by gangbangs. But since they are being paid to turn my fantasy into a reality at a comfortable distance from my fragile emotions, I can never be sure.

(A quick note on gangbangs: I watched a film in 2011 called *The Fan*

Bang, in which performer Sabrina Deep had sex with a few dozen [if memory serves] of her fans, who had been tested for STIs prior to the shoot. I was fascinated by it. The logistics involved were staggering, and I kept wondering about the etiquette and interpersonal relationships on set. For instance, was it better to be first in line, or last? Did the guys talk to each other backstage? Were there grooming standards? I was so curious, I booked an interview with Ms. Deep, who told me that she'd done around a hundred and fifty gangbangs in her time, with only about a fifth of them being filmed. She just loved them, so she did them whenever she could. The standard thinking about women who engage in this kind of sexual activity is that they're lacking in self-respect, so I asked Sabrina about hers. Her answer was well worth recording here: "You can say 'You disrespected me,' but how can you say 'You disrespected yourself'? Self-respect is like personal taste, like your own mood, like your good or bad sight: It can't be decided by others . . . Feel free to judge me in relation to your world and being and morals, but leave my own relationship with myself to myself." Also, an FYI: The stories of "fluffers" we've all heard are apocryphal *except* for on the sets of some gangbangs, where it's necessary to keep the guys prepped and ready.)

It's true that "porn sex isn't real sex," as pornographers have been telling me for years. These people are, quite literally, professionals. Smoke and mirrors—and a lot of lube application that gets edited out in the final cut—abound. It's important to realize that next time you want to try a DP (double penetration, usually of a vagina and anus simultaneously). But the sex *is still real*. The people who do it are real. And they are doing it for pay. In the sale of sexual labor there is a necessary removal of the subjective human experience from the objective performance they exchange for capital. Once that handoff is made, the performance they turned over becomes subject to the demands of the marketplace, which craves fantasy that rarely lines up with politeness.

And so we end up with categories of porn that draw attention to difference, and with porn studios that specialize in specific differences in order to capitalize on the preferences that each category represents. These niche studios, fewer in number and smaller in size than their vanilla counterparts, obey the demands of the market in which they operate as well as the politics of the industry in which they exist, and offer what they can to both consumers and performers. The tradeoff between politics, politeness, and fantasy often shows its face in titles like *Black Tranny Whackers 27*.

But this isn't a rant about the dehumanization inherent in capitalism. It's an examination of how it comes to pass that human beings with hearts and souls and voices can be distilled into a series of body parts and stereotypes which, all too often, puts them in categories that earn them less than their whiter, thinner, more able-bodied peers.

Over my years as a critic of porn as a product and a hanger-on to the industry that makes it, I found myself gravitating, as I've noted, toward feminist pornography that leaned to the far left: queer, indie fare that employed performers who didn't always fit the white, thin, able-bodied mold that the mainstream industry tended to employ. Predictably, as I was drawn to this smaller world, I began to interview and thus get to know the performers and directors who made it. I felt a kinship with those who chose the less-beaten path, or whose journeys were defined for them by virtue of their inability to fit the expectations of mainstream porn—or the mainstream world at large. I became much closer to many of these people than I'd ever dared to get with porn stars with more recognizable names and more standardized looks.

In a way, getting to know the people who didn't even bother with red carpets and VIP lists brought me closer to myself. If I'd never branched off into their corners of the industry, I'd have never gotten to where I am politically, personally, or sexually. Their thoughtful answers to interview questions, coupled with their political activism and serious *hotness*, helped me learn what gender studies in college might have, in a more exciting way than I'd probably have gotten from academia. But as I watched their careers take shape, I was forced to watch them struggle with just how difficult it is to be an "other" in an industry that's already been "othered" to hell and back by the rest of the world. Most of the people I was getting to know were plus-sized or trans or disabled or fit into any number of other categories that place them neatly into one of porn's less-public niches—those corners even the proudest of porn viewers rarely admit to peeking into. And the corners I became dedicated to learning about and advocating for.

The viewership for most niche porn is significantly smaller than that of mainstream content. With a smaller customer base to sell to, there are fewer studios that regularly shoot niche content featuring performers of color, trans actors, models of size, performers of different ability levels, and so on. And, whereas there were once dozens of companies in Los Angeles shooting most kinds of niche content, there are now only a handful for each specialty. Most of those studios don't have a lot of cash to throw around, which is the biggest reason that they often pay lower rates. And although the talent pool in any one of these categories is smaller than the more mainstream ocean of models, there are always more actors than there are scenes to shoot or studios shooting them. With a glut of talent and a paucity of roles, the inevitable occurs: *someone* is always willing to take lower pay. And, since lower rates *can* be paid, they *are*. Once a director has paid a lower rate for one transgender performer, for instance, that director will be loath to up their rate the next time. Other directors will also resist paying more than their competition. And thus the going rate for a transgender scene is lowered across the board.

A troubling caveat is that the amount of money these niches make is often disproportionate to the amount they put into production. The porn industry is infamous for its unwillingness to show the numbers, but it's been stated repeatedly by industry insiders that niche porn out-earns its mainstream competition by a large margin. Those who want to see high-quality niche pornography, faced with few options, are willing to pay more than those with more "normal" tastes. In an interview in 2011 with the CEO of JuicyAds.com, I was told, "The harder to find or the more obscure the porn is, *that's* where people are making money. That's where the demand is . . . I mean, how many teen sites are there? How many amateur sites are there? You don't have any problems finding them because everybody has *twenty* of them." But balloon-popping busty giantesses in tutus? If that's your fantasy, you'll be happy to pay whomever can provide it.

Perhaps the biggest money-making niche, particularly given its comparatively diminutive size, is mainstream trans (TS) porn. Though Venus Lux, who won the 2016 AVN award for "Transexual Performer of the Year," estimates that there are about ten companies or fewer shooting TS now—it's well-known in the industry that this type of content earns far more per scene than its competition. TS porn features predominantly trans women (trans men are more frequently seen in queer porn) paired with cisgender men, and it is the fourth most popular genre of pornography on the worldwide market. It is searched for more frequently than "butts" or "threesomes," according to the authors of *A Billion Wicked Thoughts*.

Fans of TS porn, who are overwhelmingly straight white men, are devoted enough to pay more for what they want to see, too. Evil Angel VP Adam Grayson told *International Business Times* in 2015 that transsexual porn earns more than standard porn. "Hands down, without a question," he said. "Nothing even touches it." His company can charge a full twenty-five percent more per TS movie—at the extremely marked-down wholesale level—than for a typical mainstream film, and fans will pay the increased retail price for the chance to see it. Trans performers, thus, earn more for their producers than their cisgender counterparts, scene for scene. But despite its outsize contributions to the industry, the TS segment of the adult talent pool has long faced discrimination both in pay and representation.

I won't try to make this book a primer on transgender issues, but I will take a moment to say that trans women—women who were designated male at birth, usually owing to the presence of a penis—are a diverse group. They come from every conceivable background and share virtually nothing aside from a gender identity that isn't as common as others. But mainstream porn expects that they present themselves, both cosmetically and sexually, in very specific ways. "TS girls," as they're often called, are more or less required by most porn companies to be tall, willowy, and traditionally feminine in appearance, with large breasts. They're expected to wear hyper-feminine clothing and lots of makeup, and to "pass" as cisgender women in their daily lives. But once they take off their clothes for the camera, they must be endowed with penises large enough for porn (which is to say quite large indeed), and those penises must be capable of achieving erection and ejaculation on command, like those of cisgender men in porn. Of course, there are some trans women well suited to these prerequisites, but there are many more who don't fit into this narrow definition of what a TS girl should be, according to what producers think straight white men want to see.

Tobi Hill-Meyer, a trans activist who has worked behind and in front of the camera in both the mainstream and indie segments of the industry has written, spoken, and even produced a film about her experiences with mainstream production companies who wanted her to conform to their expectations. Hill-Meyer prefers a less traditionally feminine look, but she was asked to shave her legs and wear heels to her first shoot. When the sexy stuff started, she writes in *The Feminist Porn Book*, "I wasn't allowed to be sexy the way I would be with my own lovers or partners. I had to fit an entirely different model." When she was doing a masturbation scene for her first mainstream porn shoot, she says, "After about five minutes the photographer leaned in and said in a somewhat exasperated voice, 'So, are you going to come now?' As you can imagine, that kind of pressure only makes things more difficult." Her inability to ejaculate on command, she writes, is "a pretty common condition among trans women; in fact, the ability to ejaculate is about as common (or uncommon) among cis women as it is among trans women." But the mainstream companies she was shooting for required it. One even asked her to squirt lube onto her stomach to simulate a money shot.

These expectations, of course, assume that the woman in question is comfortable enough with her genitalia to want to use them in the way the director demands in the first place, but many trans women are not, and choose to use entirely different means to get themselves off. But in TS porn made for straight men, they are expected to have penetrative sex with partners or to masturbate just like a cis man would. And while it's all well and good for a director to have an idea of what they want to shoot, it's another to expect all trans women to behave the same way to conform to that ideal. And no matter what, it's not okay to ignore the contributions of those who have excelled in the genre.

Until 2012, TS performers were largely ignored during awards season, being shunted off the red carpet without getting to the media for interviews and—familiarly—not being given a slot for their awards during the annual AVN Awards show. After decades of this treatment, performers balked, and rightly so. AVN capitulated after some of the TS performers vocally crusaded against this lesser-than treatment, and the award for "Transsexual Performer of the Year" is now presented onstage during the ceremony, while TS stars are encouraged to strut their gorgeous stuff on the red carpet along with everyone else. Meanwhile, the Transgender Erotica Awards, which were called "The Tranny Awards" from their inception in 2008 until 2013, were renamed in 2014 by event organizer Grooby after performers expressed discomfort with the terminology.

And, while there are still leaps and bounds to be made within the industry about the representation of diversity and the terminology used in reference to trans models, the use of the derogatory "shemale" and "tranny" labels has been on the decrease since outspoken trans women in the industry have begun speaking their minds. But, as Venus Lux told me, "It's up to the cisgender males to make the decision about literacy" as the genre continues to move forward with a more aware public. "There's so much of a disconnect between studio owners and performers about terminology," she said, that the issue is still fraught.

And for all this talk over TS porn, it's important to note that as far as mainstream porn is concerned, there's only one kind of trans person worth filming: trans women. Although a growing number of trans men, like two of my favorite humans, Buck Angel and James Darling, are making their own content and demanding more visibility, the trans male porn market is still virtually nonexistent. Basically, the straight white cisgender guys who run most of the porn industry don't want to deal with trans guys as sexual beings, convinced as they still seem to be that the people who buy porn all look and think exactly like they do. They've relegated trans guys to indie porn and the occasional novelty item, even as awareness of trans issues has bloomed across the American consciousness in recent years. It's depressing to see, but it's also amazing to watch as trans guys in porn develop their own markets and show the mainstream world a thing or two about what people really want.

But the world of niche porn is still dominated by inequality; similar issues are found across most niche categories. BBW (big, beautiful women) performers, for instance, are not as numerous as their thinner counterparts, but their fans are extremely loyal. Though the category itself is established enough to prove that it makes money, very few studios were willing to shoot BBW content until well into my time as a porn critic. There was no recognition for BBW actors in industry awards ceremonies. In the late 2000s, however, BBW performers with strong fan bases and a lot to say about the way they were being represented began to pop up around the industry. And when women like Kelly Shibari and April Flores pop up, they refuse to be overlooked.

April, with her late husband, filmmaker Carlos Batts, has made dozens of films and an art book, *Fat Girl*, in which April featured as a muse and fashion plate. April has written for numerous publications about her activism as a woman of size who demands to be seen as beautiful and sexy. She has performed primarily but not exclusively in indie porn projects, where larger women are more frequently portrayed than in mainstream porn, earning herself a "Heartthrob of the Year" award at the Feminist Porn Awards in 2010. And, at the inception of the long-overdue "BBW of the Year" AVN Award in 2014, April took home the first statuette—and the second, when she won again in 2015.

Not long after April's entrance into the industry, Kelly Shibari began performing when her work on Hollywood productions dried up during the writers' strike of 2007 to 2008. She told me that when a friend encouraged her to try porn, "I said, 'There's no fat girls in porn.' And he said, 'Yes, there is.' I said, 'Oh, no, it's like a circus freak thing.' At that point what I'd known about bigger girls in adult entertainment were like those postcards that you see at the beach, where there's like five-, six-hundred pound women just laying on the beach kind of blubbery, you know. It was more like a gag." She found one company—The Score Group—that presented its models with more glamor. So she sent in photos, got hired for a shoot, and began breaking boundaries for plus-size performers like she was born for it. Since then, Kelly has become an outspoken advocate for plus-size women in both pornography and the mainstream, starring in everything from educational porn films to her own self-produced content, making a cameo appearance on *Sons of Anarchy*, and becoming the first ever plus-size woman to appear on the cover of *Penthouse Forum* and in the pages of *Penthouse*.

These two performers, and many other plus-size performers in recent years, have spoken up about representation in pornography, and everywhere else. And yet, despite the great strides that have been made (you'll find much less cetacean language in the marketing these days, for example), plus-size models still have only a handful of production companies for which to work.

At AVN in 2016, Tim von Swine told me, "I've been working with a lot of plus-size girls. The plus-size girls genre is never going to go anywhere, and I'll tell you why. There's not enough companies that shoot it to put enough money [into it] for all of them to take it as seriously as it needs to be [taken] . . . I love the fact that these girls are willing to take their clothes off on camera, and get bent . . . They *love* it. They want to do more of that stuff, but there's no one around to do it."

To further salt the wound, BBW performers also earn less than their smaller contemporaries. In an article for *xoJane*, Kelly Shibari estimated that rates for plus-size scenes cap out at around four hundred for boy/girl pairings. For comparison's sake, slimmer women earn up to fifteen hundred for the same kind of scene.

Familiar supply-and-demand reasoning stands behind the lower rates for BBW performers, as it does in any niche category of pornography, and it stands up to the same level of scrutiny: It makes a modicum of economic *sense*, but that sense doesn't make it *right*. Performers in all niches have become more vocal about how they would like to be represented more respectfully, and in many cases these efforts are being rewarded by updated terminology, stronger recognition by the established industry powers, and greater visibility in the mainstream media. But across the board, niche models are still paid less by fewer studios and then marketed to consumers in ways that often go against their wishes.

Updating the terminology and representation for performers is an important step: Calling the stars of a film "differently abled," for example, rather than "crippled" isn't a particularly difficult transition, and switching out the "shemale" button on your website for "trans" presents only minor confusion for users. But categorization is still necessary, especially in the case of niche studios that cater to a specific customer base whose loyalty has been hard-earned by years of consistent output of a specific type of content. Especially since tube sites, where pirated material can be posted for free by any user, are happy to categorize videos however the person who uploads them decides to describe them doing away with categories that keep videos firmly in their given niche is not a viable option for most.

There are a few brave souls trying to prove that categorization doesn't have to be demeaning, though. Many queer porn outlets, like Pink & White Productions and Foxhouse Films, label their performers and scenes according to the wishes of their performers. And TrenchcoatX, an indie company cofounded by Stoya and Kayden Kross, has reinvented the standard porn labeling system in favor of gender nonbinary, nondiscriminatory terminology like "breasts: natural or augmented," "pubic parts: mostly internal or external," "heterosex," "the help (dildos/toys/etc.)" and so on. As reported in *The Nation*, "It is an attempt to recode a landscape of commodified sexuality that promotes retrograde categories as titillating transgressions." And, so far, it seems to be working.

The integration of different types of scenes into more mainstream content is another option, and it's one that some studios have tried. Not every scene featuring a black male actor, for instance, needs to be labeled under "interracial" because most consumers have no aversion to seeing performers of color in their smut. However, those specifically seeking that kind of scene might balk if their favorite category were done away with, leaving them casting about for the content they want. And so many sites persist with the outmoded terminology.

Perhaps a shift from within could start with payment. It would be like a dream, from a social justice perspective, if the entire industry switched to an equal-pay-for-equal work model in which everyone, regardless of their physical attributes, were paid on the same scale. Some indie and feminist porn companies already operate on this model, like Pink & White Productions. But, given the subjective nature of porn performance, this could be impossible to nail down across the wide expanse of the porn industry. What a standard boy/girl anal scene is worth to one director might be very different from what it's worth to another, depending on that director's customer base and budget. And it would hardly make sense to offer a brand-new performer the same rate as a veteran of the industry with multiple years of experience and a few awards under her belt.

As it stands, performers can command their own prices, and many do, according to experience level, skill set, and how often they want to work. But if their price is too high for directors to pay, they can be left high and dry; one must be competitive to get cast. Having a good agent to stand up for you helps with that. But base rates are base rates, dictated by supply and demand, as well as by what producers and their bosses consider appropriate. Anyone who wants to be hired as a new performer needs to get in line and work their way up. And in that line, white, thin, able-bodied women are at the front, and *everybody else* is behind them.

Cindy Gallop and her MakeLoveNotPorn.tv team are attempting to provide a new business model that could help level the playing field, if her company proves that it is sustainable and profitable: profit-sharing with performers. When profits are split down the middle between the website administration and the people doing the labor on camera—as they are at MakeLoveNotPorn.tv—regardless of their race, class, size, ability level, gender, or any other identifier, there is no way to discriminate or to cut pay from anyone. "I would urge the porn industry to have the courage to believe that you *can* do things differently, and *do* them differently . . . Within the porn industry, as I say, there is now enormous room for individual creative vision," says Gallop.

As with so many things, the most radical change may have to come from a larger shift in the way that sexual value is assigned culturally. It's no coincidence that the recognition of trans and BBW performers as important members of the porn community has come at the same time that widespread acceptance of transgender people and people of size has swept the American mainstream. With advocates like Laverne Cox and Melissa McCarthy gaining visibility in Hollywood, the movements backing them are changing the way that Americans see people who look and identify differently. Once the world has had some time to get used to the idea that white, able-bodied, skinny, cisgender women are not the only people who can be accepted as sexy, the porn industry may find itself eager to catch up with the times by expanding its definition of who belongs in "mainstream" porn, and who deserves to make competitive wages. As fervently as I believe that my friends in queer, indie, and feminist porn who proudly own their beautiful, unique bodies and desires deserve to be paid just as well as the hottest mainstream porn stars, the rest of the world has not quite caught up with our way of thinking just yet.

At the AVN Awards in 2011, I looked for my new friends from the fringes of the industry, but I was disappointed to see very few in attendance. Most of them would have been welcome at the awards ceremony as audience members, but there were very few awards available for people working in their niches, and there certainly wasn't space for them on the media-friendly red carpet outside. As the parade of "normal" people plodded across the stage before me, I sighed and downed more whiskey.

CHAPTER 16

The Gay Divide & the Condom Wars

IN THE YEARS BETWEEN my review of *East Coast ASSault* and the 2011 AVN Awards, gay porn had almost never crossed my radar. I occasionally partook of a few clips of men going at it during my guilty Internet wallows, but I had never been given any to review for the print magazine. Nor had it ever been offered by any of the companies that sent me review material for *WHACK!* I'd noticed at Exxxotica and the Adult Entertainment Expo that there weren't many gay models on hand, and it began to dawn on me that for some reason, gay porn was a mystery to me.

My inquiries were met with vague answers: "Gay porn is a separate industry," or "Our readership just isn't interested in gay stuff." I'd been willing enough to focus on straight and queer porn, since I had my hands more than full enough covering the news, politics, and pace of those segments of adult entertainment for *WHACK!*, writing reviews and set copy for print magazines, finishing up night classes in publishing, working two part-time jobs, and juggling two committed relationships. My swing party attendance had fallen off, as I'd recognized that I just didn't have it in me to write a whole book about the swinging lifestyle, and my *McSweeney's* column had wrapped up. But I'd filled the gap in my writing life by joining a poetry group that hosted costume parties, and by starting my own blog to continue where my *McSweeney's* column left off. So, though I was interested in finding out more, I assumed that my experience hadn't yet converged with gay porn, and left it at that.

It wasn't until I attended the 2011 AVN Awards that I realized just how segregated gay smut really was from the straight stuff. I'd expected there to be *some* mention, during the long evening, of the gay industry's achievements. Even a token mention, like a single award presented for best gay actor, or one of those less-exalted awards not given out during the ceremony. But as the night dragged on and I ingested whiskey to keep myself from falling asleep (not the best strategy), it became clear that no mention of gay sex was forthcoming. How odd.

Even more odd, now that I got to thinking about it, was the fact that when I'd done Internet research on most of the male porn stars I'd interviewed thus far, I'd come across quite a few old photos of them having sex with men on what were clearly gay porn sets. Yet when I talked to them about their careers or read interviews and Wikipedia articles about them, the subject of their dalliances in male-on-male action almost never came up. Something was clearly up, but I hadn't spent much time trying to figure out what.

We must keep in mind that "gay," here, does not refer—*at all*—to women. There were plenty of awards doled out for "bisexual" (two women with one man) scenes and "girl/girl" porn. But "gay" is a term, in mainstream pornography, reserved specifically for homosexual cisgender men. Furthermore, "queer" applies only to porn made outside the confines of the mainstream industry, usually blurring lines between genders and sexual orientations and rarely including cisgender men. So when I say that gay porn is its own cloistered world, I'm talking about something very specific.

In 2011, there was—and still is, as of the time I'm writing this—astonishingly little overlap between the two industries. Despite many similarities in corporate structure, performer pay rates, filming techniques, and more, they remain separated by a number of issues.

Although there are certainly exceptions to the rule, and the rule itself is changing as time goes on, the majority of straight mainstream porn coming out of Los Angeles is still filmed with a straight male viewer in mind. Most of this material is also filmed *by* straight males who, like many of their brethren in America, have been brought up with the idea that the slightest whiff of homoeroticism is tantamount to a revocation of their "man card." (God I hate that term.) As feminist pornographer Jennifer Lyon Bell told me once in an interview, "American culture is practically phobic about showing imagery of intimate male sexuality outside of a gay context," and her assessment speaks directly to the almost hysterical fear of male sensuality in straight porn, in which male actors are often pared down to torsos with penises attached, rather than human beings with feelings or even faces. Bell continued, "We've trained men to be silent and invisible during sex, and it's a damn shame." Part of what makes it so unfortunate is the fact that, over the decades, the San Fernando Valley has become a bastion of chest-pounding hetero dudes whose fear of being labeled gay isn't just a social concern. For most of them, it's a career decision to be as straight as humanly possible—any implication of homosexuality could tarnish their reputations and possibly damage their careers.

This strict delineation of sexuality has resulted in a just-as-strict separation between straight and gay porn, even though they are basically the two pillars of the mainstream porn world. Two large industries with decades of history, which operate on similar models, and that share remarkably similar internal politics. As the authors of *A Billion Wicked Thoughts* put it, "Except for the fact that the male body is the star, gay porn looks and feels *exactly* like straight porn." The main difference between them—aside from the fact that there are no women performing in the gay industry—is that men make considerably more money in gay porn because the demand for male performers there is exponentially higher. It's also much less difficult for an aspiring male performer to get into gay porn, where there exists a mirror of the "new girl" rapaciousness in the constant search for fresh faces and bodies. And although "maleness" (whatever that means) is highly prized in gay porn, there's a less overwhelming atmosphere of conservative masculinity in the air. The demand for men of different types, from domineering alphas to sweet submissives and everything in between, means that a guy who doesn't necessarily fit the no-homo mentality of the straight industry can still get hired for a gay porn shoot, so long as he can perform.

Meanwhile, landing a spot in straight porn is difficult, to put it mildly. Producers and directors are hesitant to give new talent a try, due mostly to the fact that it is extremely rare for a guy to be able to get and maintain an erection, on demand, with a camera on them, along with the eyes of a director and any other production crew that might be on set— much less be capable of ejaculating at the right time. The stable of male stars who work in the straight industry is kept small, with reliable, tried, and true performers filling in all the gaps (zing!).

"The reason why you see the same guys in porn over and over again is because you can trust those guys to come in and do [their] job,"

Tee Reel explained to me. "To be a guy working as a full-time job is very difficult. You can come in and do a couple scenes and be a part-time performer, and somebody might test you in a gangbang or a blowbang to see if you can keep your dick hard around the guys, if you can stay focused, and then they'll give you a shot working on a one-on-one. That's how most guys get in." At least one straight male performer has told me that he did his first few porn scenes for free because getting paid work was nearly impossible. In other words, the best way to land a spot in the straight porn industry as a man is to already have a track record of successful performances. But getting those successful performances in the first place can be tough. For that reason, many straight guys start out in gay porn, where the requirements are a bit less stringent. But, if he has his sights set on transitioning into straight porn, he faces the scrutiny of the super-hetero crew on that side of the fence.

Now-retired performer Danny Wylde told me in a 2011 interview that, when he started doing porn, "I wasn't working full-time at all. So I took the jobs that were available to me. Many of them came from the heavy S/M or gay sides of the industry." So that's where he worked, until he decided to try to get more mainstream straight work. "It wasn't until about a year later that I learned of the stigma attached to [gay-to-straight] crossover male talent," he said. Danny was fortunate in being able to make the leap, but some aren't.

Lance Hart, founder of PervOut.com, spent two years as a contract model for a high-end gay company. "It was great money, awesome company, all that. When my contract was up, I wanted to do straight stuff . . . And that's when I hit the wall of, 'Oh, you've done gay stuff. You can't play with us. Because gay people have cooties,'" he said in 2016.

"Cooties" is actually a good word for the situation, because the divide between gay and straight industries is in place largely due to the threat of disease, whether real or imaginary. To paint a complicated situation in extremely broad strokes, the gay industry *generally* relies more on condoms to keep performers safe, while the straight industry relies more heavily on current STI test results. This difference is somewhat in keeping with larger cultural norms. In the most sweepingly general terms, gay male culture, with its roots so firmly based in the AIDS epidemic that swept the eighties and nineties, has embraced, normalized, and even celebrated the use of condoms, and the gay porn world has taken that as its cue when it comes to sex on camera. But the straight porn industry has taken a different approach—testing instead of condoms. There is a host of reasons for this preference, which we'll discuss, but the upshot is that men who have worked in gay porn are often seen as vectors of sexually transmitted infections because it's thought that their industry does not apply testing standards as rigorously. Their reputation is not fair or accurate, but it persists nevertheless, in the manner that prejudices often do.

Danny Wylde explained to me, "My issue with the straight porn industry is that crossover male talent have been singled out as the only 'high risk' group for disseminating HIV among the talent pool. Those who participate in prostitution, intravenous drug use, and other 'high risk' activity do not seem to be taken into consideration (albeit these activities are harder to prove). Crossover talent are held to the same standards as everyone else working in straight porn. And they are just as likely, or unlikely, to participate in 'high risk' behavior off set. So when you really look at the issue, it seems that the stigma attached to male homosexuality in general trumps the concern over HIV transmission." In fact, most instances of HIV infections in the industry have been proven to come from non-industry activity, just like Danny said.

When you really think about it, it's something of a brainteaser as to how homophobia can even exist in straight porn. As director Ivan revealed to me, "You quickly get over the homophobia working in porn." He went into some in-depth descriptions of scenarios he'd seen at shoots in which supposedly straight men did things that most would qualify as further down the Kinsey scale than solidly "heterosexual." I won't repeat them here, for the sake of my readers' delicate sensibilities, but he made a good point. (And the interview is on YouTube, should you be curious.)

Furthermore, given that the porn industry as a whole is regularly pilloried by mainstream media, considered the primary vector for immoral sexual behavior in our society, it's odd to think that anyone in this marginalized industry would be eager to further marginalize others. Wouldn't it be more effective and friendlier for everyone to get along?

But, alas, pornography is something of a funhouse mirror to mainstream society—many of the issues we see in everyday life are re-created in adult entertainment, distorted and blown out of proportion. And homophobia has long been one of these outsized, wibbly-wobbly reflections. Many men in the straight industry are terrified of being seen as even the tiniest bit gay, and much of that fear comes from the debate over condom use versus STI testing. The official line on testing versus condoms from the straight industry is that consumers don't want to see condoms in porn, that the sight of latex destroys the fantasy. Recent research has shown that men of all sexual orientations tend to prefer condomless sex scenes over sheathed porn, though around thirty percent don't really care either way. But few producers are willing to bet on condoms in their content; I have heard and read numerous producers swear that condoms drive down sales. And, in such a difficult economic climate as the current one, they're not willing to take the risk.

But there are several "condom-mandatory" companies that require condoms on every set—one of these companies happens to be Wicked Pictures, one of the biggest, oldest, most respected names in the straight porn industry. Condoms are required for anal and vaginal penetration on all Wicked sets, with oral sex and the all-important "pop shot" being exempt. Wicked is one of few companies that still operates on a contract model—paying salaries to its contracted performers and promoting them, thus turning them into true porn *stars*. This is a business model that requires a huge investment on the part of the company, and Wicked's continued success is evident in its production of big-budget feature films, massive presence at industry conventions, and steady stream of awards. Clearly, condoms have not hurt Wicked too badly.

Although most straight companies claim to be "condom optional," meaning that actors can use condoms if they want to, the truth in practice is less benign. It's not uncommon for performers to ask for a condom on set and be provided with one, only to later find themselves blacklisted from that director or company's roster. Especially in recent years, with turnover rates for talent higher than ever and profits bottoming out, many companies would prefer to hire someone else next time rather than deal with someone who wants to use condoms. Some actors have reported getting into fights with directors on set that ended in tears, walk-offs, and cancellations, resulting in a bad reputation for being difficult to work with, all over wanting to use condoms. As with many issues in porn, the issue of blacklisting over barrier protection is always in flux, and I have been told more recently that this stigma is beginning to decline. But still, in such a small, sequestered industry, reputations make and break careers, so it's not uncommon for newbies to agree to work without condoms against their deeper wishes in order to safeguard future work.

Established performers who have proven themselves profitable are often able to dictate their safer sex terms more effectively, and a significant number shoot only with condoms, but for most active talent, being picky isn't as viable an option.

BUT, INDUSTRY POLITICS ASIDE, it's important to note that condoms in porn aren't necessarily the failsafe one might think. There's a reason that the term for sex with barrier protection has been modified from "safe sex" to "saf*er* sex," after all. While condoms are "highly effective in preventing the transmission of HIV," according to the CDC, they're not foolproof by any means. They aren't equally effective for every STI, especially those that can be transmitted by skin-to-skin contact, like HPV and herpes. They can break, slip off, and—especially in sustained, over-the-top porn sex—cause friction burns inside the penetrated partners' body. Latex burn means microtears on the interior of a sexually penetrated cavity, which leave a person far more vulnerable to STI transmission. If the condom breaks, and the penetrating partner has an STI—surprise! That latex burn becomes a big problem.

Due to the vigorous and prolonged nature of the sex that porn stars have on camera, furthermore, it could be argued that using condoms at all on a porn set is tantamount to using them improperly. Your average condom is not built to withstand hours of use, frequent stops and starts, or the athletic rigor of what Seymore Butts once called "circus-act sex." Particularly if there are numerous participants using condoms in the same scene, the possibility of a malfunction ratchets up exponentially—and each malfunction calls for a stop to the action, a re-sheathing of the penis in question, a water break, a bathroom break . . . By the time filming starts again, precious minutes have passed. By the end of a shoot, the use of condoms can equate to hours of extra time on set, and many more microfissures inside the body of the penetrated actors. As legendary performer (and registered nurse) Nina Hartley told *The Huffington Post*, "Shooting scenes with condoms are noticeably more uncomfortable . . . They aren't built to withstand our shoots."

Adult entertainers often have a list of reasons for preferring or *not* preferring to use condoms on camera. Whichever direction they go with, that choice should, I believe, be left up to them—not to directors, and certainly not to anyone outside the industry who lacks an understanding of the many variables. So, in order to keep performers as safe as possible with or without the use of condoms, the straight industry has put in place an ever-evolving testing protocol that strives to prevent STIs from entering the talent pool in the first place.

LEGENDARY PERFORMER JOHN HOLMES succumbed to AIDS in 1988 after having worked on gay sets where, rumor has it, he initially contracted HIV. Back then, the young and spread-out industry had no system to test its talent, but most producers did their best to ascertain the sexual health of their performers before filming. It wasn't until 1998 that the Adult Industry Medical (AIM) clinic was founded by retired performer Sharon Mitchell, who had quit doing porn to become a sexologist and health counselor. AIM became the main testing center for adult talent, using performers' test results to construct a database that could be referenced easily by anyone in the industry before a shoot. Producers collectively self-imposed a testing regimen in which all models needed to have test results no more than thirty days old in order to shoot. All sexual activity was to be logged into the system, thereby creating a network through which disease transmission could be tracked and any infected performers' sexual partners, and their partners, could be alerted and tested.

This system, called SxCheck, was still in its infancy when Marc Wallice, an award-winning performer who was rumored to be an intravenous drug user, tested positive for HIV in 1998. Rumors spread that he had been hiding his positive status for some time, and AIM set to work tracing his work history and testing his scene partners. Things were quiet until 2004, when Darren James tested positive for HIV. It was later determined that he had contracted the virus on a set in Brazil, where there is a less-rigorous testing system in place. He kept working upon his return to the US, and had infected three female partners before he tested positive. In order to contain the outbreak, the American porn industry effectively shut itself down for thirty days to reduce the risk of the infections spreading further. (If you hear about any other industry that self-imposes a moratorium on business when somebody gets sick, please do let me know about it, by the way.)

In the years that followed, similar outbreaks cropped up from time to time: Performers would test positive for HIV, the industry would shut down until all affected partners could be notified and tested, and then things would get going again. After the 2004 outbreak, however, there were no confirmed cases of transmission between partners on a porn set until 2014, when a gay male actor transferred the virus to a scene partner on camera. The actor in question had been recently tested, but using a testing method that was slower than the industry-standard RNA test. The industry duly shut down production and tracked down the actor's other scene partners to stop the spread of the virus. In this and several other cases, actors who tested positive were either gay-to-straight crossover male performers, or male performers who worked with transsexual female performers. As a result, the stigma that still haunts these actors was perpetuated.

Some studies have shown that porn actors are not at a statistically significant increased risk of STI infection than the general population, and at least one has found that the adult film talent pool is less affected by STIs than the rest of Los Angeles County. Other studies have shown different results, but the reality seems to fall somewhere in the middle; porn stars don't seem to be at a particularly elevated risk for STIs, though many would have us believe otherwise. I may be a bit of an optimist, but knowing what I know about the testing system in porn, I'd rather take my chances with going home with a porn star than a "civilian" from a bar any day of the week (and maybe, just maybe, I have). Not only are they likely to know what they're doing once we get there, they're probably going to know their STI status and be a lot less afraid to tell me about it than most of the population.

Over the years, furthermore, the testing system in the industry underwent constant improvement—testing methods and schedules were updated regularly. And in 2011, the system was working insofar as it could at keeping those inside the industry protected. But even as industry self-regulation was evolving, the AIDS Healthcare Foundation (AHF), the largest AIDS service nonprofit organization in the United States, was unrolling a massive campaign to dismantle the porn industry's testing system and impose legislation requiring condoms on all porn shoots. After the Darren James incident in 2004, AHF began to lobby the state of California to require condom use by male performers, and to register mountains of complaints against those who did not. Federal blood-borne pathogens law already mandated that barrier protection should be used between mucous membranes in places of work, but those rules were written for medical settings, not adult film sets, so they had been largely ignored by the adult film industry until AHF began raising a ruckus over the issue.

After initial attempts to force the state government's hand proved unsuc-
cessful, AHF's president, Michael Weinstein, eventually pushed an ordinance through the Los Angeles city legislature that required condoms in
permit-bearing porn films. The ordinance, which became law in 2012,
was easy for filmmakers to get around; production companies with studios on premises fell outside its parameters, and other porn producers
just didn't bother to get licenses before filming.

So, later in 2012, Weinstein became the outspoken leader of AHF's
new campaign to fund and pass Measure B, a ballot initiative that required
condoms in all licensed porn movies filmed in Los Angeles County. It also
required that production companies obtain and display health permits,
which would require them to incur significant costs. Given the shoestring
budgets of many small studios in the age of online piracy, this did not go
over well. Nor did the fact that AHF spent over two million dollars on
backing the initiative and countless man-hours on the collection of more
than three hundred thousand signatures to get it on the ballot. Two million
dollars, critics said, could have been used to fight AIDS—the supposed
mission of AHF in the first place.

But Weinstein's, and by default AHF's, fixation on condoms has fa-
mously been aimed at adult entertainment, and in the past decade that laser
focus has been applied via ballot initiatives, lawsuits, lobbying, and rumored
underhanded tactics in order to force barrier protection onto porn actors.
The fight has been continuous, unrelenting, and frankly peculiar in its fe-
rocity. At AVN in 2016, Wicked contract star jessica drake summed it up
nicely: "One man, Michael Weinstein, seems to have a very personal agenda
against the industry. And so instead of running the AIDS Healthcare Foundation, and . . . helping people with HIV, or helping prevent the spread of
HIV/AIDS, he seems to be focusing all of his efforts on taking us down."

Porn industry bloggers have speculated that Weinstein may have financial ties to condom companies. Others think that he may be seeking
to take over the industry's testing apparatus or to name himself the czar
of set inspections—either of which would mean AHF could land hefty
government contracts and fatten up Weinstein's paycheck. Whatever the
case may be, I think Nina Hartley summed it up most succinctly an interview when she ranted, "The push for condom use is strictly driven by
PC bullshit, tainted by old-fashioned Puritanism, by people with a political agenda who are skeeved out by porn."

This fixation on putting condoms on performers came amidst AHF's relentless hassling of the industry's primary testing clinic, AIM. Weinstein and company produced public spectacles outside the clinic in Sherman Oaks, and called out the clinic's refusal to share patient STI status with county health officials and violation of federal HIPAA laws by sharing STI status within the porn industry. In February 2011, AIM's private database of performer STI status, birth dates, stage names, real names, home addresses, and more, was breached. A website (which I will not name here because I don't want to drive any traffic its way) appeared, exposing the private information of over twelve thousand industry workers, both past and present, along with derogatory language, photos, and more. Although some of the information, it was argued, had to come from elsewhere, it was widely agreed that the majority must have come from AIM's patient database. After the ensuing flurry of lawsuits and hysteria, AIM closed permanently in May 2011, leaving the industry bereft. The Free Speech Coalition—the industry's premier trade organization—stepped in, creating the FSCPass system, which now takes responsibility for the collation, dispensation, and security of performer test records that are routed to it from several FSC-approved testing facilities. Many attributed AIM's slip-ups to its near monopoly on industry testing, so it is hoped that more testing clinics on the scene will lead to a more democratized testing landscape.

I followed all these developments with horrified fascination. From my perch in New York, it boggled my mind that anybody would be so cruel as to target an industry that already bears the brunt of our nation's neuroses about sex, disease, and privacy. Model April Flores recalled of her experience being outed, "We're already out there so much. Can't our [stage] name just be our name and have some level of safety?" Porn actors were fearing for their lives as their fans and potentially stalkers learned their home addresses and phone numbers. Retired performers' new careers were threatened when bosses discovered their former jobs. The health of thousands of people was put in jeopardy by the shutdown of the clinic. A multi-billion-dollar industry was sent into a tailspin, and my moonlighting as a porn journalist was in jeopardy, to boot. I wrote frantically about the goings-on in LA but found little in the way of interest or readership; the industry-insider politics weren't as fascinating to the layperson, I discovered, as they were to me. And though no concrete link was ever established between the AHF and the disgruntled former porn worker who seems to have published the leaked information, rumors flew that the timing of the leak coincided a little *too* neatly with AHF's attempts to discredit the clinic. The leak was all that AHF needed to renew its efforts to force the porn industry to do something it didn't want to do: force all its performers to use condoms.

In 2012, the Free Speech Coalition galvanized in an attempt to stand against Measure B, and numerous other trade associations, publications, and porn industry icons spoke against it. The "No to Government Waste" campaign produced ads explaining that enforcing condom regulations in porn would be a waste of taxpayer money, not to mention potentially fatal to the porn industry, which brings in significant tax revenue to the city of Los Angeles, its county, and the state of California. AHF promptly launched its own "Yes on B" campaign, trotting out HIV-positive retired performers as paid spokespeople and unveiling billboards around Los Angeles.

The battle raged for months, but in the end, most voters in Los Angeles County just didn't know much about the testing protocols that the porn industry used. They didn't understand that condoms are all well and good, but that many models choose not to use them for solid reasons. They only knew that they'd seen commercials and billboards exhorting them to "protect" adult film actors. And so almost fifty-seven percent of voters, when presented with Measure B on Election Day, took it at face value. And it passed. And AHF patted itself on the back and looked forward to Cal-OSHA levying fines against the industry.

Pornographers began to decamp to Las Vegas, Phoenix, Tampa, and Miami to get away from the draconian law. Applications for adult film permits in LA county dropped by ninety-five percent. Vivid Entertainment filed a lawsuit against the county health department, claiming that Measure B was a violation of performers' free speech. A district judge only sort of agreed—condoms, he decided, were not a violation of free speech, but, "Given that adult filming could occur almost anywhere, Measure B would seem to authorize a health officer to enter and search any part of a private home in the middle of the night, because he suspects violations are occurring. This is unconstitutional." Vivid considered the ruling a victory, but nevertheless filed an appeal to attempt to solidify their First Amendment claim. The federal Ninth District Court agreed with the lower court about the unenforceability of Measure B, reaching a settlement in March 2016 that made Measure B pretty much moot.

But, in 2013, HIV showed its unwelcome face yet again. Over the summer, four performers tested positive. Production was halted industry-wide for a total of almost twenty days as several generations of scene partners were tested—none of the transmissions were found to have occurred on an adult film set. But then, in December, another male actor tested positive for the virus, leading to another weeklong industry moratorium. After all these tears in the fabric of the rigorous testing system, many in the industry began to rethink their stances on condoms and testing. Industry-wide, testing protocols were ratcheted up to a fourteen-day maximum between testing and shooting, which is still in place. Currently, many actors who work without condoms require their partners' test results to be no more than a few days old. Industry-approved tests now use the Aptima HIV-1 RNA Qualitative Assay test for HIV, which can detect HIV RNA in human plasma as early as ten days after exposure to the virus. Most industry testing panels now also include screenings for Hepatitis B and C, trichomoniasis, and syphilis on top of HIV, chlamydia, and gonorrhea. And, though no testing protocol will ever be one hundred percent safe, neither will sex with condoms. It's not a safe world we live, or screw, in. But the porn industry is doing as much as it can to protect its own.

THE AIDS HEALTHCARE FOUNDATION, however, was not satisfied with Measure B's unenforceable status or with the porn industry's travails. In early 2013, AHF sponsored AB 1576, a bill that would have mandated condom use in adult films across the state of California. In late 2015, the Cal-OSHA Standards Board decided to take a look at a complaint that AHF had lodged back in 2009, objecting to the lack of state-level regulations specifying how blood-borne pathogen laws should affect the porn industry. These regulations, collectively called §5193.1, would have required a laundry list of impractical concessions pushed onto the industry in order to avoid worker exposure to potentially infectious bodily fluids. The regulations would have required barrier protection for all genital-to-genital contact, as well as skin, mouths, eyes, and all mucous membranes that might come in contact with infectious fluids—fancy talk for gloves, dental dams, plastic outfits, and eye protection. In effect, it would have turned every sex scene in California into a medical fetishist's dream, and everyone else's nightmare.

On the day of a public hearing on the matter in February 2016, most of the adult industry shut down, and well over a hundred workers—actors, producers, and others—took an unpaid day off. They flew, bussed, or drove to Oakland to speak on behalf of their industry. After a long day of impassioned anti-legislation pleas, mixed with weepy tales of woe from several former performers who contracted HIV while working in the industry (all of whom had been paid by AHF to attend the hearing—and none of whom actually contracted HIV on an adult film set), the board voted to table the guidelines and work with the adult industry to find regulations that would be more feasible and appropriate. The industry celebrated a major battle won, but steeled itself for the war to continue.

AHF, undaunted, was already preparing for the next clash: yet another ballot initiative, slated for the November 2016 election, which would not only require condom use at all porn shoots in the state (again), but also allow private citizens in the state of California to file suit against pornographers for reported violations of existing condom laws. These private individuals would thereby be able to obtain, via the public record, the private information of all the porn folks sued, thus reducing the safety of the industry further.

The Free Speech Coalition led the charge against Proposition 60, funded almost entirely by dues charged to its industry members. It spearheaded an ad campaign that denounced Prop 60 for encouraging harassment, and porn stars and advocates took to the streets in rallies that called out AHF for its meddling.

The industry was so on edge after years of relentless hounding from AHF that, at an XBIZ panel led by the FSC to discuss the legal issues on the slate in early 2016, I was called out by the panelists as an outsider. My credentials were questioned, and I was asked, point-blank, if I was there to spy on the meeting for AHF. When I answered that I was an independent journalist, just there to do research for a book, I was permitted to stay on the condition that I turn off my recording equipment. Later, when the Cal-OSHA hearing in Oakland over §5193.1 was going on and I was looking for live tweets, I discovered that I had been personally blocked from the FSC's Twitter feed, having apparently been labeled a meddler and possible mole.

Prop 60 was defeated by fifty-four percent of California voters who had no patience for the idea of their taxes being used to force condoms onto porn stars' bodies. But things are still tense when it comes to condoms in porn. The truth of the matter is that most mainstream producers of straight porn just don't *want* to film with barrier protection. Whether that's due to concerns for performer safety or fears of losing money hardly matters. What is at issue is the fact that, if condom-mandatory legislation were to be enforced in Los Angeles, many producers would move their businesses elsewhere, thus further decentralizing the industry. Or they'd go "underground," shooting off the books in hidden locations to evade regulations. Both of these options would dilute the standardized testing protocol, making it more difficult for performers to get tested easily and effectively, and much harder for the test results to be consolidated and made easily accessible to directors, producers, and actors. With a less-centralized land base, peopled by producers fearful of making their whereabouts known, the porn industry could easily fall into practices that put performers' health and safety in much greater jeopardy. The industry is notoriously difficult to corral as it is, with no union and several trade organizations that often butt heads. If the testing system were to fall by the wayside due to regulations that imposed condoms and took control of STI testing, it's not a huge leap to imagine a reversion to the outlaw days of the early eighties, before porn became legal in California.

The advent of PrEP—a drug that prevents the transmission of HIV in users—has helped to allay some of the fears and dangers that hover around this controversial topic, but of course the decision to use it must be made on an individual basis, so it can't be assumed that it will make the porn talent pool impervious to infection. And PrEP doesn't prevent the transmission of other STIs, so testing for active porn performers remains important for the safety of the performers.

All logistical talk aside, it's important to point out that pornography is a for-profit *entertainment* industry—not the documentation of private sex lives, nor a vast library of sex ed videos. While it's all well and good to want performers to be protected from on-set STI transmissions, the adult videos we all watch are peopled with rational, thinking, consenting adults, most of whom take their health and safety so seriously that they routinely pay out of their own pockets to submit to twice-monthly blood tests. Those tests cost around $200 a pop, and the grown-up individuals who pay for them have the capacity to make their own decisions about what they put on, and in, their bodies. I'll refer back to Nina Hartley's excellent words: "The risk of any one activity can never be reduced to zero and after a certain point it becomes cost-ineffective to attempt it. Living includes taking risks. People in adult entertainment have assessed those risks and do what they can to mitigate them."

Producers, whether they're right about it or not, are largely convinced that putting condoms in their scenes will eviscerate their sales. Christian Mann of Evil Angel told the *NY Daily News* back in 2012 that condom legislation for the industry was basically an attempt to "compel an industry to create a product that the market doesn't want." It was, he and others thought, a veiled attempt to drive pornography out of business. Pornographers were having a difficult enough time making profits without another drain on their cash flow being forced on them by legal bodies that didn't understand their unique business needs. Their goal was to entertain their customers with fantasies that they manufactured, not to be the pinnacle of sexual responsibility for the world to follow.

The push to force condoms into sex scenes reeks—if you ask me—of a sex-negative culture that doesn't know how to educate its children about safer sex practices, looking to an entertainment industry for sex education. It's an oft-cited fact that children are being exposed to pornography via the Internet at earlier ages all the time. The last statistic I heard ominously whispered that the average American now sees porn for the first time at the tender age of eight. In a country where parents who grew up ashamed of sex have no inclination to bring it up to their kids, porn can seem like an easy out. There's plenty of it out there, and the kids are going to see it *anyway*. Wouldn't it be handy if porn were required to show them how to have *safer* sex, so that parents could avoid the conversation altogether?

But the porn industry does not exist to educate children who are neither legally nor financially able to support it. Porn is made for paying adults. Not only is the viewing of pornography by children illegal, it is counter to everything that the porn industry stands for. Pornographers don't *want* kids to view their products any more than they want those products to be pirated and streamed on the Internet for anyone to watch. Nina Hartley said it bluntly way back in 2010, and it continues to be true: "Porn is not designed to be sex education . . . It's entertainment, and it's not our job to teach safer sex techniques. It's people's personal responsibility to educate themselves, assess the risks at hand, and act accordingly. People's safety is their job, not ours."

I spoke to rock star and friend of the porn industry Dave Navarro just after Measure B passed in 2012, and he summed up the porn-as-education idea perfectly. "If I'm watching a scene and it's a boy/girl/girl scene, and [at] the end of the scene, they all turn to the camera and go, 'And remember! Only *you* can prevent forest fires!' I'd want my money back! You know what I mean? Like, what is this, like 'The more you know' in porn?"

It may be unsurprising that most pornographers are not interested in making their films into PSAs for sexual health and wellness, but there are some for whom education is part of the mission of porn-making in the first place. For years, indie pornographers—particularly the queer and feminist among them—have been offering quiet but disruptive alternatives to the gay/straight divide in everything from aesthetic preference to diversity to—you guessed it—safer sex practices in order to better represent diversity in porn and to display that safer sex is hot sex.

In an interview for my blog, queer porn actor Vid Tuesday said, "Queer porn is very pro-barrier, which makes the performers feel very safe. A lot of mainstream genres rely on testing because so much is done bareback, but a lot of queer porn uses barriers for even oral sex and fingering, and makes an aim of showing and sexualizing safe sex practices." (It's a remarkably effective tactic; once surgical gloves, for instance, become equated with hot queer sex on camera, it's astonishing how quickly our Pavlovian responses set in. I don't personally engage in much sex that calls for gloves, but just the snapping sound they make when Jiz Lee puts them on for a queer sex scene gets my juices flowing.) Queer porn actors adhere to similar testing protocols as the straight industry, as well, which makes their safety at work possibly *better* than either the gay or straight mainstream industries.

By allowing actors to engage in the sex they want, with whom they want, and making barrier protection of all kinds available on every shoot, with no negative repercussions for those who choose to use them, and *also* encouraging up-to-date STI test results, directors like Alyx Fox in New Orleans and Shine Louise Houston in San Francisco have been breaking down the stigmas and traditions of old-school porn. In providing performers who don't want to do just "gay" or "straight" porn an outlet for their considerable talents, they produce groundbreaking work that refuses to be categorized neatly and succeeds nicely in turning people on while turning a profit. Feminist porn shoots can rarely pay as much as mainstream gay or straight shoots, but many performers are happy to exchange some profit for the ability to have more honest sex and to feel free from unwanted labeling. The queer and feminist porn world is far from perfect, but in some respects, at least, it seems to have a leg up on mainstream porn.

One hopes that an inclusive, safer, and ultimately *hot* lesson can be learned by all concerned as porn looks forward to a legislative-battle-ridden future. Gay or straight or neither or both, pornographers are all facing massive changes from every possible side of their industry, and only unification may be able to save it. It may be time for the gay and straight and queer industries to consider what they have in common.

Despite the bifurcation between gay and straight porn industries, the barriers in place for men looking to transition from gay to straight porn are ever so gently being torn down. Multiple award winner Ryan Driller, for instance, doesn't hide the fact that he got his start in gay porn. "When I got into the industry, I was seeking everything out, and they [gay studios] were the first studios to approach me. I turned them down for months and months because I'm not gay. And I'd never done anything with a guy. So it wasn't in my realm, and it definitely wasn't what I was looking for. But as I did more research, I saw that there were a lot of other guys before me that had done it. So, I didn't call them back, but when they called me back, and they kept throwing more and more zeros [into] those numbers," he accepted and began working regularly in gay films. Once he had gotten his name out there and earned a reputation for reliable performances, he began to get calls from the straight industry, and he has been happily working in it for years now. "It's still an issue with every guy who does it, who tries to cross over," he added. "As much as it was presented to me as 'This is how you get into the industry,' it was also 'This is how you *don't* get into the industry.'" His success in the mainstream straight industry might be a signal that times are changing.

Other signals are popping up around the industry, too. In 2013, AVN initiated the GayVN expo in Las Vegas, which takes over the Hard Rock the weekend before the AVN convention. The two shows run into one another, and while I personally still find it discouraging that they're separated, it's a nod toward change that the industry's most recognized trade publication has made the two events as seamless as they have. AVN has stepped up its coverage of gay industry news, as well, now including gay news items on its website's front page and in its print magazine.

Other industry organizations and events are making subtle changes, as well. XBIZ, which is something like AVN's younger, hipper cousin, has integrated gay-industry-oriented panels and seminars into the rosters of its numerous yearly conventions, blending gay and straight issues on its website, as well. And even Exxxotica, the smaller cousin to both of these organizations' trade shows, has added SW!TCH, an LGBT showcase that welcomes performers and personalities from the gay side of the industry to its conventions.

Of course, none of this means that it's any easier, exactly, for men to work in the gay and straight sides of the industry as they please. And it hasn't exactly ended the weirdly outdated-yet-relevant debate over testing versus condoms. But any step in the direction of acceptance and integration, I believe, is a good one. And although it pains me to say it, sometimes, in porn, you have to be willing to take what you can get.

CHAPTER 17

The Feminist Porn Awards

THE MONTHS BEFORE AND AFTER the 2011 AVNs had been revelatory. I was pulling the majority of my income from writing set copy and reviews for the print magazines that had gotten me into the porn industry in the first place, but I was increasingly frustrated with them and the industry they represented. The more I questioned the way things were in mainstream porn, the more I gravitated toward the diverse territory of indie, queer, and feminist pornography.

Each of these adjectives—indie, queer, and feminist—encompasses its own hunk of the landscape, with many overlaps and just as many variations between the genres. Indie porn embraces a wide variety of styles and ideologies, from kink content to art films to bizarre-o parodies of cult favorites (my favorite: *Faster, Pussycat! Fuck! Fuck!*). Indie porn, moreover, tends toward the showcasing of bodies and sex acts that mainstream porn eschews, whether due to concerns over obscenity or the bottom line. There's a DIY aspect to indie porn that goes beyond low budgets—a sort of bare-bones realness that reflects the filmmakers' need to show their visions as part of a lived experience that must be shared. When I talked to Clark Matthews, the director of the short film *Krutch*, which swept the Cinekink film festival in 2013, about his indie pornmaking debut, he summed up the indie mindset: "Especially with video technology being what it is today," he said, "it's totally fruitless to sit around and say, 'Why aren't other people telling *my* stories better?' Just do it yourself. There's so much authenticity to it."

Queer porn is a specific subset of indie porn for the most part, which often pushes the boundaries of what sexual behavior can be documented even further. Queer porn usually features performers whose sexual and gender identities don't fit into the neatly binary categories that mainstream porn prefers. Gender designations and the sex acts that usually go along with them in straight porn are tossed by the wayside in queer porn, in favor of whatever the performers want to do, no matter their identifications or body parts. It's all good. And it can level the playing field for performers of all types, from cisgender blondes to disabled transgender women of color. That isn't to say that no categorization happens in queer porn—naturally there are films that focus on different groups (like trans men, women of size, and so on), but the differences between performers feel much more celebrated than exploited in most queer porn I've seen.

And feminist porn . . . Well, feminist porn is sort of the umbrella under which I decided to lay out my towel in 2011, and where I've happily stayed ever since. Feminist porn is a broader field than either "indie" or "queer" porn, but it's easy for indie and/or queer porn to *also* be feminist. Due to the ever-changing evolution of what "feminism" means, it is open to almost anyone who identifies as a feminist and who makes porn ethically according to the feminism they espouse.

Feminist porn has never been interested in anything short of a revolution in the way our society treats sex and pleasure. From Betty Dodson's drawings of women masturbating in the 1960s and her decades of running Bodysex Workshops in which she helped women examine their sexual responses; to the sex-positive performances of "golden age" feminist porn stars (and artists and publishers and activists) Annie Sprinkle, Veronica Hart, Veronica Vera, Candida Royalle, and Gloria Leonard who created a support group for like-minded feminist sex workers in the early 1980s; to Susie Bright's anti-establishment erotic magazine for women, *On Our Backs*, in the mid-eighties; to the late eighties' Pink Ladies Social Club in California started by Nina Hartley, Angel Kelly, and Jeanna Fine; and forward through the decades since, feminist-identified women (and trans folk, non binary people, and men) have been making pornography and championing a philosophy that subverts patriarchal standards. Their aim has always been to educate the world about the unexplored power of female sexual agency—and really any sexual agency that doesn't conform to cisgender, heterosexual male standards—in a world that seeks to repress it.

There is no agreed-upon designation of what makes porn feminist, nor is there an easy-to-use directory of companies, directors, or performers who fall under its auspices. Its ambiguity is due largely to the fact that almost anyone making porn anywhere could be making porn that ascribes to feminist standards, without even knowing it. But despite its nebulousness, "feminist porn" has more or less coalesced as term for a body of often independent, frequently artistically motivated, politically active, sometimes queer, and largely feminist filmmakers, sex workers, and activists. Not all of them see eye to eye; as Shine Louise Houston, the woman behind Pink & White Productions and *The Crash Pad* put it to *Rolling Stone* in 2016, "You say feminist, and then you get into what's feminist and everybody fights." As in many progressive movements, there are struggles within the group about what "the rules" should be, how terminology should be deployed, how money should be handled, and so on. Feminist pornographers, furthermore, are far-flung. They're spread out globally.

In 2013, The Feminist Press published *The Feminist Porn Book*, a collection of essays by pornographers and scholars who participate in or study the medium. In it, many of my new heroes wrote on their varying ideas about what it means to be a feminist pornographer, and the editors of the book offered the following definition: "Feminist porn uses sexually explicit imagery to contest and complicate dominant representations of gender, sexuality, race, ethnicity, class, ability, age, body type, and other identity markers. It explores concepts of desire, agency, power, beauty, and pleasure at their most confounding and difficult, including pleasure within and across inequality, in the face of injustice, and against the limits of gender hierarchy and both heteronormativity and homonormativity . . . Ultimately, feminist porn considers sexual representation—and its production—a site for resistance, intervention, and change."

Meanwhile, the Feminist Porn Awards, held yearly in Toronto by the feminist sex shop Good For Her, judged submissions according to a list of criteria that held feminist porn must show the following elements: "Actors are treated with respect, paid fairly, given choice and ethical working conditions, [and] empowered in their work; directors collaborate with and incorporate the actor's own sexual desire and fantasies (making for better scenes too!); it expands the boundaries of sexual representation on film and challenges stereotypes especially of women and marginalized communities; realistic pleasure is depicted." Good For Her further specified that feminist porn could be or include: "edgy or soft;

high production or low; storyline or none; straight, queer, cis, trans, bi, or a combination thereof; made by, for and includes people of any gender/ sex, size, age, race and ethnicity, ability, orientation, and desires (including men); and of course is hot!"

That's a lot to bear in mind, but I also really like director, performer, and educator jessica drake's simplified version: feminist porn, she believes, could be as simple as "treating people the way they should be treated."

All three of these definitions are overviews of exactly the things I was looking for in my professional smut in 2011. I've already mentioned the difficulty in putting too high a priority on "authenticity" in adult film, but it would be silly not to note that one of the most defining features of feminist pornography is the ongoing *pursuit* of authentic pleasure in its performers.

Most mainstream porn aims to portray a fantasy version of sex that does not exist in real life. In this idealized world, penetrative sex lasts for at least half an hour, erections are immediate and long-lasting, women achieve orgasm quickly and easily, unprotected sex has no repercussions, and anal sex is effortless. (Pro tip: Those oh-so-easy-looking anal sex scenes in pornos? Contrived. As Madison Young told us, most porn stars do at least one, sometimes several, enemas before they shoot, and after having spent a considerable time relaxing the orifice with a butt plug before shooting.) Performer and director Seymore Butts once informed me, "I see it as it's happening in the raw, and in the raw it's not anything like the finished product." Of course, there's nothing wrong with enjoying the finished product's glamor; escapism is important in today's world, I believe. But it's vital to realize that these fantasies, reproduced *ad infinitum* by mainstream pornography, don't exist in a vacuum. That's why they have concerned critics of the industry for decades, and especially over the last ten years as people who use this particular brand of fantasy as their guide to sexuality might be getting incorrect notions about what's expected of their bodies, their partners, and more.

And that's why feminist porn is important. Whether or not true authenticity in pornography can ever be achieved, it seems worth striving for, to remind us fallible humans that sex can take many different forms, not all of them athletic, toned, and heterosexual. While feminist porn also offers fantasy sex that sometimes does and sometimes does not look more "real" than mainstream fare, its attempts to portray pleasure in accessible and—yes—authentic ways makes it stand out. It's an alternative to mainstream pornography that can give the savvy consumer a more nuanced understanding of what sex can be.

My review of *The Crash Pad* had been like a springboard in the search for more porn that reflected its makers' interaction with the questions I was now ready to ask about the implications of pornography on the world. Since I'd breathlessly (and naively) extolled *The Crash Pad*'s many virtues for *WHACK!*, I had talked my way into screener copies of feminist porn films from studios that prided themselves on tossing out old, tired tropes in favor of fresh perspectives. The material I was seeking out and writing about looked to me like porn that wasn't just made by smart people, but made for a smart audience, as well. (I'd argue that actually, the majority of porn is made by intelligent people, but that much of it is marketed to what its makers consider the lowest common denominator.) I'd been so impressed by the performances in these films that I had also begun to seek out their stars and directors for interviews. I was able to publish most of these at *WHACK!* But sometimes my questions went places that didn't fit the magazine's brand; I wanted to explore the depths of feminist porn and its importance, to look at the differences between queer feminist sex on camera and its counterparts in mainstream porn and examine why they mattered. *WHACK!* wasn't the place for these questions, and although I could ask them freely on my blog, there wasn't much of a readership for them.

So I started looking for places where I could write about alternative porn for a wider audience in a blatantly feminist way. In late 2010 and early 2011, there were not very many of these outlets, but I eventually became a contributing writer to feminist porn star, director, and artist Madison Young's website TheWomansPOV.com. The site was a mish-mash of reviews, op-eds, interviews, and links to Madison's art, docu-porn, and straight-up-porn films. It was all feminist, gleefully queer, often beautiful, sometimes hilarious, and exactly what I wanted.

Through TheWomansPOV, I gained access to more feminist and queer films, directors, and performers, and was able to go in-depth on the topics that obsessed me. For instance: Why was there so little porn shot from a female perspective? (Luckily for me, as the website's name hints, Madison was making her own series of *hot* women's POV films, and I got to see a lot of them.) What *was* the point of feminist, indie porn showing people fellating strap-on cocks, since those cocks didn't have nerves in them? And why *did* these strap-on blowjobs so often look just as hardcore as mainstream gonzo porn blowjobs coming out of LA? Wasn't that regressive? (The short answer I got from the several feminist filmmakers and performers about this question was, simply, that what constitutes a feminist sex act isn't what it looks like—it's how the people performing it feel about it. Queer porn maker Courtney Trouble, to whom I turned with my quandary, informed me, "Part of the reason that I like giving super-sloppy gaggy blowjobs is because I *like* to be dominated. And so, like, the act of 'being forced to do it' is part of what's hot to me." Performer Syd Blakovich, who also helped me wrap my brain around the idea, chimed in: "We are deciding what we do and how we want to do it, what makes us hot. And if . . . our core erotic themes revolve around the idea of subjugation, then the act of subjugation itself can become an empowering act if we are willing and consenting parties to it.")

Interviews like these were my self-guided version of Gender Studies 101, with a focus on porn and feminism, and as I dove into them I also compiled a list of grievances with mainstream porn. The list was augmented by an ongoing series of talks I was having with entrepreneur, feminist, and all-around rabble-rouser Cindy Gallop. In 2009, Gallop had given a TED Talk in which she told her stunned audience, "I date younger men, primarily men in their twenties. And when I date younger men, I have sex with younger men. And when I have sex with younger men, I encounter, very directly and personally, the real ramifications of the creeping ubiquity of hardcore pornography in our culture." She had noticed a marked tendency in these younger men, she said, to re-create what they'd seen acted out in porn. Unnerved, Gallop—a business veteran with years at the helm BBH US, a leading ad agency in New York, and the founder of tech start-up IfWeRanTheWorld.com—decided to do something about it.

She developed MakeLoveNotPorn.com, a simple site that pointed out, in adorable cartoons and with plain language, that while in porn most women *love* facials, in the real world, they might not. And similarly, it revealed that not every woman is comfortable with anal sex, or a variety of other acts that might seem normal in porn. It suggested, in most cases, *asking* about these things before trying them in the heat of the moment.

A simple enough idea, it would seem, but one that needed a champion. And Cindy Gallop was a champion indeed. Her TED Talk and website became two of my favorite things, and I quoted her line about "the creeping ubiquity of hardcore pornography" as sex education in America in one of my *McSweeney's* columns. Shortly after it was published, I received a social media missive from Ms. Gallop, and we began a series of conversations over e-mail (and, to my delight, in person at her lavish, art-festooned Black Apartment in Chelsea) about the ways in which the porn industry could be held to a higher standard.

Since our time brainstorming, Gallop has gone on to launch MakeLoveNotPorn.tv, a website that strives to "do for sex what social media has done for everything else." At MakeLoveNotPorn.tv, users are able to upload videos of their own sex—"in all its glorious, silly, beautiful, messy, reassuring humanness"—for curation and sorting by Gallop's team. The videos they keep are posted for members to watch—at five dollars per video per three-week rental period. During that time, users are encouraged to watch the videos as much as they want, to share them with friends, to enjoy them, and talk about them on the site. Gallop seeks to normalize the everyday sexual experiences of regular humans, show the world what real-world sex and real-world pleasure look like, and to let people watch it, think about it, and talk about it freely without shame.

Gallop's goal is to not only enter the once-empty space between pornographers and consumers, but to make that space welcoming and exciting for the rest of the world to enter. Her aim is to create "an open, healthy dialogue around sex and porn, which would then enable people to bring a real-world mindset when they view what is essentially artificial entertainment. The entire message of MakeLoveNotPorn boils down to one thing, which is just simply: 'Talk about it.'"

As my interest in alternative and feminist porn deepened, in March of 2011 I attended Cinekink, "The Kinky Film Festival," in New York City, and my horizons in sexy filmmaking exploded. Cinekink was in its eighth year of celebrating kinkiness on camera. From a documentary about the International Mr. Leather pageant to adorable shorts about pissing to hardcore porn vignettes, the festival explored kink in a big, dark theater in the East Village for a long weekend every year.

I was nervous but excited about my first experience watching porn in a theater with strangers, and was delighted that in doing so I felt very little awkwardness and even less judgment—the crowd at Cinekink was comprised of perverts like myself, and nobody was sneering down their nose at me for getting turned on by the bisexual three-way in Kimberly Kane's *My Own Master* or crying during the documentary *Bucking the Trend* or applauding wildly for *Kink Crusaders*. We were all of one mind, and I was so rapt in my enjoyment of the atmosphere and the vast amount of information I was soaking up about kink lifestyles of all kinds, that I nearly starved myself over the course of the weekend, unwilling to leave the premises for long enough to get meals.

Heightening my rapture was Cinekink's tradition of combining the Saturday afternoon porn showcase with a panel discussion to which filmmakers and performers were invited. To my delight, the 2011 panel convened to discuss ethics in pornography—the very topic that had been on my mind for months: How do pornographers go about making their films in such a way that nobody has to feel gross after leaving the set, or the computer or television?

They each had their own ideas about these topics, of course, but every answer centered on treating performers with respect, and allowing that respect to come through in the finished product. Paying everybody on the same scale, regardless of race, size, ability level, or gender identity; refusing to pigeonhole models according to their body parts or ethnicities; allowing anybody to work with anybody; pairing performers who specifically chose to work together; providing food, water, and other amenities backstage; having a variety of sex toys, condoms, lube, and other accessories available for performers to use as they pleased; and establishing clear consent at as many junctures as possible throughout the process of filming.

The concept of consent really struck a nerve for me. I had never heard it discussed so openly before, though the topic had been brought up in my interviews and writing, and I think that panel at Cinekink really set me on a track of thinking that I haven't yet left. A path that beckoned me deep in my gut, as a direct answer to the gnawing anxiety over the morality of the material I'd been ingesting for years. I never explicitly equated my decision to watch porn professionally with the processing of my personal trauma, but looking back at the directions in which I took my career, it's obvious to me now that I was looking for something to get me through the tendrils of shame, fear, and sexual dysfunction that clung to me after I was assaulted. The panelists were talking about one of the most fundamental issues at the heart of all pornography, and one that had called to me even though I hadn't understood it: How does one establish clear, enthusiastic, and ongoing consent for those involved in producing pornography, and how does one then make that consent clear to viewers?

One of the biggest pitfalls of online porn piracy has been, as Cindy Gallop pointed out in the TED Talk that brought us together, the obfuscation of the fantasy element in porn. In a full-length porn film with opening titles and credits at the end, background music, and a title all attached to the main event, it's difficult to get around the idea that the movie is a fully packaged product, deliberately constructed for your edification. But, like Sinnamon Love said in interview, the millions of consumers who watch pirated material are "losing out on the commercial packaging of the product and the understanding that, you know, I didn't just go to a bar and pick up three guys and have sex with them."

With video clips stripped of their trappings, it's easy to forget that the actors *are* in fact actors, that their paperwork was signed, consent given, and money exchanged. In some cases, it can be difficult to imagine that all these forms of consent were given, especially if the scene involves hardcore sex, power exchange, depictions of force, or any of a number of other acts that can come across as edgy. A consumer can walk away from a viewing session wondering, "Did I just watch something unethical?"

The most obvious—yet often overlooked—answer to these dilemmas, of course, is to *always pay for your porn* so that you can see the bells and whistles that establish your smut as the constructed fantasy it's meant to be. The more porn you purchase, the more people can continue to make, with more consenting actors. But the questions go much deeper for those who are in the business of making porn that they can feel good about, and that their customers can feel comfortable watching— even consumers who might see that content without having paid for it. The more I thought about the implications of consent upon a finished product, the more I realized that although many of the producers whose work looked "mainstream" did not label themselves as "feminist" pornographers, their ethics and on-set strategies lumped them firmly into that category.

Consider, for instance, how consent in a porn scene is complicated when performers don't know who they'll be having sex with until they arrive on set. Sure, the abstract idea of a boy/girl scene with some spanking and dirty talk sounds fun, but what if you arrive and discover that your costar, whom you've never met, has poor hygiene? (And this is not a hypothetical situation: I've heard this complaint from many an acquaintance who makes porn.) It may seem like a no-brainer to instead cast performers who know each other and/or want to work together, thus ensuring fireworks on set, but relatively few producers go to the extra lengths required to make it happen, which puts that kind of thoughtfulness squarely into the consent-driven feminist sphere.

Jenna Haze, for instance—one of the most decorated mainstream porn stars of the late 2000s—told me that for movies she directed for her company, the connection between actors was top priority. "I cast [performers in] my sex scenes based on who they want to have sex with," she told me in an interview in 2011. "I love passion. I want to see two people really get off on each other." Though most would classify her productions as mainstream porn, her feminist tactics were on display in the sizzling chemistry between performers. (Further upping her unlabeled feminist cred, Jenna also informed me that she *never* used Photoshop for any of the content on her website or DVDs: "I think it's false advertising!") The same could be said for numerous other filmmakers who operate mainly out of LA and shoot with mainstream aesthetics and talent.

The ideas that nestled into my brain at Cinekink began sending out roots that would occupy my brain for years. Feminism in porn, I began to realize, equated largely with consent. And consent was my new gold standard, whether expressly advertised or quietly worked into the production process. I wanted to find more of it.

SUFFICE IT TO SAY THAT by the time April 2011 rolled around, I was foaming at the mouth in my eagerness to attend the sixth annual Good for Her Feminist Porn Awards in Toronto. I had finagled press passes on the promise that I'd write about the event for *WHACK!* and my blog, so I grabbed my passport and rented a car for the nine-hour drive north with Matthew in tow, conveniently labeled my "camera guy" to warrant his press pass.

That weekend, I was flabbergasted by the authenticity (yep, I said it!) and accessibility of the humans who made up this community. Over the course of our weekend in Toronto, Matthew and I were welcomed warmly and openly by the people whose work I had been watching breathlessly from afar. I was able to approach the stars whose performances had inspired me, the movers and shakers behind the disruption of pornography . . . and they were really nice! A lot of them even knew who I was! I couldn't believe that my little column and blog and magazine were actually being noticed, and by the people I most wanted to notice them! I was in heaven.

At the Feminist Porn Awards ceremony—which, I'd like to point out, was held in the Berkeley Church on Queen Street—there was a sense of inclusion and camaraderie that surpassed anything I had felt at any other porn-related event. After the ceremony, the floor was cleared to allow for a gigantic dance party at which porn stars and commoners mingled freely. Jiz Lee, the star of that fisting and squirting scene that had so confounded me in *The Crash Pad*—said hello, having remembered me from Cinekink, and actually took me outside so that we could hear each other talk more freely.

I looked back on my time in Vegas a few months prior, when I'd been part of a group—along with Cindy Gallop, whose coolness towed me along in its wake—on board a Burning Angel party bus to an exclusive party where we got to sit in the roped-off section with the porn stars and drink fancy booze. And, though it had been a mostly fun evening, I remembered feeling very distinctly the "you're not one of the cool kids" vibe that I remembered all too well from middle school. The Burning Angel crew was all perfectly nice, but nobody was interested in talking to me or sitting near me or really doing anything to extend friendship my way. I'd had similar feelings in most other situations I'd found myself in with porn stars. Behind closed doors, I'd established a pretty solid rapport with several performers who also enjoyed, er, herbal remedies in hotel rooms. But I wasn't allowed on the inside—not in public. And that was okay, but it made me really despise conventions, awards shows, and all that jazz, where my natural introversion made the awkwardness of our public interactions excruciating.

But the Feminist Porn Awards crowd? Engaging. Friendly. Welcoming. The accessible and not-too-expensive bar may have upped my love for the environment, but I'm willing to bet that I was no drunker when I left that night than I'd been when I left the AVNs. And the feeling I took back to the hostel with me was very, very different from the one I'd grumpily borne out into the Vegas night a few months before. No, the FPAs were different. The entertainment was better—drag performances, boylesque dancing (burlesque, but, you know, with men taking off their clothes), and *so much glitter*. The outfits were weirder. The people were more interesting to look at. The atmosphere was welcoming. There were no cross-armed bouncers in sight. There was no velvet rope. Everyone was smiling and hugging.

Nikki Darling, who performs in both the mainstream and the queer, feminist, kinky sides of the industry, told me that, to her way of thinking, "The adult industry as a whole is kind of like high school, so we all sit at different tables. So I guess a lot of the queer, Bay Area, kinky [people] are kind of like the weird theater geek table . . . We're the weird table over in the corner. I like that table! That's the table I sat at when I was actually in high school!"

You may be unsurprised to discover that I also sat with the weird theater kids in high school, and maybe that's one reason why I felt so at home at the Feminist Porn Awards. These were my *people*.

*With April Flores on the red carpet at the Feminist Porn Awards in 2013, with
our respective awards* (PHOTO COURTESY OF THE AUTHOR)

In the arms of my biggest porn crush, Keni Styles, in Miami in 2011—I have no memory of this moment (PHOTO COURTESY J. VEGAS)

CHAPTER 18

Making It in Miami

THE SPRING OF 2011 PASSED in a whirl of porn conventions and conversations with agents and lawyers about media deals. Contract negotiations for my pilot had wrapped up with an even-handed, if not exactly magnanimous, pilot deal, but no co-writer had turned up. The lack of female TV writers in LA was just as profound as it had been the year before. An interesting juxtaposition, I thought, with the porn industry. Although its "boys club" reputation is warranted in many ways, porn is comparatively welcoming for women who want to succeed in business, from writing to directing to producing. (Wicked contract star and award-winning director Stormy Daniels told me that she loves directing—"Come on, you get to yell at boys with their pants down *and* get paid for it! It doesn't get any better than that!")

But not so in Hollywood, where boys still rule the roost. I considered finding a female *porn* script-writer; the Hollywood folks would have no idea what to do with us. I had a feeling that writing talent from the Valley might have more to teach the big production studio than anyone would expect, but, sadly, I knew the idea would never fly. Any porn talent the TV company would want, I felt certain, would be "starring-as-themselves" novelty items in skimpy outfits, on camera and *not* behind it. Nobody at the big kids table would go for my idea.

Meanwhile, *WHACK!* had teamed up with a man we'll call Moe (if you picture a much younger version of *The Simpsons* bartender and replace his apron with a goofy T-shirt, you're not far off), who claimed he could get us advertising revenue if we made him part of our team. We obliged, as we'd so far had no luck earning any money on our venture. The position we'd placed the magazine in—the unoccupied middle ground between the porn industry and consumers—made us a conundrum for online advertisers. We weren't a porn site, and we were at this point non-explicit (aside from the occasional boob) because we wanted consumers to be able to read interviews and reviews anywhere. But we weren't *not* a porn site, either. Many of our analytics implied that *WHACK!* was frequently an accidental click during a frenzied mastur-bation session—our top search terms were the names of porn stars we'd interviewed, and although people often did stay to read the articles, we weren't exactly what many were looking for. So advertisers didn't know what to do with us. Adult companies couldn't use explicit ads on our site, but non-adult companies didn't want to touch us with a ten-foot pole, lest their reputations get besmirched.

In short, we'd been laboring on the magazine for years and had made *zero* dollars on *WHACK!* We loved working on it, but we had funded every bit of it thus far by scraping the bottoms of our very shallow pock-ets. Almost every cent I earned went to *WHACK!*, minus rent, groceries, and health insurance. I dragged my lovers to strip clubs (not too difficult to manage) and sex industry events instead of taking them on real dates because I didn't have the time or money to do both. Matthew and Jenn were usually happy to oblige, but my life had been devoted to making my career in porn journalism work rather than, you know, having a life.

In effect, Moe's promises to find advertisers and other forms of monetization for the website were pretty appealing. But I didn't trust him. I made my discomfort known to the rest of the *WHACK!* crew, pointing out that he didn't seem to have a plan so much as a desire to hang out with porn stars. But the others voted me down, so we started meeting weekly at Moe's apartment in the East Village. It wasn't long into this association that I realized that his neighbor was a porn star friend of ours—a sweet lady who I'll call Alexa—and that they had been sleeping together. Which was all well and good, as far as I was concerned, but I recognized that he had gotten it into his head that, if he and Alexa teamed up with us, we could all turn a profit. And I wasn't convinced that he actually knew how to facilitate that.

Specificity in planning notwithstanding, Moe was gracious enough to throw in some cash and some smooth-talking that landed us our very own booth at the Exxxotica expo in Miami Beach, Florida, in May of 2011. Moe paid for our booth and promised us spending money if we could get ourselves to Miami and find a place to stay. So I, along with

j. vegas and our IT guy, Jordan, bought plane tickets and reserved beds at a hostel near the beach.

I flew to Orlando, then boarded a puddle-jumper to Miami. As I located my economy seat, I glimpsed a very large pair of sunglasses and the sweep of an abundance of dirty-blond hair as it flounced over a small shoulder. A light voice speaking to the large tattooed man with a shaved head in the other seat; I saw neck tattoos. The woman beside him turned her head just enough to show her profile—my favorite performer and a close friend of *WHACK!*, a prominent porn star who I dubbed "Jennie Hart" in Chapter 8.

I leaned forward and whispered, "Jennie!" between the seats just as the plane taxied onto the runway, unable to get closer because of my seatbelt.

She looked up. "Lynsey? Oh my god!" She leaped up—during take-off, clearly without her seatbelt on, for all the plane to see—and turned around to get a better look at me. "I'm so glad you're on this flight! I'm *so* bored!"

She introduced me to her bodyguard, who I'll call Graham here because I don't remember his real name and because Graham seems like an excellent name for a bodyguard. Jennie knelt on her seat, facing backwards, with her arms hanging over the back of it, while we chatted. She'd been signing autographs in Orlando for a few days, and she was now looking forward to Miami, where she was signing at the expo and hosting a few parties over the weekend. After a while, she sat down and checked her phone (which she had clearly not set to Airplane Mode). She was saying something to Graham and scrolling an app when suddenly she went still.

After a beat of silence, she shout-whispered, "SHIT. Shit."

She sprang back up in the seat, her eyes wide with panic. "*Shit.* Oh my god. Lynsey. I left *my fucking clothes* in Orlando. All of my designer clothes. In the dresser at the hotel!"

She turned around and sat down, silent.

Graham turned to me with a not-very-concerned expression, winked, and held up his hand with fingers splayed. Then he did a silent, measured countdown on his fingers: Five . . . four . . . three . . . two . . . one . . . And right on cue, Jennie began to chant, "Oh my god. Oh my god. Oh my god." She sped up incrementally until she was whispering

"Ohmygodohmygodohmygod" like a prayer, her breath coming faster, her pitch climbing several octaves.

What followed was an epic forty-five-minute meltdown that I recall now with fondness. For the remainder of the flight, Jennie told me in detail about the contents of her three-thousand-dollar travel wardrobe. She demanded Graham call someone right away and have the items shipped or driven to Miami. When Graham refused, reminding her that he couldn't make calls during the flight, she began frantically texting and tweeting. Her emotional state jumped from fear that the housekeeping staff would steal her designer collection to quiet, to stoic calm, back to optimism that somebody in Orlando could bring it to Miami, and then right into rage at Graham for not having checked her drawers because he knew how forgetful she could be. There were tears.

The moment the plane touched down, Jennie was on her phone, taking a moment before the Orlando hotel's front desk picked up to berate Graham for not already being on *his* phone, too. The two of them were still in their seats, trying to figure something out, when it was my turn to leave the plane, so I filed out with the other passengers—every last one of whom knew exactly what had happened to poor Jennie, since she had given approximately zero fucks about sharing her misery with the plane. When I made it to the gate, I called Jordan, whose flight landed shortly before mine.

As I hung up, Jennie appeared out of the jetway with a small roller suitcase in tow. She was nibbling on her lower lip, and when she saw me, she ran to me and threw her arms around my shoulders as she broke down into sobs. She had cried on the plane, but this was different. Her grief felt deeper now. She was ugly-crying. Utterly breaking down.

We sat down as she tearfully explained to me, in hushed tones, that she was under a lot of stress in her personal life. Her new boyfriend had approved of her career when they got together, but now that things were getting serious between them, he was feeling jealous. He wanted her to consider quitting porn to settle down with him.

"I love my work," she told me as I held her hand. "I've worked so hard for this career. I don't want to give it up! And I *love* what I do! It's made me who I am!" But she didn't want to lose her boyfriend, either.

Feeling as if I had suddenly been tossed from the shallow end of Jennie Hart's acquaintance pool into the deeper waters of confidante territory, I muddled through soothing answers, but the more she talked, the less muddling I needed to do.

I tried to put myself into her (one remaining pair of) designer shoes: Jennie is about a year older than me, which in May of 2011 put her at twenty-nine years old. She had been working in porn for a full decade—most of her adult life. She'd won numerous awards from every industry group that gave them out, become one of the most recognizable porn stars in the world, and started her own production company. She was a walking triumph, having found a job she loved, grown into it, grown up with it, and succeeded beyond her wildest dreams. She worked around the clock, maintaining the vessel with which she performed (her small but beautifully proportioned body), perfecting her brand, feature dancing, signing autographs, managing her company, and now writing, directing, producing, and performing in her own films, all while keeping a dynamic social media presence to interact with her millions of fans worldwide. Her star was still, almost impossibly, on the rise a decade into a career that most predicted would last only months.

I looked at the beautiful, intelligent, successful woman sobbing in my arms, thousands of miles away from her home and her stupid jealous boyfriend. I felt certain that this boyfriend benefited from her career more than he realized; Jennie very likely provided him with a lifestyle he couldn't begin to expect on his own. And the work she put in was exhausting. She was depleted. And she was under far, far too much pressure.

I wanted to punch her selfish boyfriend in the head. What kind of jerk signs up to be the significant other of a dazzling woman like Jennie Hart—a woman who is *world famous* for her fierceness and sexuality—and then gets petulant about the career that allows her star to shine so brightly? What kind of self-entitled prick would *dare* approach her, much less work himself into her life and her heart, only to decide that the career she has poured her heart, body, and soul into is too threatening? What an absolute turd.

As Jennie began to gather herself, Graham came down the jetway to tell her about the phone calls he'd been making to get her things back. They both thanked me for my support, and we went our separate ways.

That afternoon, as Jordan, vegas, and I were settling into our hostel, I got a text from Jennie, inviting us to the penthouse she was sharing with her best friend Joanne at a luxury hotel farther down the beach. The three of us basically tripped over each other's feet on the way to hail a cab, and we spent the late afternoon enjoying beers and weed in a palatial suite overlooking Miami Beach with two of the world's most successful porn stars. Jennie had arranged to get her things from Orlando; she would have her wardrobe later that night.

She invited us to a VIP party that evening, where we lounged around an outdoor courtyard filled with palm fronds and candles, watching a few brave souls swim in the pool despite the chilly night air. We were waited upon hand and foot as we schmoozed with the top talent in the adult industry, with Jennie periodically updating me on the mission to save her clothing. By the time we left, it had been recovered—in just one suitcase, which Graham proudly wheeled by us with a grin and a wave. I felt like *WHACK!* had accomplished something, after years of trying. Not success, exactly, but maybe acceptance. We had been admitted into the cool kids' club. It may have just been that I was in the right time and the right place with the right star having a panic attack, but I preferred to think that our hard work and passion for porn had been integral, as well.

THE NEXT MORNING, WE arrived early at the convention hall to set up *WHACK! Magazine*'s first-ever booth at an industry convention. Moe, although he showed up hours late and only provided us with a third of the spending money he'd promised, had secured a large corner spot just inside the doors, directly across from the LA Direct talent agency booth, where some heavy-hitting performers would be signing throughout the weekend. We set up a signing table for our "booth babes" (Lexi Love, Angel Vain, and Trina Michaels), arranged all the swag we had brought with us—stickers, magnets, and other cheap-o goodies—and settled in for the long weekend.

At the party the previous night I had seen my first male porn star crush Keni Styles come in, and I'd commented to a few people about how attractive I found him. You might remember Keni from Chapter 14—the only actor of Asian heritage to make a big name for himself in the history of American pornography. I had struck up a sort of Twitter flirtation (or, at least, my version of a Twitter flirtation, which consisted of asking him for an interview repeatedly) and had been praising his performances in reviews. I enjoyed his chemistry with female performers, his charming

smile, and his British accent almost as much as I enjoyed his physical attributes, which were more than enough to win me over in the first place.

I don't remember how, but word of my crush got around, and he was
brought over to the *WHACK!* booth by a friend and introduced to me.
In typical confident-porn-guy style, he was relaxed but slightly goofy in
an extremely appealing way, while I furiously blushed and kept asking
him about an interview. I probably could have stuck the camera in his
face right then, but I was too tongue-tied to get my shit together, so I told
him I'd catch up with him another time. Then I studiously avoided him
for the rest of the day. Smooth, I know.

On Saturday night, we accompanied Jennie and her entourage to the
party she was hosting at the Fontainebleau hotel's nightclub. Adorned in
our discount-rack best, we walked into a massive nightclub with some of
the biggest porn stars in the world, feeling very much like this should all be
happening in slow motion, possibly with explosions happening behind us.
We proceeded straight to the VIP section overlooking the dance floor, where
we got blitzed on bottle service. Moe and Alexa joined us, making out in
the corner the whole time, and vegas, Jordan, and I danced the night away.

When I woke up at the hostel on Sunday, my voice was gone. I've
been prone to laryngitis my whole life, and my three solid days of drinking, shouting at strangers at the convention, moving between Miami's
late-spring humidity and arctic air conditioning, and Saturday night's ex-
cesses had combined to leave me *sotto voce* for the duration of the expo.
As I descended to the hostel's bar/lobby, I realized I couldn't remember
much of the night before. I did, oddly, recall walking back to the hotel
with vegas and Jordan, and demanding tacos from a street vendor at 3:00
a.m. But most of the party, after our dramatic entrance, was gone.

When I found vegas and Jordan, I tried to croak out a question about
what the hell had happened. They laughed at my hangover. "What are
you even doing here?" vegas demanded. "I can't believe you didn't go
home with Keni!"

I shout-whispered, "Keni Styles?" He nodded. I was confused. "He
wasn't even at the party."

He raised one eyebrow and whipped out his cell phone, pulled something up, and shoved it in my face. It was a photo of me, drink in hand
and with a shocked look on my face, in the arms—like, literally being held
several feet off the ground in the arms—of a hugely grinning Keni Styles.

I had no memory of this event.

"You two really hit it off last night," vegas gloated. "You should have gone back to his hotel with him."

To this day, I don't remember what went down that night. After thinking very hard, I could vaguely recall Keni arriving and eventually dancing with me, but not that he'd picked me up. I wondered if our dancing had been sexy or silly. In my sensible way, I imagined I must have decided to leave the party rather than throwing myself at a porn star I'd just met. I didn't want to make the rather gross assumption that his friendliness or career decisions left him open to my sexual advances. I'm sure I threw in the idea that, with two romantic partners back in New York, I shouldn't indulge with a virtual stranger, lest they be upset.

But looking back, I wonder if I just cock-blocked myself. If he'd actually been interested. And whether my partners in New York would have been that upset if I'd gone for it and brought home an amazing story of coital bliss with my biggest crush in porn. After all, we were already in a polyamorous relationship—Jenn regularly had dalliances on the side and told me all about them. Matthew wasn't so open, but he was remarkably laid back about my crazy lifestyle.

Sigh.

Lynsey G: missing out on the fun stuff, on purpose, since 1983.

CHAPTER 19

Losing It to the Tubes

WE GOT BACK TO NEW YORK on the 23rd of May, and on the 25th I had lunch with the management team of apexart, a gallery in Tribeca. It was a non-traditional space that did not sell works for profit, but rather invited thinkers to curate shows based around themes. The gallery's director had been considering doing a show about pornography for years, and had read my *McSweeney's* column. He was interested in my point of view and wanted to discuss the idea of me curating a show for the gallery.

I was ecstatic. Stepping into the middle space between the porn world and the not-porn populace had attracted curious looks at first, but now I was luring people out to stand there with me and make connections of their own. Here was my opportunity to invite people into the middle with me in a physical setting, in public! I'd now come full circle, from providing customer service at a high-end gallery uptown to curating my own show downtown.

Setting to work on the art show was an exhilarating but challenging experience. How could I make my show inviting, but also pack a punch? Porn was nothing new to the art world, the director cautioned me. Presenting it in a way that invited discussion rather than blasé sensationalism was the challenge. But we didn't want to move too far away from the shock angle, either—sex does sell, after all. I was cautioned not to be so professorial that the subject matter became uninteresting, but neither to revel too much in the salaciousness of the material. The trick was to find the middle ground, as always, to place myself firmly in the center, and from there to show what I saw. The validity of my perspective on pornography, really, doesn't come from my closeness to it, but rather from the distance I have maintained from both the industry *and* consumers. How could I show the world the things I saw from my tenuous position between porn and public?

The answer came to me almost immediately when apexart first contacted me, but it took months of back and forth before I felt confident in it, since it didn't involve me curating so much as *creating* an art show: I would interview people about their personal relationships with pornography. Performers, directors, producers, critics, consumers. The interviews would then be cut up and arranged into short documentary films, which would be shown at the gallery in the spring of 2012.

As I began to prepare for the show, I received an e-mail from my TV and book agents informing me that they were dumping me. The literary agent said that my columns, essays, and sample chapters just weren't translating into a book-length work the way that she had hoped. The TV agent said that she didn't see any future in working with me as a client for other projects, but that she would continue to service my TV deal, since her agency also represented the production company (a detail which no one had told me previously). Although the TV deal had been signed and my (meager) option money had been paid, the team was no closer to finding a co-writer for my pilot than they'd been on day one, and the idea was clearly beginning to go stale for all involved.

I wasn't surprised. After my initial whirlwind of new-girl adulation and a few post-signing months of bliss, I'd been hearing less and less from the producers and agents who had lauded me as the next big thing in Hollywood. I was writing more than ever, for more places than ever, but my new stuff wasn't getting as much of a response as the column at *McSweeney's* had. It made sense: I had been a pervy outlier in the *McSweeney's* world, as I now was in the Tribeca art world, but amidst the clamor of online publishing I wasn't making much noise. I had tried pitching to larger publications, but had gotten no bites, so I continued to dedicate my energy to *WHACK!* rather than pursuing prominent bylines. My agents, with clearer understandings of writers' career trajectories, had noticed what I was up to, and they dropped me.

I'm sure it's bitter grapes that makes me wonder how much of their hesitation in more actively representing me came from a fear of judgment for being aligned with pornography. It felt as if it was okay for me to write about pornography in a literary magazine, with one eyebrow constantly raised. But when I got into the details of blowjob techniques in porn films for my less-exalted publications—look out! Nobody wanted to read about the implications of fellatio upon the cultural concept of gender relations. They wanted to read about the time I went home with Keni Styles after a party at a huge night club in Miami. But I didn't have that story to tell.

At any rate, I didn't have much time for reflecting on my bruised ego. I, too, had read the writing on the wall and had summarily started an internship at a major publishing company, which, within three weeks, turned into a full-time job for the company's premiere genre paperback imprint. Mainstream publishing turned out to be an interesting place to find myself. After watching the adult entertainment industry battle death by technology for years, I was familiar with the symptoms I saw there: dropping profits, resistance to change, polarization, and conglomeration. Just as the porn industry had seen its formerly astronomical profit margin shrink as content was pirated, publishing had been in a free fall as bookstores closed, e-book sales skyrocketed, and other forms of media pushed books toward the bottom of the pile of consumer preference. And yet, in this climate of drastic technological shifts, publishers were still hesitant to make changes to catch up.

When I entered the publishing industry, e-books were an afterthought for my imprint, which still operated primarily in romances, murder mysteries, and thrillers—the exact genres that had been selling well as e-books. But nobody had time, in their panic over the changing publishing landscape, to devote to prioritizing e-books, even as brick-and-mortar sales opportunities continued to shrivel and digital publishing flourished.

Sound familiar?

In light of these changes, the publishing industry was shifting in opposite directions. On one end, independent publishers were popping up and taking advantage of technology that enabled them to reduce the time, cost, and overhead needed to publish books. Self-publishing was also booming, and mainstream publishers were buying fewer books to keep their bottom lines satisfied. This DIY mentality mirrored that of small, independent pornographers (many of them feminist and/or queer) who had taken the opportunities that cheaper, higher-quality tech offered.

Meanwhile, publishing behemoths serviced the other end of the spectrum, consolidating as sales continued to slow and the media shrieked over the death of print. About a year and a half after I started working in publishing, two of the biggest publishers in the world—Penguin and Random House—announced that they would merge, thus combining workforces and taking over an enormous share of the world's publishing market in an effort to combat the threat of Amazon usurping the book-buying public, the means of distribution, and even the means of production. In a striking parallel, porn was witnessing the beginnings of its own, darker, slicker, conglomerate behemoth: a corporate machine that was growing every day, gorging itself on profits from the very piracy that was breaking down the rest of the industry.

THE ENTITY THAT IS NOW called MindGeek was started in 2003 in Montreal, where college friends Ouissam Youssef and Stephane Manos teamed up with a friend from the competitive Foosball circuit, Matt Keezer, to start some porn websites. When they did well, the group created Mansef, a holding company for their expanding enterprises, including a high-end pay site called Brazzers featuring content they contracted from producers in America. Brazzers specialized in big, often-augmented boobs—an aesthetic that had started to wane before Brazzers revived it—and high production values. I'd reviewed Brazzers films for both the print magazine and WHACK! and praised their quality, though I was never a fan of the plastic, blonde, tan-lined look they pushed.

The Brazzers family of companies expanded quickly, with JugFuckers, RacksAndBlacks, and more appearing in quick succession. A second network of sites popped up soon after, called Mofos, which specialized in less manufactured-looking performers—soon I was reviewing films from TeensLikeitBig, which had a more natural aesthetic and tended toward more extreme sex. (I preferred the Mofos content, generally.)

But even as Brazzers was growing in size and credibility in the porn industry, its cofounder Youssef was branching out in a different direction: tube sites. Internet porn piracy takes many forms, but by far the most popular tactic—and therefore the most draining on the industry—is tube sites. Taking their moniker from YouTube and modeling themselves after their namesake, porn tube sites allow users to upload pornographic content for free, and to watch it to their heart's content, also for free. This means that anyone with an Internet connection can post amateur videos of themselves having sex (legal, so long as everyone involved consents), or scenes they've recorded from porn films (totally, completely, utterly illegal—and far more frequent than the former; "amateur" porn on tube sites is almost entirely comprised of professionals pretending not to be). Tube sites display whatever their users upload unless a Digital Millennium Copyright Act (DMCA) takedown request is filed by the copyright holder, in which case it will be taken down in due course. But pirates act fast, and there are so many of them that most porn companies that try to counter them fight losing battles with diminishing resources, given that people are now able to watch their movies for free instead.

So, when Youssef purchased the domain Pornhub.com in 2007 and added the tube site to the Brazzers family under the name "Interhub"—a separate company owned by the same people—he was getting into bed with porn's biggest enemy while continuing to produce porn via Brazzers. Even as Mansef was paying porn crews, directors, producers, and performers to create new content for sale, that content was being pirated and uploaded to a growing family of free tube sites that Mansef also owned, and its advertising revenue was being funneled to Interhub. The Mansef/Interhub team had a simple strategy: Make money on traditional porn production *and* porn piracy, keep it quiet, and laugh all the way to the bank. As consumers flocked to the tube sites for their free and nearly limitless content, profits were dropping across the industry—except for over at Mansef, where business was still shockingly good. Rumors spread, and the Brazzers team—who had never been on a porn set but who were quickly becoming porn tycoons—were treated with suspicion.

In 2009, the Secret Service seized over $6 million from two Mansef bank accounts for suspicious activity. In short order, Mansef and Interhub's assets were sold to Fabian Thylmann, a German programming wiz who, overnight, become a porn overlord. At the time of purchase, he already owned several porn sites (including Xtube), and when he acquired Mansef and Interhub's operations, he renamed the conglomerate Manwin in 2010.

I had heard a few grumbles about the newly dubbed Manwin by the time it went on an acquisitions spree, adding small companies to its roster by the bucketful. By July 2013, the company had acquired tube sites YouPorn, GayTube, SexTube, TrannyTube, and RedTube, effectively cornering the market in porn tube sites, since it already owned several of the biggest. By that same date, Manwin had also acquired Twistys, Digital Playground, and Reality Kings, some of the premier porn site networks in the world. It additionally controlled the online operations of industry titan Wicked Pictures and the online and television operations of Playboy.

In under a decade, Manwin had become *the* primary player in the adult industry and showed no signs of slowing down.

According to many in the industry, particularly outspoken antipiracy advocate Stoya, Manwin's modus operandi is to allow porn piracy to undercut producers' profits to such a degree that those producers are willing to sell for peanuts. Once small companies have been purchased, they are allowed to continue creating content, but their profits are constantly sucked away by the tube sites, which still feed into the larger conglomerate. In effect, Manwin is making money no matter what, and the hundreds of people working for the company's content-production side simply have to make do with less, since the people paying them are also the ones stealing from them. As Nate Glass of the anti-piracy company Takedown Piracy told me in 2016, "It would be as if Twentieth Century Fox owned the Pirate Bay!" (Or, in the publishing world, as if Amazon owned Penguin Random House *and* used book stores.)

In 2013, Manwin had become public enemy number one in adult entertainment, but since so many still were still on its payroll, there was little to be done. Thylmann sold his stake in Manwin to Ferras Anton and David Tasillo, who had been with the company for years, and they renamed it MindGeek. These two now quietly oversee a gigantic share of the porn industry—a share so big that most in the business, along with plenty of journalists, have called it a monopoly. But the day that governments around the world start to care about monopolies in smut is still far off and, in the meantime, the holdouts still remaining independent have continued to seek out new avenues for money-making that can either cut MindGeek out of the equation or make peace with the looming Big Brother of porn.

By the time I hit AVN in 2011, the effects of tube sites were already being felt, although Manwin (which hadn't been renamed MindGeek yet) hadn't reached its zenith. The AVN expo in 2011 was much smaller than the year before. People were reporting drops in profits of up to eighty percent. At the awards ceremony, an anti-piracy PSA starring prominent industry faces was played, to raucous applause, and a number of acceptance speeches included pleas for viewers to pay for porn instead of watching it on the tubes. These entreaties didn't go unheard: The AVN Awards were being broadcast on Spike TV, which, ironically, was owned by—you guessed it—Manwin.

Since then, the trend has continued, even escalated. To my dismay, in 2012, the Adult Entertainment Expo was even smaller than the year before, and had been moved to the Hard Rock Hotel and Casino—a smaller venue well off the Strip. By the last quarter of 2014, production in Porn Valley was down seventy-five percent from 2008. *The Pornography Industry* author Shira Tarrant estimated in 2016 that at least $2 billion was being lost to online piracy, largely via tube sites, every year. MindGeek is now rumored to be one of the top three consumers of bandwidth *in the world*, with much of that mouthful going directly to its tube sites—of which it currently owns eight of the top ten worldwide. MindGeek has reported that its sites get over a hundred million views *every day*, with the vast majority of those views coming from the tube sites and a tiny percentage transitioning into paid subscriptions to its many pay sites or click-throughs to advertisers. Tube sites have become so ubiquitous that many studios upload trailers and clips as promotional material in the hopes that even one out of a thousand viewers *might* click the link to their pay site and make a purchase.

Studios that have managed to avoid the MindGeek leviathan must try to outmaneuver it while still eking out a profit in a market that just keeps shrinking. Given that most production companies own many sites that feed into one another, ownership in the industry is quite opaque, which means that whether industry workers want to steer clear of the monopoly or not, it's difficult to make a living *without* working for MindGeek. Some of the performers I've spoken to can't tell me whether they've shot scenes for a MindGeek company because they don't actually know. Others refuse to even speculate—they choose not to talk about MindGeek at all, lest their words get around and they find themselves blacklisted by the biggest bully on the playground.

There is resistance from the grassroots, however. A startup called Takedown Piracy entered the scene in the spring of 2009 when Nate Glass, a salesperson for an adult production company in LA, decided to do something. "I kind of took it as a personal challenge, and I have a total hero complex! I saw people I knew getting laid off, I saw us downsizing," he told me. And he thought, "This is not justice! This is not right!" So he set about developing digital fingerprinting technology that would identify copyrighted content by scanning tube sites and pinpointing unique markers for each studio. His company generates and sends DMCA takedown notices to the site illegally hosting its clients' content. They started in 2009, and as of the time I'm writing this, Takedown Piracy has removed over fifty million copyrighted videos from free websites on behalf of their clients, and has worked out deals with a number of tube sites to block those clients' pirated content in the future. Takedown Piracy has made a noticeable dent in the mountains of pirated porn in the world, and Glass is hopeful that dent will grow.

And, for better or worse, the tube site model may soon change, if MindGeek's latest innovation takes root. At the end of 2015, Pornhub introduced Pornhub Premium, a Netflix-style, $9.99-per-month subscription service that entitles members to faster, higher-quality streams of all the content available for free on the rest of the site, as well as exclusive full-length films produced by Pornhub's partner studios. As of February 2016, the Premium package also offers Pornhub original content. It launched with *Full Holes*, a *Full House* porn parody that, frankly, looked god-awful to this porn journalist. (But I've never been a big fan of the *Full House* franchise, so don't take my word for it.)

The tube site subscription model has yet to prove itself, but it's another double-edged sword for the rest of the adult industry. On the one hand, it offers a pay-for-your-porn, Netflix-style model from the biggest tube site of them all, which could be a boon in that it's reintroducing consumers to the idea that pornography is a product with monetary value. And, for studios who partner with Pornhub to shelter their content *behind* the paywall, it could help to keep piracy at bay. However, so far there have been no plans announced to kick any of that $9.99 per month back to the industry in a meaningful way, which leaves adult industry workers in more or less the same position they're in now.

The monopoly isn't all bad, of course. MindGeek's flagship tube site, Pornhub, is so profitable and so widely recognized as the biggest porn site in the world that it has taken the opportunity to give back to its users in quirky, sometimes delightful ways. In 2012, Pornhub launched a month-long "Save the Boobs" campaign by donating one cent to breast cancer research for every thirty "big-tit" or "small-tit" videos its users streamed. Shortly thereafter, the company launched the Pornhub Cares initiative, which has since made charitable donations to reforestation efforts (donations based on views of the "big dicks" category—get it? wood?), domestic violence (via a clothing line cofounded with domestic violence survivor Christy Mack), and whale conservation (one cent per every 2,000 videos streamed). They've even started a $25,000 scholarship, awarded to the winner of an essay contest every year.

In early 2017, Pornhub launched the Pornhub Sexual Wellness Center, a sex education site that brings together sex experts and doctors to school the masses on issues ranging from basic sexual anatomy to gender issues to sexually transmitted disease, and more. The move was roundly lauded by porn fans and mainstream media as a responsible answer to the fact that pornography serves as sex education for many of the tube site's viewers. Pornhub's vice president Corey Price told Refinery29, "As a leading provider of adult entertainment, we thought it important that we also offer a platform on which carefully sourced information about all aspects of sexuality be made available to our viewers." But adult industry insiders were skeptical—one of the primary reasons that so many people are learning about sexuality from porn in the first place is because they can watch it easily and for free. Illegally. On Pornhub, where the vast majority of the fare available was filmed with the intention of entertaining, not educating, in exchange for legal tender. But now that it's available for free, it's serving both purposes. And rather than cracking down on copyright violations in an effort to get pornographers paid, Pornhub has made itself a one-stop shop for education and smut, theoretically eliminating the need to look elsewhere—say, pay sites or VOD sites—for sexual material online.

Pornhub has also leveraged its popularity into brilliant ad campaigns that inhabit a solid middle ground straddling salaciousness, titillation, humor, and wry winks to the public acknowledging that porn is a secret we all share. In other words, MindGeek has dropped its consumer-facing brand directly into the space I myself have been trying to occupy for years by bringing people together to talk about porn in a real way. With its sixty-four million hits a day in traffic, Pornhub is in an incredible position to collect and process information that the world has been wondering about for years. And it recognized its potential, launching Pornhub Insights in 2013. Looking at every imaginable metric for porn consumption, the company has examined porn viewership during various sporting events and holidays, the correlations between income and porn-watching habits, political divisions and porn use, marijuana in porn searches, and more.

The results of these data-crunching and processing efforts are fascinating, to say the least (just a nibble: "lesbian" is far and away the most searched-for word on the site, and Kim Kardashian is one of the most popular porn stars—even though she's not a porn star), and could be of immense value for pornographers. But more than that, Pornhub is demystifying the dirty habit that we almost all share. By giving us feedback on our habits and laying them out for all the world to see—and doing it in a friendly, SFW way—they're clobbering the stigma surrounding porn use. (For instance, one of their biggest reveals has been that easily a quarter of their registered users are female—and then breaking down what these female viewers are watching. The results are riveting. Did you know for instance, that women are 122 percent more likely to search for gang-bang porn than men, at least on Pornhub?)

But it must be stated that, just as algorithms on Facebook and Google cultivate the consumer tastes that they then cater to, so too is MindGeek steering its viewers. All this data collection on the part of Pornhub is likely part of a larger effort to direct users to content they'll enjoy, much like Amazon's "You Might Also Enjoy . . ." function that introduces shoppers to similar products. Those suggestions don't come up arbitrarily—the site is tracking your interests and comparing them with those of millions of other users. The end result is, as Shira Tarrant put it, "You're being spoon-fed a limited range of pornography . . . Online-porn users don't necessarily realize that their porn-use patterns are largely molded by a corporation." With this wisdom in mind, one starts to question the prevalence of, say, "teens" as a search term, or "MILFs." Are we really all thirsty for these two age groups, or have we entered into a feedback loop that tells us these categories are popular, so we must want to watch them, so they continue to get made? It's a question that I couldn't begin to answer, but it makes me look a tad askance at the information Pornhub puts out.

Still, it's interesting to watch the porn monopoly's prize website—and possibly the industry's biggest enemy—going to such lengths to be a good citizen. And, skeptical though I may be, I can't help also being impressed. But the cynic in me must ask: Wouldn't it be nice to see them spending as much time and energy on giving back to the community upon whose backs all of this data—and money—is generated? While MindGeek is making us feel a little better about watching porn, most of us are still getting it for free—from MindGeek. For the industry, that means that there is still less work to go around, and less money. Studios are still failing, rates are still falling, and the public doesn't much care because they're getting all the porn they want free of charge, as well as a winking pat on the back from the Pornhub Cares folks.

In December 2016, superstar adult performer Nikki Benz tweeted that she had been assaulted on a Brazzers set by the director, Tony T., who had choked her during a scene that she said "wasn't supposed to be a rape scene," but in which she had been pushed well past her limits. She'd called for a cut multiple times, she said, but filming had continued. Her eight hundred fifty thousand Twitter followers, who call themselves the #BenzMafia, were outraged and began immediately calling for justice, denouncing Brazzers and Tony T., and pulling their memberships from the company that had employed Ms. Benz as a brand ambassador and contract star. Brazzers backpedaled, publicly siding with Ms. Benz while also denying culpability. Tony T., you see, was an independent third party, contracted to film a scene according to his own whims, which would be purchased by Brazzers if it met their requirements. Brazzers reported that they would not purchase the scene, nor would they ever work with Tony T. again. Yet the statements rang hollow: Nikki Benz was one of the biggest stars in the industry, with one of the largest fan bases, and she was unwilling to be mollified. The company was so big, they maintained, that they clearly didn't care about the well-being of the people at the bottom: the performers themselves. Nikki Benz, known for shooting high-end, mostly vanilla scenes, should never have been paired with a director like Tony T., whose career in porn started as an aggressively dominant male performer for hardcore gonzo companies and who had earned himself a reputation for aggression on set. Whatever he was planning to film with Nikki Benz, Brazzers should have seen the writing on the wall well before they booked their biggest contract star to work on one of his sets. As performer Gen Padova told me shortly after the incident, "It was Brazzers's responsibility. There's a contract there. You take care of that person who is representing your company. That's a lot on the line. You're the largest and the most successful company in the industry, and have been for years, you'd think you'd be a little careful with something like that."

The fallout is still raining down on the largest of MindGeek's production outfits. Tony T. and Ramon Nomar, the director and performer who Ms. Benz called out, have filed a defamation lawsuit for unspecified damages. Tony T. has categorically denied the truth of the allegations, even showing the raw footage of the scene in question to a small group of industry insiders in an attempt to clear his name. Still, many performers have come out publicly in defense of Ms. Benz and to add their own stories to hers: Brazzers, it seems, has a history of hiring producers who mistreat female talent on set, then silencing their complaints by withholding pay and pressuring performers to stay quiet. A huge company's word, the thinking seems to go, will be valued above that of a mere porn actor. But the tables may be turning: nearly a million angry fans on Twitter and an increasingly loud outcry from the people on whose bodies the whole of pornography is created are refusing to let MindGeek live this one down.

And in the meantime, performers and independent producers have been finding workarounds to stay free of MindGeek's tightening fist. The result is an intriguing post-apocalyptic porn landscape. Since 2010 or so, I've been witness to some truly genius changes in porn. Just as Amazon's dominance and large-publisher conglomeration has left a space for indie publishers to proliferate and self-publishing to flourish, the corporate titan of porn has encouraged small producers and performers to think creatively and find more ways to make money.

Kink.com is an excellent example of independent success. Started in 1997 as Cybernet Entertainment and renamed Kink.com in 2006, the company is dedicated to, as its mission statement attests, "demystifying and celebrating alternative sexualities by providing the most ethical and authentic kinky adult entertainment." With its focus on the wide world of kink, ranging from simulated water torture to fucking machines to standard bondage and domination and everything in between, Kink has managed to do well by filming specialized content that MindGeek doesn't have a particular interest in owning. (The company's production efforts don't make much in the way of kinky content, and Pornhub isn't very interested in fringe material, which it offloads instead onto MindGeek's smaller tube sites.) With its ever-evolving focus on the ethical treatment of models and other workers, Kink has set itself up as a progressive force within the industry, aiming to expand and improve at every juncture. The company also pays well—slightly less, on average, than a standard mainstream company might, but more than smaller companies can afford.

Many independent studios have taken a hint from Kink.com's success and specialized in fringe content that doesn't fall under MindGeek's purview. Back in 2010, industry veteran Debi Diamond, who had just returned to porn after a fifteen-year hiatus, told me, "To stay in the game you must be creative and serve up fresh niche content," and that has only gotten more true with the continued role of piracy. At most industry gatherings I have attended in recent years, new faces I've struck up conversations with have often told me that they do fetish work, ranging from balloon popping to farting to foot fetishes—for themselves, from home, with extremely low overhead costs. "With hand jobs, pegging, foot fetish—that stuff—there's less constraints, so you can shoot more of it in a day. It's easier on your body, and there's zero, zero, zero chance of anybody passing [an STI] on to anyone," says Lance Hart of kinky porn and payment company PervOut.com. Companies like his are too small for MindGeek to notice, and they shoot content that MindGeek doesn't particularly want, anyway. And because the tube sites host relatively few fringe offerings, the increasingly kinky public finds content where it can—very often paying small producers for it in the process. (It's worth noting that this doesn't mean that fringe content *doesn't* get pirated or put on tube sites, merely that this happens less frequently to non-mainstream content.)

Specialization at a small scale has proven itself a more sure thing for performers than shooting old-school porn scenes in the new millennium, and porn has morphed to meet the needs of its fans as well as the wallets of its smaller producers. As Danny Wylde told *Forbes* in 2017, from his perspective as a retired performer, he can see "the reality that performing is no longer a way—for most people—to make a lot of money." Even performers who frequent the mainstream LA porn studio circuit have branched out into alternative revenue streams for the extra cash and the control it can give them over their careers.

Performer websites, for instance, began to revolutionize the way adult actors made money as soon as the World Wide Web began displaying photos. Nina Hartley told me in a 2010 interview for *WHACK!* that performers had "more leverage and power, in that they can learn how to run their own websites and keep more of the money for themselves" than in the past, and since then that trend has deepened. Almost every performer has their own website today, as well as a phalanx of social media profiles, giving them more power over their image and finances. With the ability to produce and display their own images, models can monetize their own content and make money on their terms.

But websites are just the tip of the porn iceberg. In a 2016 study, Heather Berg, a professor of women's studies at the University of California, Santa Barbara, found that of the eighty performers she interviewed, nearly all were making money outside of prerecorded porn scenes. "For all but the most popular performers (and then usually for only a short term)," she wrote, "there are simply not enough film performance gigs to sustain an income." Anything from phone calls to used lingerie to Amazon wishlists can be sources of income for porn stars these days.

"There are a lot of girls who do webcamming and make a lot of money," Nikki Darling said to me in 2016. "There's starting to be a lot of multiple revenue [streams] or multiple hustles. I think ten years ago, you could be a full-time porn star and you could really make money and a good living. But with the rise of the Internet and piracy, and how easy it is to get content for free, there now are all these alternatives that are widening your net." A few weeks before I spoke to her, at a panel at the XBIZ conference, four out of seven models affirmed that they made fifty percent or more of their money from sources other than filming traditional porn scenes.

As sex scenes have grown ever more passé, consumers have developed a taste for interactive, custom-made content that connects them directly to performers. As such, webcam shows that put models into one- on-one, or one-on-a-few, contact with fans have exploded in popularity. At the Adult Entertainment Expo in 2016, Christopher Ruth of the Fine Ass Marketing agency told me candidly that he estimated easily fifty percent of the industry's profits now came from camming. There are a number of big webcamming companies that operate on a variety of brilliant payment models, but the long and short of the camming industry is that models— sometimes porn performers, sometimes not—do sexy things on camera for a group of onlookers, and the company hosting or producing the cam show takes a cut of their profits. Cam shows are prized for their interactivity, with viewers able to type messages to the model during her show, to take her into a "private" room for a more intimate experience, and to suggest ideas for what the model should do next, or just to say hi. The camming industry has maintained its edge by keeping up technologically with the trappings that can help their industry, notably with the finest in teledildonics (long-distance smart sex toys) and every new iteration of high-definition filming and viewing technology, including virtual reality.

But webcamming isn't the only game in town for adult models to make money between filming porn scenes; clips are another performer favorite. With videos ranging from a few minutes to full-length porn-style sex scenes, most clips are produced by models themselves for their fans— either solo or with partners, in any configuration or niche they want. The videos are loaded onto "clip stores," either on one of the many large clip websites that host content and take cuts of the payments, or directly on the performer's website (using one of these large website's interfaces). Nikki Darling told me, "The amateur clip type of thing is kind of where, from my vantage point, I see a lot of porn going." For the performer, it's an opportunity to make money and take control over their labor. And for the interested consumer, it's worth noting that purchasing clips from the performers that make them is often relatively inexpensive.

Clip stores are a good source for independent income, but Nikki says that they're not all that simple. "I think it can be beneficial, and it does widen your net of income . . . You're picking up different skills. You're learning how to edit, or you're speaking to people who know how to edit. You're figuring out how to upload and shoot . . . It's entrepreneurial in a lot of ways, because you're making yourself a business and figuring out what's best for the business and what your market is." Moving behind the camera is an excellent source of not only cash but agency in the adult entertainment industry. In today's MindGeek-dominated landscape, entrepreneurship may be the best way forward for performers like Nikki, whose careers are diversifying every day. From creating custom videos and photos for fans, to sending those videos and photos over mobile apps like Snapchat for pay, to monetizing social media streams using new apps like FollowPlus, to paid private Skype video calls, to text message sex via companies like DreamLover, the possibilities abound for a savvy performer to make a living without shooting for MindGeek at all.

Live, interactive possibilities also abound, like feature dancing at gentlemen's clubs, educational speaking engagements that are opening up to sex workers in the 2010s, public appearances at night clubs and elsewhere, and, of course, one-on-one sessions with clients. For adult entertainers of the kinky persuasion, work as a professional dominatrix can be extremely profitable. For those with less specialized tastes, short stints at legalized brothels in Nevada bring extra attention and cash to the brothels *and* the performers. And, though it's still taboo to speak of, private escorting gigs are—and have long been—standard practice for many.

As Exxxotica New Jersey approached in the fall of 2011, the ways in which escorting and industry events dovetailed weren't at the forefront of my mind, preoccupied as it was by the pending art show. *WHACK!*

was planning to attend the expo in full force, and we were in talks to put together a red-carpet, media-heavy party in Manhattan the weekend of the show. We hoped to invite press outlets to take photos and ask questions of the industry royalty in attendance. We'd also, of course, give said royalty lots of liquor and shuttle at least a few to the event in limos.

We were extraordinarily lucky to have a generous pro-domme friend hooking us up with all of this, as to date *WHACK!* had not made any money. Under the guidance of our "business guy," Moe, we had gotten a website redesign and a booth at Exxxotica Miami, but no more. His behavior had become more and more erratic, with *WHACK!* always coming in last place behind whatever other schemes he was running. As time went on it became clear to me that he was a drug dealer who knew a lot of people in business—*not*, as we had been led to believe, a businessperson who did a lot of drugs. As Moe began showing up hours late for meetings, sniffling more and more during our chats, and failing to come through on any of the things he'd promised, we got tired.

Tensions grew, and by mid-October they reached a breaking point. Over beers at a bar one night, we told Moe that we thought it was time we parted ways. He had, after all, shown up almost an hour late for a meeting *across the street from his apartment*, so by the time he arrived, we'd had it. We wanted to be polite; j. vegas and I had prepared a whole list of talking points that we wanted to communicate in order to figure out how best to end the relationship to everyone's benefit. But, after vegas got a few sentences into his prepared spiel, Moe stormed out of the bar without looking back. Bemused, the rest of us finished our beers. Then, the texts started coming. I don't know where he went after he left, but for hours after *we* departed, vegas and I were barraged with text messages. With vegas, he wheedled and whined, trying to get back into good favor. With me, however, he let loose. He called me a variety of—in Moe's defense—rather creative names and accused me of sowing discord amongst the team, blaming me for everything. I'd never felt more confident in my slightly paranoid but on-point creep radar.

At any rate, as we approached Exxxotica New Jersey in November, we were leaning heavily on friends who were better off financially than we were to make our party happen. We were excited—this would be a gala event that would attract media and fans and put the *WHACK!* name at the top of the "cool" list at that year's convention. Despite Moe's shenanigans, we were maintaining a good rapport with many companies and performers, and in the week leading up to the convention we had a healthy list of confirmed A-list attendees for our party. We made it clear to them that we were hoping they would arrive, walk the red carpet, get their pictures taken, have a drink, and then feel free to stay for the evening or head to other engagements as they saw fit.

We sent press releases to every media outlet we could think of, billing our party as an Exxxotica-weekend event. We hadn't gotten the convention to partner with us, as they had official, branded parties running at the hotel in Edison, so we were careful to avoid any confusion over whether the convention itself was involved in the party. However, when the media got hold of our press release, headlines implying that our party was an official Exxxotica-branded event began to circulate. We attempted to alert the media to the mistake, but nobody seemed to care.

Until I got a phone call from an extremely prominent adult star. We'll call her Alyssa Lane. I had interviewed her in a hotel room in Manhattan a few months prior, and we had gotten along swimmingly. She was such a huge name in adult film that the interview had gotten a *lot* of attention for *WHACK!*, and we had maintained a good rapport with her since. But Alyssa had gotten word of our press-heavy event and read the erroneous headlines, and she flew into such a rage that she called me at work to scream at me for ten minutes. I had no business calling it an "official" Exxxotica after-party, she said. I was diluting the brand, and disrespecting the convention by taking models away from the *real* Exxxotica after-parties. Furthermore, the performers who attended might miss other important appearances in New York because of our party. They might drink too much and end up hungover the next day, then be late for their signing obligations at the convention. In short, she told me that the party we were throwing was disrespectful and unprofessional.

I tried to counter her shrieks, but she was not interested in hearing anything I had to say. And, over the next few days, we got word that Alyssa was on the warpath, alerting her friends and at least one talent agency that we were up to no good. Soon, performers began backing out of our party. By the time we left the convention on Saturday evening, our two limos were full of adult stars, but nobody else was coming. The *WHACK!* crew and I drove our friends' beat-up cars into the city and arrived at the red carpet just ahead of the limos. We did some red-carpet interviews and managed to attract a decent press turnout, but the party was not nearly the star-studded extravaganza we'd been hoping for.

In the aftermath of our letdown, our domme friend, who had kept her head high throughout the debacle, explained to me why Alyssa Lane had gotten so angry she'd blocked most of the performers from our red carpet.

"Alyssa is a madam," she told me, point-blank. "She runs girls every time there's an event in New York, and so does the guy at the talent agency that slammed us. If their girls came to our party instead of escorting on Saturday night, they wouldn't be making their pimps any money, and pimps don't like that."

I was floored. The concept of porn stars doing escort work was not unfamiliar to me; I'd often wondered about performers' sudden trips to New York, and I'd heard oblique references to "private" work, but mostly when performers were assuring me that they didn't do it. Those who did, they said, were liabilities because the unprotected sex they might have with outsiders could bring disease back into the porn industry. The fears of STI transmission from escorting work aren't unfounded. A number of actors who have tested positive for HIV in the past decade were later revealed to have been escorting on the side. One of the most difficult issues around testing in pornography is the fact that when people aren't on the clock—or on camera—it's impossible to keep track of what they're doing with their bodies. That's why the testing protocols for performers are so strict. Unless they were to get new tests literally every day, which would be prohibitively expensive and might leave the talent pool completely drained of blood, there's not much room for making the rules stricter than they already are.

Anyway, despite the risks, performer escorting is a big business, and as time goes on, more appear to be partaking. As the industry continues to shrink, everyone is looking for extra cash. And few alternative revenue streams pay as well as escorting. Because of their celebrity status within the world of sex work, their relative scarcity in the escorting market, and their business acumen, porn stars can charge exorbitantly for private bookings, with hourly rates reaching into the thousands. I can't confirm the rumors I've heard about royalty in the Middle East procuring the services of porn stars for tens of thousands of dollars a night, but I can say that I've heard those rumors from enough different sources that I believe them to be true. In a climate where the average female performer earns about half her income from porn, a flight across the world and a night being wooed by some of the richest men in existence in exchange for twenty grand can be an awfully compelling proposition.

But it's important to recognize, as well, that not all porn actors are "stars" capable of racking up tens of thousands for a night out with a fan. Many porn models do private sex work for other reasons that are as diverse as the people themselves. With the porn economy in the state it's in, working in porn and even moonlighting as a cam girl while picking up paid text messaging on the side doesn't always fulfill some models' needs, whether professionally, emotionally, or financially. A large number of them started out in private sex work—stripping, domming, doing phone sex, camming, or escorting—before branching out into porn, and vice versa, some out of necessity, others out of curiosity, and many others for reasons we will never know, nor should we presume to judge.

Escort, writer, porn actress, and educator Christina Cicchelli told me once, "When it comes down to it, most of us enter this workforce for money, for a place to stay or for a bite to eat . . . When I first began in the industry I didn't really plan it and didn't consider being a stripper or a call girl as a career. I just knew I needed money and I would rather dance and entertain clients than work at the mall." There are many in the sex industry with similar stories.

Although prostitution is illegal everywhere in America except for Nevada—and even there, only under very strict regulation—some of the stigma that comes with private sex for pay is beginning to dissipate, ever so slightly. In the past few years, sex workers of all stripes have become more vocal, especially on the Internet, forming online communities and support networks, speaking up for themselves in droves, and shining much-needed light into their field of work. Naturally, not everyone who does private sex work is willing to come forward and demand respect from the public, given the stigma they face and the fact that their work is currently criminalized, but those who do are making great strides in visibility for their industry. Efforts like the Red Umbrella Project have brought the experiences of sex workers to the public in storytelling and film as sex workers begin to unite for common goals. And the best part? People are beginning to sit up and take notice.

Of course, the old second-wave-feminism, sex-negative view of sex work as inherently exploitative still exists, and it may be dominant in most of America. But a new generation of articulate, empowered, and increasingly outspoken sex workers are speaking up for their work, their rights, and their struggles to an ever-more-compassionate and educated public. They argue that sex work can be just as legitimate and non-exploitative a means of income as any other, that outdated ideas about sexual morality are behind the continued criminalization of most forms of sex work, and that that criminalization and the surrounding stigma contribute to the majority of the risks that sex workers face—not the job itself.

Porn stars in particular are getting more reverent treatment from the public. A growing number of colleges and universities have begun asking performers to speak to students at campus "Sex Week" events and in classes on topics ranging from sexual representation to empowerment to sex education. In 2014, Routledge began publishing a brand-new, peer-reviewed academic journal called *Porn Studies*, dedicated to the important discourse about porn in our culture. Trade publications, too, are showing interest in hearing from the people who actually *do* sex work instead of from wallflower journalists like me. Ten-year veteran of the porn industry Aurora Snow's ongoing work for *The Daily Beast* is an excellent example, as are Andre Shakti's smart and pithy columns for *Cosmopolitan*. Former performer, director, and producer Tina Horn recently wrote a book, *Love Not Given Lightly*, about her experiences and those of her friends who have done professional sex work of various kinds, and she's gone on to write for numerous websites about her experiences. And these few are just the tip of a growing iceberg of outspoken sex workers building audiences around the world. In short, while porn and escort work are still taboo subjects, neither is quite as hush-hush as it once was, and the crossover between the two types of work is starting to come out of the shadows.

In a way, this evolution makes sense. With fans more focused than ever on interactivity with porn stars, being accustomed as they are to being able to tweet to them directly, follow them on Twitter and Snapchat and Facebook and Instagram, to meet them face-to-face at public appearances, it's only natural that some fans want to engage with them more, shall we say, personally. Interactivity is the new face of porn, and it doesn't get much more interactive than a date. Apparently, those dates and their thousands-an-hour payments were more important to the likes of Alyssa Lane and others who managed the escorting careers of porn models than those models showing up at a red-carpet party for *WHACK!*

Hard at work just before the opening of "Consent" at apexart in March 2012
(PHOTO COURTESY OF APEXART)

At the live taping of Ultimate Surrender in late 2011 . . . everybody won!
(PHOTO COURTESY OF THE AUTHOR)

CHAPTER 20

Porn, Art, and Obscenity

As 2011 DREW TO A CLOSE, I began conducting interviews for my art show, which I'd decided to name "Consent." I felt it was important to emphasize that, when we get involved with pornography, our participation is a consented-to agreement—a relationship between pornographers and consumers. I hoped that in some small way, the videos I would create might bring porn insiders and outsiders together and remind visitors of our shared humanity, and our shared sexuality.

I started the filmmaking process by purchasing a cheap video camera on the gallery's dime and setting out to interview people in New York. I tracked down a few near-strangers I'd met at parties and through mutual friends—those who I had been introduced to as "the porn girl" and stuck around to talk to me. I also recorded conversations with a number of close friends, detailing what porn meant to them. I included a few professional friends, as well: Cindy Gallop, of course; a former adult scriptwriter named Dan; one of the writers for *WHACK!* whose perspective had always intrigued me; some poetry acquaintances; a fellow porn critic; and three adult performers who lived in the city—industry veterans Sinnamon Love and Brittany Andrews, as well as the then-novice Natasha Starr. There were others I'd have loved to get on camera, some for very personal reasons. But I decided to limit my list to people I had never slept with (with one exception, but I'll never tell who that was), for fear of losing my focus on the art show in pursuit of my own libidinous curiosity.

But my libidinous curiosity, it turned out, may have been my greatest strength in these interviews. I started every interview with the same, quite personal, prompt: "Tell me about your first experience with pornography." The answers were stunning. Not because the stories themselves were riveting (though some were) but because first times are formative experiences, particularly first experiences with smut. One of my subjects described the experience as "a feeling of shock . . . Something powerful was happening in my brain." Everyone remembers their first encounter with porn, because it can color your outlook on sex for the rest of your life, depending on how much that first experience teaches you. But nobody had ever asked most of my subjects about this indelible first experience. Once they got started, the floodgates burst *wide* open.

Although I'd already spent years writing about the diversity of sexual desires in the world, the interviews I collected for "Consent" really began to drive home just how correct I had been. Particularly with regard to first encounters with pornography, people's responses and takeaways were wildly divergent. Most of us, upon our first encounter with this new, scary yet exciting source of pleasure and guilt, had nowhere to go with our new-found discovery. Friends might be alerted, but the adults in our lives who might have provided context for porn were rarely told about our illicit peeks into the things we tried not to imagine them doing behind closed doors. One interviewee said that she began watching clips of anal porn in her early teens. "I was really aroused by it, but I was embarrassed that I was aroused by it," she revealed. "I would have been destroyed if my parents figured out that I was doing that." And so she just internalized it and let it color her experience of sex for years. When she found out a high school boyfriend watched a lot of porn, she said, "I started observing it more deeply . . . This is the really kinky shit to do. This is the way to be *special*."

For some subjects, porn provided not just a template for sex, but a deeply conflicting outlet, as well. One woman told me, for instance, that she had never been able to orgasm while watching porn unless something violent was happening in the scene, and that guilt plagued her. She had tried to quit watching it, she told me, but she also had difficulty reaching orgasm with a partner; porn was her most reliable tool for climax. "I think that the porn that I watch is harmful to me," she said. A victim of childhood sexual molestation, she had a conflicted relationship with pornography in which she both relived and took control of the trauma in her past by watching smut that mirrored her own experiences and feelings of anger.

Her story, upsetting though it was, reflected a trend. For many of my interview subjects, porn was a source of great shame. But, as one of few things in modern culture that is usually kept private, their relationship with porn was safe from prying eyes and was thus, in a weird way, freeing. In a porn viewing session, viewers could let go of the walls they construct around their formative traumas, their darkest desires, their fear of discovery. In many ways this sounds healthy; wouldn't we all love to let go of our baggage, even for a short time? But the taboo around pornography, and often the types of porn that these people consumed, made their relationships with the medium fraught.

For others, the taboo around porn was its draw, and this fascinated the hell out of me. Personally, I've always been intrigued by the forbidden, but not so much in order to revel in it as to break down the socially constructed walls that make things forbidden in the first place. But some of my subjects enjoyed pornography, as consumers or creators, *because* of those walls. For them, porn felt like a playground where they could drop all expectations. Porn was a gleeful opportunity to indulge in the things they knew they weren't *supposed* to like. For performers and producers, the act of making a taboo form of entertainment liberated them from the rules of a Puritan society, and they used their freedom to push every limit to near the breaking point—as a point of pride, as a form of art or activism, or just for the fun of getting away with it.

Others saw porn as just an interesting but atypical diversion—something they'd tried but never found compelling enough to make a habit of. These interviews were short, but I was amazed by them. I suppose, had I grown up in an environment in which sex were *not* the most forbidden topic, perhaps I'd never have been so drawn to pornography. Most of those lacking interest in porn came from open and accepting backgrounds, in which shame didn't enter heavily into the dialogue about sex. I envied them in a way, but then I also cherished the dark and forbidden rush I felt when I watched porn, even after years of doing so professionally. I'm not sure if I would trade places with them if I could.

A shared theme among interview subjects was that *very* few had ever purchased pornography. Those who had actually shelled out legal tender for smut tended to be older and had made most of their purchases before free porn became readily available—via magazines, videos, or visits to porn theaters. Of the younger interviewees, a few more fiscally responsible souls had subscriptions to one or more membership sites, but most did not. Several blinked at me, uncomprehending, when I asked them about paying for porn. One said, "I guess it just doesn't seem worth it. I can find enough for free that it doesn't matter."

What was most frustrating was that many of these subjects also complained about not being able to find porn that they liked. Some complained about production quality, others about content on tube sites, but they were united on the fact that finding *good* porn was difficult. I intimated to them that if they did a bit of research and spent a bit of money, they'd be able to find something more edifying, and to ensure that more of it got made. The responses I got were mostly polite, a few incredulous.

"I tried to pay for pornography for the first time," said one disgruntled guy I spoke to, "and I found that the movie was unavailable for digital download, and they wanted me to pay twenty bucks to get a DVD shipped to me. And at that point, I was like, 'Fuck you. I've tried to do a transaction, and you're being a dick about it.'" He gave up and had never again attempted to pay for porn.

Eccentricity was not unexpected in these interviews, but eccentric *trends* were a fascinating surprise: Several cisgender men informed me that they saved their favorite porn, but not in the way you might expect. They didn't download entire videos, but rather still shots or short clips that they handpicked from their favorite moments of a porno. As they were watching, they'd hoard these moments to a cache on their computers. It was a time-honored ritual that they indulged in as they neared climax, amassing gigabytes of the most orgasm-inducing moments of their masturbatory forays. But when I asked them *why* they did it, they had no reason at the ready. They didn't even go back to their smutty cache to enjoy what they'd saved. Their sometimes-massive stockpiles of pornography just sat on their hard drives, never to be enjoyed again.

This phenomenon confounded and sort of obsessed me—and to date, it still does. Were these men saving their favorite moments because they felt a need to gain a more personal connection the people on the screen? Did the act of clicking "save" cement the glorious moment of release in their subconscious? I'll probably never know, but I wonder how many people out there engage in this little quirk.

The one thing that banded everyone together, from performers to critics to tube site frequenters, was that they *loved* talking about porn once I got them started. Some of the interviews went on for over an hour, and I *loved* conducting them. My overwrought schedule was exhausting, but I was so excited to be talking to people about the issues that had obsessed me for years that I hardly noticed.

In October, I flew to the Bay Area. My primary goal was visiting a friend in Oakland, but I'd also arranged to meet with a personal hero of mine, Madison Young, as she was setting up an art show for her queer, feminist art collective, Femina Potens. Madison had begun her porn career as a mainstream porn star and rose through the industry's ranks in LA before branching out into more indie and feminist projects. She prided herself for bringing feminism to mainstream porn by visibly enjoying the hell out of her scenes, refusing to fake orgasms, and supporting her art space in San Francisco with the earnings from her anal scenes in LA. At Femina Potens, she had cultivated a community of like-minded queers, feminists, and progressives under the banner of art and revolution, and had then begun to direct and perform in queer, feminist performance art that often ventured into pornographic territory. When I met her, she was also running TheWomansPOV.com, and she had just given birth to her first child.

We met at a gallery space in the Mission District and plopped down on the floor, the white walls reflecting the midday sun and the space echoing with music blasting from a radio down the block. My friend Leigh, with whom I was staying, filmed our interview, which turned into a rambling conversation about our childhoods, philosophies, desires, and fears. And porn and art and feminism. And bondage and kink and fetishes.

Madison showed me the bruises covering her ass after a recent caning session and brimmed with joy while she told me about the experience. She caressed her still-full-from-pregnancy body as she talked about her love of rope, the ecstasy she found in relinquishing control, the joy she felt during rough sex. She referred to the mainstream porn she used to make as "fast food porn" and spoke of the deeper, more nourishing fare she and others in San Francisco were making. She spoke of art and porn as one and the same, both parts of an evolving mystery, and as the interview wore on into its second hour, I felt her excitement about these topics seep into me.

A day or two later, Leigh and I ventured back into the Mission to visit the Armory—the home of Kink.com and the epicenter of American kink pornography. I had scored two press passes to a live taping of Ultimate Surrender, a sex-wrestling event in which competitors grappled while performing sex acts on one other for points. When the bout was over, the winner got to fuck the loser. All in front of a cheering crowd of onlookers, and, of course, the cameras, which streamed live to paying customers around the world.

Leigh and I were nervous. Both feminists, but with different degrees of comfort with pornography and live sex, we weren't sure what was in store at Ultimate Surrender. I was worried that I had dragged my sweet artist friend to a horror show of demeaning activity. We sat in a holding room near the building's main entrance with other audience members, taking in the architecture of the massive structure. Built nearly a century earlier to resemble a medieval castle, the Armory had served as an armory and arsenal—and occasionally a prize-fighting arena—until 1976. It was purchased in 2007 by what is now the largest kinky porn company in the world. (The Armory's reign as kinky porn's stronghold came to an end in 2017, when Kink.com decided to move production off premises in favor of renting the aging building out for events and office space. The company still owns the Armory and is continuing to produce porn in several cities around the US.)

It's an interesting melding of entertainment, sex wrestling. In many interviews I've done, porn performers have told me that they enjoy doing extreme porn not because it feels good so much as because they wanted to prove that they *could*. Toughness is sometimes worn like a badge of honor. When Katsuni told me in 2010 that, in porn, "The key of success is a balance between will, strength, pleasure, and intelligence," there was a reason she put "will" and "strength" at the front of the list.

In pornography, going big is a way to get noticed, too. Houston, a self-described "porn superstar," set a world record by having sex with 612 men in one day at the filming of *The Houston 500* in 1999. When I asked her about her motivations for going so over the top, she told me simply: "I was making history, becoming an even bigger star, dominating the porn world . . . I wanted to be the biggest porn star in the world and that's what I did." Her feat required physical stamina and true grit that I'll never be able to approach.

Toughness can also be a mark of dedication to making great entertainment. Kaylani Lei, a tiny but powerful performer, said to me during an in-

terview, "I can be my little four-foot-eleven self and take a mean, big
in a scene. Granted, I'll be sitting on ice later that night or walking fur
the next day, but hey at least we got a great scene!" Women like Kaylani
feel that sometimes gritting one's teeth to get through a scene that pushes
their limits can provide a reward in the form of an excellent product.

For others, extreme porn functions as a physical paring down of the
self into something more free and honest. Oriana Small—formerly known
as Ashley Blue, the queen of extreme porn in the mid-2000s—told me
that, "With people there watching, it felt like a wrestling match. Like I
was strong." For those who enjoy using their bodies athletically, porn is
an excellent fit. Or wrestling. And most amateur wrestling doesn't pay
as well as porn-wrestling, so, hey, why not?

But then again, why?

When they let us into the arena, Leigh and I took advantage of our
press passes to nab front-row seats, setting up the camera we'd brought
and reading our pamphlets while wishing we had known in advance that
the event was BYOB. We were about to witness a featherweight tag-team
event, our informational pamphlets told us—the first of its kind. We'd
signed paperwork to confirm that we realized our faces might be live-
streamed to the world, as well as waivers cementing our understanding
and comfort with what was about to take place. The emcee explained
the rules: Points were awarded for sex acts performed on a member of
the opposing team. Basically, the goal was to pin or otherwise immobilize
the opponent, then disrobe, lick, tickle, kiss, fondle, face-sit, smother, or
finger her for points. The first team to amass a winning number of points
got to choose an appropriate sexual punishment for the losers.

Leigh and I settled in with trepidation, bemoaning our sobriety, as
the games began.

What followed was, to put it simply, *way* more fun than we expected.
The wrestlers genuinely enjoyed themselves, with screaming orgasms
forcing a pause in the action several times during taping. When Team
Blue eked out a victory over Team Yellow, the winners brought in two of
Kink.com's best wrestlers, Isis and Donna, to help deliver a twelve-
minute, hardcore, strap-on gangbang that included all manner of deprav-
ity and ended with several squirting orgasms from Team Yellow as the
crowd roared its approval.

In the end, I'm pretty sure everybody won.

BACK IN NEW YORK, I upped my commitment to interviewing. I recorded primarily in people's homes to help set them at ease. This meant I was running all over New York City, usually after work on weeknights, and occasionally doing several interviews back to back without time for dinner—all while juggling my already overloaded schedule. I was, in a nutshell, a complete wreck.

One night just before Thanksgiving, I left work to attend happy hour with one of the gallery's staff members. She took a good look at me and told me I needed to slow down. I agreed, then went out to conduct two interviews in a row. Over the course of the evening I had about three drinks but no food. I left my last interview at around 11:00 p.m. and boarded the subway back to the Bronx, so exhausted that I was afraid to sit down for fear of falling asleep and missing my stop. I leaned against the doors of the 5 train and put on my headphones, keeping my brain active with a podcast . . . until suddenly I woke up.

On the floor of the train.

There was a man standing over me, saying, "Miss? Are you okay?"

I was confused. I had no memory of losing consciousness, but I suppose that's how passing out goes. The man, assisted by another who had joined him, helped me stand back up. "You should sit down," they said.

"No, I'll be fine," I answered, leaning back against the door and trying to make sense of what was happening. I was frightened, but mostly embarrassed. When I'd woken up, my face had been smooshed into the subway floor, and I wondered vaguely if I'd fallen in a really unattractive way. Had people seen my nose crunch up like a pig snout? I glanced out the door as we slowed down to stop at 96th Street. I was almost home . . .

And then I woke up. On the floor. Again.

This time the two men helped me to a seat. There were plenty of them available on the late-night train, and I felt silly for not having just taken one in the first place. Now a fuss was being made over my dumb mistake.

I looked at the doors again. They were open, and we were still at 96th Street. I felt my heart rate quicken—how long had we been here? How long had I been passed out?

Oh. Dear. God. Horrified, I realized that I was the "sick passenger" slowing down the train! The sick passenger that made hundreds, even thousands of people late to their destinations as other trains backed up behind mine, while I sat on my butt waiting for a medical crew to arrive and cart me off to a hospital! I was holding up every one of those people who just wanted to get home to their families and beds.

I looked around. Everyone was watching me.

I couldn't be the sick customer. I refused to be *that guy*. Someone, sounding far away, told me, "We'll call an ambulance."

And then the idea of a hospital visit confronted my reeling brain. A New York City emergency room is basically the last place any sane person wants to be. Hours in the waiting room, hospital staff who hate their lives and their patients, harried doctors, insufficient care. A whole night in the hospital, missing work the next day, maybe having to cancel interviews, all followed by an astronomical bill. I was lucky enough to have great health insurance through my new employer, but even that wouldn't entirely cover a visit to the ER; I could be in debt for months or years.

I stood up in a panic, yelling, "No! I'll be fine. I'm just going to get off the train." I patted my skirt down and stepped onto the platform. As one of the train crew came out to implore me to wait for medical attention, I shook my head. "No, thank you! I just need some air!"

I got out of the station as fast as I could, bursting into the humid late-autumn night. I was embarrassed, terrified, and still confused. The cold air and moisture revived me enough that I could wander the Upper East Side for a few minutes, getting my breathing under control, before finding a cab, calling Matthew, and bursting into tears.

I ARRANGED TO TAKE THE month of December completely off from *WHACK!* and this lightened my burden considerably, but I kept up my breakneck schedule of interviewing people in New York for apexart, working my full-time job, writing for dirty print magazines, and dating two people. In January I flew to Los Angeles to collect interviews from more porn performers. My month off from *WHACK!* had been moderately restful, and I had regained enough energy to be excited about renting a car and touring the city on my own. The interviews went swimmingly, and the majority of my subjects agreed on one thing: They loved sex, and they had found a legal industry in which that love was rewarded.

April Flores, with whom I spoke in her living room, told me that although she'd never intended to make a career of it, she'd discovered in her first shoot that porn empowered her, and she'd decided to stick around for the self-love as much as for the paychecks. "I got tired of reading and hearing that porn degrades women, because I've never felt degraded in this field. I always say that I felt much more degraded as a receptionist than I did—ever—in porn," she told me. Adult film had given her a more positive body image, too, as a plus-size woman. "Porn doesn't give women bad body image. Life does," she said. "We are assaulted, as women, with these images of what we should be to be happy. I don't think it's porn. It's life." At that point she had starred in several movies her husband, Carlos Batts, had filmed, and worked with a number of feminist, queer, and mainstream pornographers, all while spreading a message of body positivity for plus-size women who, like her, wanted to feel sexy in their skins.

Nyomi Banxxx confided that she adored her job. Of course not every shoot was the best experience of her life, she granted, but despite her successes in other fields—modeling, beauty pageants, acting, vocal performance, mainstream filmmaking—porn was the only place she wanted to be after six years in the industry. "I love this industry. I love everything about it," she told me. "It allows you to become an individual. It allows you to be able to brand yourself. It allows *me* to have learned myself sexually."

Kelly Shibari visited my hotel room to talk before she drove to Las Vegas to prepare for AVN. She tried porn on a whim and found it a safe place to experiment sexually with partners who knew what they were doing. She realized that porn was, as she put it, "a great way for me to get laid by people who are never going to call me afterwards!" Kelly has since gone on to be the first plus-size woman to appear in *Penthouse*, and a PR professional for the adult industry.

Sinnamon Love, in our earlier interview in New York, had shared Kelly's sentiments. On a porn set, she said, there were other professionals on hand to help if anything went wrong during a hardcore or kinky scene. "The opportunity porn presented," she said, was "to explore certain types of fantasies on camera in an environment that was safe and consensual and that allowed me to feel protected. I felt like, 'I can have sex with these guys, and there are people there that are watching what's going on. It's not going to get out of hand.'"

One afternoon, I called Oriana Small to confirm our interview, and she instead invited me to the photo shoot she was doing that afternoon. I had recently finished reading her memoir, *Girlvert*, a retelling of her days as the reigning queen of gonzo porn, when she was the star of the JM Productions series *Girlvert*. In that series, she had gleefully tricked other women into brutal threesomes, tear-inducing punishment, and more, while playing the role of a bratty teenager with a sadistic streak. Her brand of porn had always upset me, but her book *floored* me. It's difficult to describe, but it revealed to me some part of the human psyche that I'd witnessed, yet been unable to process before.

After what I'd read and our correspondence earlier in the day, I expected to enter a porn set in the hotel I'd been summoned to. So when I walked into a tiny room strewn with vintage clothing and makeup, I was surprised to find Oriana, in a black-and-white checkered skirt suit with her lips painted to match, on her back with her legs splayed as another model, Audrey Bernal, stood over her in a latex French maid outfit with a chainsaw held aloft.

The legendary kink photographer Eric Kroll was responsible for the mayhem, and after attempting to find a place for me to watch events unfold, he instead invited me to take part in the shoot. In short order, I was clad in a gold bodysuit, holding Oriana's arms down while Audrey dribbled a homemade concoction of grape jelly, salsa, ketchup, and water over Ori's vulva and thighs. She was attempting a blood-spatter effect, but ended up with a more menstrual-looking scene while Eric snapped photos of our ridiculousness.

It was a surreal afternoon. We got lunch afterward and talked, but Oriana didn't have time for an interview. I did, however, get some diverting photos e-mailed to me a few weeks later, and a Skype interview with Oriana that I used for the show.

AFTER A FEW DAYS, I left LA and drove to Las Vegas. I'd figured that AVN would be a perfect time to collect interviews—with porn stars gathered like fish in the proverbial barrel—but discovered that I had grossly misinterpreted the situation. During AVN, everyone is running from shoot to signing to public appearance and back, booked to the gills. An hour-long, sit-down video interview in a quiet place was not an option for most.

But I did manage an interview with Danny Wylde, a performer with whom I'd grown close to through some of my correspondence with Cindy

Gallop and whose nihilistic perspective intrigued me in the same uncomprehending way as had Oriana's. Danny worked occasionally in queer and
feminist productions, but spent the majority of his time in Los Angeles,
where his status as a bisexual man who had starred in gay, straight, and bi
porn made him a rare figure. We had a great talk in his suite high above
the Strip, talking about the need for an open dialogue around the pressures
that porn places on male performers. "Just fairly recently, I almost failed
a scene for the first time in the last couple years," he told me. "I don't think
that ever gets easy. I think as a man, especially when it's your job . . . from
a self-esteem point, or just self-worth, even, it's very emotionally draining
to fail a porn scene." Male porn actors' rock-hard and fail-proof erections,
he wanted to assure viewers, were not to be taken as easy, much less realistic. As a matter of fact, a few short years later, Danny was forced to quit
performing when a mishap with performance-enhancing drugs brought
him to the emergency room. He was told by doctors that if he continued
to use these pharmaceuticals, he risked inuring himself so badly he would
never be able to have an erection again. He quit the business and has gone
on to work behind the scenes and as an author and subculture icon.

I went back to my cheap (read: smelly) hotel and ordered cheap (read:
terrible) room service that evening instead of lingering outside the awards
show. I had considered getting tickets to the AVNs and trying to nab a
date on my solo trip, but after a week of chasing porn stars around multiple cities, I was so tired I didn't even want the (awful) wine that came
with my dinner. And I had been disheartened by the state of the convention. It had been moved from the sprawling Sands to the Hard Rock
Hotel & Casino, and I didn't see the move as a positive one. The Adult
Entertainment Expo and its attendant Adult Novelty Expo were big
enough to take over every one of the smaller venue's convention halls,
with some booths spilling out into the hallways between them, making
the show floor a bewildering maze of wall-to-wall people. I had wandered
the aisles alone, looking for familiar faces and often getting lost.

I collected a few video interviews for *WHACK!* as I wandered the
floor, until I came upon the same pro-domme friend who had recently
helped us with the disastrous party in New York during Exxxotica. As
we chatted, I noticed a man in a large cowboy hat ambling by.

When I turned to look, there was a pair of light, grayish-blue eyes piercing back into mine from a jovial face I recognized: Max Hardcore. The man

anti-porn zealots point to when they're screeching about exploitation, degradation, and coercion. The man who more or less invented the term "skull fuck"—an oral sex move in which the fellator is forced onto the fellatee's cock by a hand on the back of the head, usually forcing the cock down the throat until tears and gagging are produced. The guy who made his models call him "Mister" in knee socks and pigtails, and, in some cases, syphoned his bodily waste into their various orifices—mouths included—on camera. The guy who had just been released from a thirty-month federal prison sentence for disseminating obscenity. *That* guy.

He and his case had fascinated and repelled me for years. Obscenity trials in pornography are relatively rare, given that porn is not strictly illegal, but under the second Bush administration they had picked up significantly with the Department of Justice's new Obscenity Prosecution Task Force, formed by Dubya himself. Bush was so focused on prosecuting pornographers for obscenity, in fact, that after he was sworn into office, adult entertainment lawyer Paul Cambria, together with porn industry leaders, developed a list of sex acts and themes that pornographers were encouraged to avoid in order to duck obscenity charges under the new administration. The Cambria List isn't a set of rules so much as guidelines that include nearly everything we're used to seeing in porn today—degrading dialogue, double blowjobs, facial cum shots—and has been criticized for discouraging normal, healthy acts that like male-to-male contact and interracial sex. However, the list also cautions against a few acts that have remained taboo, and which Max Hardcore enjoyed filming: shots with the appearance of pain or degradation and peeing indoors, to name a couple.

In the Dubya years, several others had gone to court over their work, but Max Hardcore was a different animal. I'd become a little bit obsessed with him, and had interviewed several performers who had worked with him—Oriana Small among them—to find out what made him tick. I'd been told that he was a friendly, soft-spoken guy with kind eyes. But that sweet-tempered reputation just didn't match up with his films. Make no mistake: I'm not just talking about hardcore sex. I'm talking about hiring very young women who are often new to the industry, putting their hair in pigtails, dressing them in clothes that make them look younger, requiring them to talk in baby voices, and asking them to pretend that they are twelve years old. I am talking about Max, who usually starred in his films, urinating on his costars, fisting them without apparent consent, inserting specula into their orifices, talking them into eating their own vomit. Max Hardcore was literally the monster in porn's closet.

But although his work horrified me, I wasn't sure I could agree with him being locked in a federal penitentiary for making what he considered artistic expression, no matter whether I *liked* that expression or not. As performer and artist May Ling Su, who had worked with Max Hardcore by her own request, told me in an interview, "Max Hardcore may not have started out thinking he [was] going to make videos to challenge authority. I think he just made videos he wanted to make. It was the law that made a political statement out of him. What that means for us is up to us. Do we shrug our shoulders and say, 'Serves him right for being so deviant. No one should do anything beyond the norm'? Or do we say, 'This is wrong! No one should go to jail for consensual sexual expression, on camera or off'?"

I suppose Max Hardcore represented, to me, the limits of artistic expression being pushed to their furthest extreme, and then peed on. But had those limits been *broken*? All his paperwork was in order, with I's dotted and T's crossed. His costars were duly paid for their performances, and none had ever pressed charges or testified against him. Some starred repeatedly in his films—clearly they were as excited by his shocking exploits as he was. May Ling Su told me that she enjoyed the experience and consented to everything that happened, which left me with little footing to feel disturbed by what had gone down, other than my own squeamishness. She told me, "Consent. That's the line. It's obscene when the participants are below the age of consent. It's obscene when the participants are coerced or drugged against their consent. Obviously there are videos that depict non-consensual sex or underage sex, played by consenting adults, and those can be scary and sexy and it messes with your mind. But I want to know that it's all in the realm of play, and that in real life it's being carried out by responsible adults."

So, did Max Hardcore's films merit an obscenity conviction, or merely a pass from those who were too weak in the stomach to handle them, like myself?

Unable to get his case out of my head, I had written to him in prison in 2010. He responded with a five-page letter handwritten on lined notebook paper that he'd turned into stationery. "Max Hardcore," it said at the top, "America's Most Wanted Pornographer (TM)." There was a 3x5 photo of him behind bars in a trucker hat and tank top with an acoustic guitar in his hand and a toothy smile on his face. Clearly Photoshopped, it gave the impression of a simple, all-American guy wrongly imprisoned on a trumped-up charge.

The letter complained, in high-minded language, about the failure of the justice system in persecuting an artist like himself. Despite his lawyer's "inspired interpretation and logical explanation of the US Constitution," he said, the 11th Circuit Court had denied his appeals, and he remained behind bars for "making religiously immoral motion pictures which were too tawdry from the poor people of Tampa to tolerate. It should also be stated," he went on, "that there were never any allegations of anyone who was compelled to perform in any of my movies. Also, no one in Tampa, Florida, where I was prosecuted, had protested my productions." That much was true—he had been convicted not because people had objected to his films, but because the Bush-appointed task force had purchased several of his works online and had them mailed across state lines to Florida. These films were meant for distribution somewhere in Europe, where obscenity laws were more lax, and were not marketed for an American audience. How the feds were able to worm their way out of entrapment for that one, I don't understand.

His letter continued: "Equally unsettling is that a jury of my purported peers would be unable to understand the importance of free expression as a fundamental human right. They sentenced me to forty-six months in prison, along with a fine of nearly one hundred thousand dollars, simply because my movies had somehow violated their mysterious 'community standards,' which are nowhere written down. As a result of this outrageous travesty of objectivity and open-mindedness, I am being held against my will [in] very substandard conditions here at the decrepit La Tuna Federal Correctional Institute."

As dramatic as his wording may have been, I had to admit: Max Hardcore had a point.

HERE'S THE THING ABOUT obscenity laws in America: To call them "vague" is to give them a lot of credit.

Firstly, what qualifies as obscenity is material that does not merit protection by the First Amendment, and can thus be censored. However, there is no standard metric for what constitutes obscenity across the nation, leaving each federal district, state, and community therein free to decide what it finds un-protectable, and for the courts in that district to set their own precedents.

If the material in question passes over state borders via the post, said material comes under federal jurisdiction and can be tried at the same level for obscenity, thanks to the Comstock Act of 1873. The vast majority of pornography is now, of course, distributed electronically, which has fluffed feathers on both the porn and law enforcement sides of the obscenity issue. There's no real standard in place yet that specifically applies to online distribution—which is one happy reason why many sex acts have become normalized in the Internet age.

One hundred years after the Comstock Act, in 1973, the Supreme Court instituted the three-pronged Miller Test. The Miller Test is our most current rubric for determining what is obscene, and it is at once frustratingly imprecise and beautifully nebulous. A work can be considered obscene only if it meets *all three* of the following conditions: (1) The average person, applying contemporary adult community standards, finds that the matter, taken as a whole, appeals to prurient interests (i.e., an erotic, lascivious, abnormal, unhealthy, degrading, shameful, or morbid interest in nudity, sex, or excretion); (2) the average person, applying contemporary adult community standards, finds that the matter depicts or describes sexual conduct in a patently offensive way, (i.e., ultimate sexual acts, normal or perverted, actual or simulated, masturbation, excretory functions, lewd exhibition of the genitals, or sado-masochistic sexual abuse), specifically defined by the applicable state law; and (3) whether a reasonable person finds that the matter, taken as a whole, lacks serious literary, artistic, political, or scientific value.

The first two prongs of the test are held to local "community standards," while the last is held to a broader standard of what a "reasonable person of the United States" would think, so as to avoid giving any "community" too much sway over a ruling. And the third prong provides some safety for pornography because, according to the Miller Test, most pornography with a storyline can't be proven to have *no* literary or artistic value. Gonzo porn remains in murky territory—there is limited context for the sex and therefore more room to push community standards past the third prong. Max Hardcore's work, as material that pushed well past what most communities would consider acceptable limits, straddled many of these blurry lines.

Hardcore had been a target for obscenity prosecution for over a decade before he was convicted. His first trial, for child pornography, was called off when the Supreme Court ruled that adults portraying children in films were protected by the Constitution. In 2005, his offices were raided by the FBI and several computer servers were seized, but no charges were made because, ostensibly, nothing illegal was found. Finally, when his company, Max World Entertainment, Inc. was indicted by the Department of Justice Obscenity Section in 2007 on five counts of transporting obscene matter by use of an interactive computer service and five more counts of mailing obscene matter, Hardcore was found guilty on all charges and, in 2009, carted off to La Tuna, from where he wrote to me in 2010. He was released in July 2011, and he attended the AVN Expo in January 2012.

WHEN I SAW HIM, I froze. I turned to my friend and whispered, "That's Max Hardcore! What do we do?"

"You should interview him," she said simply.

I screwed up my courage, turned on my heel, and walked right up to my nightmare. When I introduced myself he displayed a vague memory of my letter, and when I asked him to talk to me on camera for *WHACK!* he was happy to oblige. He offered to film it himself, as he was experienced with POV camera handling (shudder), but instead I handed it to my friend, and off we went.

What followed was probably only about five minutes of chatter, some of which was lighthearted banter about what he planned to do now that he was out of prison (answer: make more films), and some of which went deeper into his motivations (answer: art and freedom of speech—which did not really constitute an answer, per se) and his feelings about having been sentenced (answer: outraged and shocked, naturally). I don't recall many details, but I do remember looking at his incredibly white teeth as he grinned his way through the exchange, and his blue eyes wandering over my body when he offered to cast me in one of his films. He reminded me of a shark—always smiling, but cold.

I walked away trembling. My friend handed me the camera and I mentally logged myself one point in the badass category. When I got back to the hotel room, however, I checked the footage: There were a few fumbling seconds showing my feet facing Max's on the bright casino carpet, but then it cut off. Apparently my shaking hands had incorrectly pointed out the buttons, and the entire interview had been lost.

In the years since then, Max Hardcore has fallen out of the public eye. He now has a Twitter account, from which he posts links to his old videos, but beyond that I'm not sure what he's up to. I think I spent so much time trying to figure out what it was about him that so compelled and terrified me that I ended up learning more about myself, and about porn, in the process. It wasn't Max himself that was so enthralling to me—it was what he represented.

Max Hardcore made porn that married two things Americans love: violence (both physical and emotional) and sex, in a way that could be labeled as dark. He brought in an element of brutality that, to my mind, does not easily fit into the category of erotic entertainment. As a pacifist, I found Max's work abhorrent because his definition of pornography was at odds with my idea about what porn could and *should* be. In my idealistic way, I'd been building a case for the ways in which porn could be empowering for those who make it and those who watch it. I'd gotten warm fuzzies during interviews when people said things like, "Sex is one of the most empowering things in the universe, and also one of the most beautiful. It should be celebrated and showcased" (Raven Alexis, in 2010), and I'd taken that sentiment to heart.

I'd been cultivating this middle space, hoping that we could all get together there and shake hands. I still believe in the importance of that space, and as more people have stepped into it, I've seen the value it holds for many of us who have been victims of the negative attitudes our culture feeds us about sex.

But not everybody *wants* that middle space. We don't unanimously look forward to breaking down the barriers between "them" and "us," and we don't all think that pornography *needs* to be healthy. As I've said before, lots of people like porn *because* it is taboo. They enjoy the thrill they get from watching people do things they're not supposed to. Furthermore, some people really, legitimately love to degrade and to be degraded. Many find a safe and legal vent for those impulses in pornography that reflects their darkest desires. Max Hardcore made some of that pornography. And that doesn't make him the citizen of the month, perhaps, but it also doesn't make him an outright monster.

If there's anything that the process of interviewing people about their experiences with sex and porn has taught me, it's that no matter how open-minded, how expansive I want to be, I'll never get it all. Everyone *is* different, and when it comes to sex, they are *so* very, very different. I will never be able to wrap my head around why Max Hardcore would film women drinking his urine out of one of their own body cavities. But Max Hardcore will probably never be able to understand what I find so compelling about watching a woman receive cunnilingus from a POV camera angle, either. I feel a little confident in saying that one might be objectively less upsetting than the other, but I'm not here to judge. I'm just here writing about it, and asking others to talk about it, too.

HOLY MOLY, I WON A FEMINIST PORN AWARD!

CHAPTER 21

Winner

WHEN I RETURNED TO NEW YORK, preparation for "Consent" went into overdrive. I got off the plane and headed directly to performer Brittany Andrews's apartment for an interview, rolling my suitcase behind me. I was immediately thankful for Brittany's talkative nature, since my brain was scrambled and possibly numb after so many interviews during my trip. An industry veteran of almost two decades, she had been flirting with retirement for years, moonlighting as a DJ, but she had stayed active enough to know exactly how she felt about modern porn. As a 2008 inductee into the AVN Hall of Fame, her status was so cemented that she was able to demand condoms in her scenes with no ill effects to her career, and she had been a staunch advocate of condoms in porn for years. She was likewise vocal about the deleterious effects of hardcore gonzo porn: "It's a shame that you've got young men who think that this is how sex is supposed to be," she fumed. "And you see young women thinking that . . . this is how women are to be treated in the bedroom—not like goddesses, but like dirty fucking whores that you slap around." She threw her hands in the air in frustration.

After the interview, I went home to the Bronx to shower and change, then hopped the subway to Queens to j. vegas's apartment to start editing the videos. His skill at video editing and our established working relationship made him the obvious choice for this process, and he and his new wife (they'd married in the summer of 2011 and there had been *one hell* of a party) had just welcomed a daughter. Our available time for working was limited to nights and weekends after we both finished work, and even further constrained by the baby's sleep schedule, so we needed to use every precious moment to the best of our ability.

We had less than two months to edit over twenty-four hours of footage into four short films, each one coherent enough to hold together around a theme. I'd landed on four ideas that came up in almost every interview: the porn *industry* as people see it from inside and outside; how porn fits into *society* at large; the thorny issues of *morality* that come up around pornography; and the *reality* of porn in people's lives. I'd also decided to drop in clips of explicit sex performed by the people I'd interviewed—I didn't want the art show to end up too removed from the topic at hand. There are plenty of documentaries already out there featuring talking heads getting high-minded about pornography. I wanted the subject matter and the discussion to coexist.

I went to vegas's small apartment every evening after work for the next two months, and most weekends, as well. We'd work from my arrival around six until ten or later, finding the right clips, cutting them, piecing them together until we'd formed the structures of films. Some, like the Madison Young interview, had to be heavily color-corrected and sound edited before they were usable. Two of my interview subjects had requested that their faces not be shown, so we overlaid much of their footage with porn—we preferred hardcore sex to a blank screen.

I still needed an interview with myself for the show to be complete. As the self-described occupant of the middle ground between porn and the public, I wasn't approaching these films as a documentary filmmaker —not really. I'd been asked to curate a show from my own perspective, and though the work of making the videos clearly reflected it, other people's words did not. I didn't see a point in remaining objective, and I was honestly curious about how I would answer some of the probing questions I'd asked my subjects.

Through apexart, I was introduced to the former producer of a successful TV series about sex—a show so popular that many of my interview subjects had referenced it as a formative part of their sexual journeys. This woman, who I'll call Sharon, had interviewed hundreds, if not thousands, of people over several decades. Although the series had come to an end, she still worked for the same cable network and had an office in the Grace Building next to Bryant Park, where she invited me for our interview.

I was all nerves walking into the offices of one of the biggest television companies in the world. After my brush with TV fame in LA, part of me still clung to the hope that interest in my story might be revived. Maybe Sharon would see something in me and pitch my ideas to her network. I let myself briefly envision calling up my old agent and smarmily telling her I'd gotten a better deal.

I'd provided Sharon with a list of standard questions I asked my subjects to get things started. But she didn't use it. Instead, she subjected me to an interrogation about my motivations for being involved in pornography. She was trying to get to the deep, dirty truths beneath my smiling exterior. It was the type of interview I'd have liked to conduct with Max Hardcore. But I was not Max Hardcore, and try as she might, Sharon couldn't expose my hidden well of dark secrets because my secrets were not very dark and they were already on the table.

It's a sticking point I've come up against a number of times, but never as pointedly as in this interview: People assume that I have an agenda behind my work. That I really want to make porn myself or that I'm just in it to sleep with the porn stars. But for me, neither of these is a motivation. I have, almost unavoidably, considered doing porn to see what it's like on that side of the camera and to discover if I'm brave enough to handle it. A reporter can't really know her subject matter unless she immerses herself, right? But honestly, I'm *not* that brave, nor am I that dedicated a journalist. And, alas, I'm just not an exhibitionist. I might get a thrill from getting nude in front of a camera—and I have done so as a model—but having sex in front of people just isn't something I'm interested in. It never has been.

And as far as sleeping with the porn stars? I won't deny that the prospect is enticing, but I *will* deny that it has ever been my motivation for writing about the porn industry. If it were, the payoff would not begin to match the huge input of time, money, and energy that I have poured into my work. I've seen my share of starfuckers circling porn performers, and I've always wrinkled my nose at them, perhaps unjustly. There's nothing *wrong* with lusting after one's favorite porn star, since that's the point of what they do, but coming up with sneaky ways to get private access to them so I can proposition them just isn't my style.

Some people assume I'm acting out in response to some darkness in my psyche or my past, in the same way that they believe all porn stars were molested as children. I can admit that, yes, I *am* turned on by pornography—it's *designed* to turn me on. And yes, I am coming from an extremely repressed background, which makes my interest in smut perhaps more pointed. And, yes, I was raped as a young adult, which likely provided some impetus to work through my own trauma by watching a lot of sex. But as far as an inner darkness leading me down this path? Not as far as I can tell. Then again, maybe I'm just not self-aware enough to see the darkness that lurks inside me.

Whatever the case, seekers of my hidden perversions aren't going to get very far. I'm a pretty open book. I find porn *interesting*. As a subject of study, pornography is one of the least understood forms of entertainment from both a production and a consumption point of view. In my time writing about porn, the industry and how society views it have both changed measurably. But we still know far less about how smut impacts us as a society than we do about most things. Billions have been spent on the search for the perfect facial exfoliant, but we hardly talk about why we find facial cum shots so compelling. I find this discrepancy strange, so I've devoted myself to promoting porn as worthy, even important subject matter.

As I answered Sharon's questions with the above sentiments, I sensed her frustration growing. I wondered if she was hoping I'd burst into tears as I recalled a buried childhood trauma. As she kept wearing me down, I grew frustrated, too. My only secret was that I was *already* worn down. I had little patience for her antics, and I could only offer what I had to give. After about thirty minutes of unsatisfying back and forth, we ended the interview. She shook my hand and brusquely informed me that they'd get the footage to apexart soon.

I got word a few days later that Sharon's video was unusable. The minicassette on which the interview had been recorded, at her request, was a mess. Sharon had recorded my interview over something else, and the resulting video quality was low, with those little lines of static fuzz you might remember from VHS days. The audio was completely drowned beneath a low buzzing noise.

Sharon's office apologized about the tape, of course, and offered to do another take, but I couldn't find a time that worked for both of us. Truthfully, I didn't want to be subjected to her interrogation again, and in our e-mail exchanges she grew more and more curt. She finally ended by telling me that she frankly didn't understand why I wanted to have myself interviewed, because she couldn't see how it would contribute to the films anyway. In other words: "You're not interesting, so leave me alone."

I've come up against similar dismissals a few times in my career, and I've only recently been able to take a deep breath and get over them. I'll never know what it is about me that puts people off—particularly other women who work in journalistic roles in my porny world. But I've been introduced, sometimes wined and dined, chatted up, befriended, invited to parties, and otherwise made overtures to by women who do similar work, and in the majority of cases, my reception grows cold shortly thereafter.

I've come to believe, after many let-downs, that, like Sharon almost said, I'm just not that interesting. I'm not here to swap stories about porn star make-out sessions, or to brag about my publications, or to indulge in industry gossip. I'm interested in the larger picture . . . that middle ground. And, though it pains me to admit it, a lot of people find the middle ground dreadfully boring. Sharon was joining a long list of people who found me tedious because I didn't have anything incendiary to say. She may have also found my dullness something of an intimidation: Was it possible that pornography didn't need to be a den of sin and degradation, and that my interest in it could be, actually, benign?

I was pissed that she'd wasted my time, but I didn't have enough of it left to fret. I instead asked a friend to interview me, and our chat was a great addition to the art show films, if you ask me. So, Sharon, if you're reading this? Kiss it. I'm plenty interesting for my own needs.

I KEPT MAKING THE pilgrimage to Queens to sit beside vegas and direct his edits for the next two months. We forged from raw footage four films that explored human experiences with pornography. They weren't achievements of great finesse, as most of the footage was grainy or blurry or blown-out, but they reached into the minds of their subjects and broached the difficult issue of pornography in our lives. I was proud of our work, particularly given our extremely limited time and resources.

Two days before the show opened, vegas and I watched our working cuts of the films and then set them to render while we downed celebratory beers. We'd had a delicious meal cooked by his wife, and I was set to be back in Penn Station around nine to meet an artist with whom I'd been planning a photo shoot for months. I'd taken the next day off work to run all the necessary errands and get myself prepared for the show, so this artist and I were planning a late-night photo shoot in an empty subway car, knowing I wouldn't have to be up early the next morning. I thought some modeling would be a good way to let loose and work off some nerves.

But when vegas and I checked the renders, we were horrified to realize that something was *very* wrong. The sound was off in every single video, and some of the visuals glitched out, replacing the people on the screen with ugly bars of bright green. We frantically tried to fix them, playing with levels and layers and clips, but every render turned up the same. We finally discovered that one of the porn video files, from which we'd put at least one clip into every film, was corrupt. And now, so was every film. Because of the way we'd saved our progress, we had no versions of the films from before we'd added the infected clips remaining, so we couldn't go back and rebuild. And we had about forty-three hours before the show opened.

I texted the artist, who was already waiting for me at Penn Station, to say I didn't know when I would get there or if I could do the photo shoot. He assured me he would wait as long as he could, and vegas and I got back to trying to fix the films.

Somehow I kept myself from crying, possibly because I was so exhausted I didn't have the capacity to produce tears. After much trial and error, we discovered that if we removed all the clips from the video at fault and took out *every* caption introducing *every* interview subject, we could mitigate the effects of the corrupt file. This meant that there would be no written indication of who all of these people flapping their jaws about pornography *were*. It was a disaster. But we didn't have the time to put the captions back in, and the attempts we made only further screwed up the files. We'd have to do without. In a fortunate twist of fate, the show materials, website, and brochure already included labeled still shots of the interviewees, so those who were paying attention would be able to identify the speakers.

I resigned myself to subpar videos and left j. vegas to finish rendering the files. I took the last Long Island Railroad train from Queens into Manhattan to meet the artist, who had sat in TGI Fridays, bless him, until it closed—and saved me a margarita in a Styrofoam cup. We went back to my apartment, but instead of finding an empty subway to shoot in, I proposed we drink whiskey until we passed out.

And so we did.

This artist, who is perhaps predictably now my fiancé, called out of work the next day to help me run errands for the art show. Really, he stayed with me to keep me from having a complete breakdown. I'd rented a car to pick up the DVDs from Queens and cart them—along with my oversized trunk full of porn DVDs, which were to be displayed at the show—to the gallery in Manhattan. I was so on edge that traffic made me twitchy, and so worried about not getting the car back in time that I nearly hyperventilated, but he stayed by my side and fed me soothing words, kept me laughing. When it was all said and done, I took him out for sushi to say thanks.

We had been in contact for months, so he wasn't a complete stranger, but still, the fact that this person I hardly knew would give up an entire day to keep me sane when I was at my anxious, overwrought worst stayed with me. That he never even got the photo shoot we had spent so long planning, and never complained about it, spoke even louder.

In the months that followed, he and I got closer, and I eventually realized that the bond we were forming was something that needed to be cemented. I broke up with Matthew shortly after the art show opened, not in order to date this artist I'd met, but because the artist made me realize that I could expect more fulfillment out of my romantic attachments. Matthew and I had been friends in high school, lovers in college, and we had pretty much been dating for ten years. The magic had long since been replaced with comfort, but the more I examined that comfort, the more I realized that it had been strained for some time. He had agreed with my relationship with Jenn more out of necessity than approval; he knew I wouldn't let her go, and since he was pursuing a PhD and had very little time for romance, he'd been able to handle it. But tensions had run high, and he had occasionally shown his cards, which read that he didn't like sharing me.

Meanwhile, Jenn's life had been shifting dramatically. She had quit her job at a research lab early in 2012 to pursue her artistic dreams, and although I supported her decision and tried my best to keep up with the changes she was making, her life was increasingly devoted to late nights and a different lifestyle than my own. In the summer of 2012, we decided to amicably end our romance on the grounds that it couldn't be sustained by seeing each other once a month for lunch.

I'm happy to report that I've maintained strong friendships with both Matthew and Jenn, who stuck with me through some truly incredible years, and who I continue to value as some of the best people in my life. And I'm now engaged to this incredible artist who swept me off my feet the day before my art show went up on March 21, 2012.

THE OPENING OF "CONSENT" was one of the biggest in the gallery's history, with hundreds filing through the doors, photographers wandering the premises, and booze flowing. The videos weren't beautiful, but they played well enough, and the viewing stations were packed. I was proud, and so relieved that I couldn't stop smiling.

In the essay I'd written for the show's pamphlet, I'd said, "'Consent' is my attempt to turn up the lights in the space I occupy by documenting and presenting what the world looks like from my point of view. I've brought together conversations with the 'insiders' and the 'outsiders,' footage from the movies I've reviewed, images of my friends and colleagues in the industry, and my very own porn collection, sourced from my years of being given review material. I want to show you what my empty space is like, and invite everyone to join me in here." And I was thrilled that all these people had taken me up on my offer. They stood around the gallery, taking in my films, discussing them, and letting themselves be seen in what was once my nearly private domain.

Friends from around the country came to see the show, and my older sister even flew in from Colorado to check it out. My parents endured me sending them a brochure, but declined to visit the city on the grounds that they would be more upset by it than proud.

WHEN THE SHOW CLOSED in May, life went back to what passed for normal. I kept showing up for work, blogging, and maintaining *WHACK!* But I could feel myself slowing down. The pace at which I'd been living for five years was catching up with me. I noticed an uptick in the activity of the rheumatoid arthritis I've had since I was a baby. I was frequently fatigued and achy, so I took a lot of pain relievers. And then my stomach started hurting. My doctor told me I was developing an ulcer, prescribed me some preventative medication, and upped my dose of injectable immunosuppressants so that I could take fewer pills.

I'd received a stipend for the art show, but it had quickly gone to medical bills and credit card debt. I found myself scraping by on my measly publishing salary with swiftly diminishing health to maintain other activities. My budding relationship with the artist gave me a fresh perspective, and I had to admit that I was simply doing too much. I couldn't keep it up.

So, one evening in July, I invited j. vegas out for a drink, and we decided to let go of *WHACK! Magazine*. We'd nurtured our beloved project for almost four years, and it had blossomed, but we had never made a single, solitary dime on it. Instead we had poured thousands of our hard-earned dollars into it, and we'd had some wonderful times. But we both needed to move forward or we would drown. After a few bittersweet beers, we hugged and parted ways.

The next day we turned control of the magazine over to one of our writers, who lived in Europe and had shown extraordinary devotion to the *WHACK!* cause. He took care of it for a while, but then he abruptly moved to Brazil, got married, and let *WHACK!* slide. It still exists on the Internet, and is currently in the process of being repurposed into a photography website by a talented artist. Most of the old material was deleted when the site went to Tumblr under new management, but I had very luckily saved all of my *WHACK!* writings on my own website, where they can still be read if one digs through the archives.

I also quit my remaining print magazine jobs. The first magazine had stopped asking me for reviews when Charles—the guy whose butt plug I mistook for a paperweight—discovered that I was still working with vegas, whom he despised. I'd parted ways with the "barely legal" magazine after discovering that their photos came from unknown and likely illegal sources in Eastern Europe. And the other magazine, for which I'd continued writing set copy about boobs, was getting closer to bankruptcy every day. When I told my editor that I couldn't turn in any more copy until I was paid for three months' worth of work, he responded that he was personally filing suit for unpaid wages the next day.

Because I have never mastered the art of *actually* doing less, but I excel at telling myself that I will learn, I immediately began sending new (uncorrupted) edits of the films from "Consent" to film festivals and awards shows. A shortened edit of "Morality" was played in the summer of 2012 at the YANS & RETO festival in Manhattan, and a full edit at Cinekink the following spring, where I had been promoted from a press attendee to the red-carpet interviewer of filmmakers and performers.

I also sent a re-edited copy of "Society" to the Feminist Porn Awards. I had no expectations, given the amateur quality of the film, so I was both shocked and giddy to discover that it was on the list of nominees for the April 2013 show. That year was also the inaugural Feminist Porn Conference, to be held at the University of Toronto the weekend after the Awards. I resolved to scrounge up the funds to get to Toronto, where as a nominee I could rub elbows with an elite group of smart and sexy visionaries.

The Feminist Porn Awards had been moved from the church to a much larger venue, the Royal Cinema, in the year I'd been absent. With a gigantic crystal chandelier above and a crowd big enough to pack the theater, the experience felt more formal this time around. Compared to the ever-shrinking AVN expo and awards, the growth of the FPAs was striking: Feminist porn was getting *big*. The previous year, queer and feminist porn websites had swept through the nominations at the AVNs, and feminist porn panels had begun popping up at number of mainstream industry conventions. A cadre of queer and feminist pornographers had walked the red carpet in Vegas, their tattooed, pierced, plus-sized, unenhanced, trans, and proudly *outré* appearances drawing lots of attention. Articles and podcasts and questions about the feminist, queer, and indie genres were abounding online, and interest was expanding. And, subsequently, the Feminist Porn Awards were exploding.

The ceremony was interspersed, as before, with comedy, burlesque, and BDSM demonstrations that kept the crowd limber, and I kept drinking to calm my nerves. The Feminist Porn Awards didn't have a set list of nominee categories; instead, you were alerted that you or your work had been nominated, and that was that. I didn't know when my prospective award might pop up, or whom I was up against. After a few hours passed and I'd heard no mention of my name from the stage, I assumed I hadn't won anything. So, when the Honourable Mentions category was announced, I was pleasantly tipsy, relaxed, and getting a little sleepy.

And then someone on the stage said my name. As a clip of Sinnamon Love—talking about how she'd never seen porn before she was *in* it—played on the big screen, I floated to my feet and onto the stage as if in a dream. I was drunker than I'd realized, and completely unprepared for this honor. I had no speech in mind, no inkling of what I was supposed to do up on a stage with a trophy (a Crystal Delights glass butt plug on a stand with a magnetic bunny tail attached, and a plaque with my name on the front) in my hand, before a crowd that suddenly appeared much larger than it had from the floor.

I don't remember what I said. I was too overwhelmed. I'm pretty sure I thanked the interview subjects for allowing me the honor of recording them, and j. vegas for editing it, and probably said something awkward and drunken and silly, because that's how I roll. *Me.* Winning an *award.* For my dinky little art film. In Canada. With the coolest people in the world.

WHEN I DISPLAYED MY Feminist Porn Award in my apartment in the Bronx, I felt like I'd reached a pinnacle. In my line of work, the possibility of topping myself seemed farfetched. Instead of setting new goals, I reflected on the path that had brought me to that moment onstage in Toronto. I'd begun on this path by stumbling into it and blithely deciding to keep on walking, but along the way I'd learned volumes about the industry, the world, and myself. I'd done more healing and exploring than I'd have managed otherwise, and arrived at a place where I felt more confident in myself, my sexuality, and my place in the world than I could have dreamed.

As I looked at the landscape of porn, I was delighted to note that things had changed since I'd begun watching it for pay. From a doomsday scenario of nose-diving profits, decimated distribution chains, subpar products, and crash-and-burn tactics on screen, I was noticing pinpoints of light breaking through the smoke: feminist pornographers, queer pornographers, indie pornographers, new technology, performers making themselves independently profitable, better testing protocols, and ingenuity at every level were starting to clear the rubble from the Internet's blaze. Green shoots of ideological shifts and changing paradigms were poking up through the ashes as porn's unrelenting drive to survive kept pushing onward.

Of course not *everything* was coming up roses: MindGeek continued
to eat up smaller businesses and undermine those who refused to be swal-
lowed. More allegations of serial assaults have popped up in the industry,
most notably the previously-discussed allegations against director Tony
T., who has been shooting for multiple companies—especially Brazzers,
of the MindGeek family—for years. The AIDS Healthcare Foundation
was rolling out seemingly unending legislative initiatives to force intrusive
regulations on adult models' bodies. More STI outbreaks popped up in
Los Angeles—including one involving my old heartthrob, Mr. Marcus.
The feminist porn community underwent upheavals as the landed gentry
at the top of the pile began infighting over who was more politically correct, to such an extent that in 2016 the Feminist Porn Awards took a hiatus, reconsidered its goals, and morphed into the Toronto International
Porn Festival in 2017.

And with the Trump administration's conservative ideals now firmly
in control of the White House—with none other than Reagan-era anti-
porn zealot Ed Meese as part of the transition team—porn in America is
facing uncertain times. Operation Choke Point, the Department of Justice's 2012 initiative that aimed to cut off money to select industries online—notably including pornography—is still in effect. The Republican
party named pornography a "public health crisis" in their 2016 platform,
and shortly thereafter several states passed resolutions along the same
lines. One of these states, Utah, may pass legislation allowing consumerss
to sue porn producers for undefined "harm" inflicted by their products.
And, after eight years of President Obama's leadership during which
there were no federal obscenity trials, Donald Trump and his attorney
general, Jeff Sessions, have vowed to take up the fight against smut once
more. Which is especially ironic, considering Trump appeared in a 2000
softcore porno called *Playboy Video Centerfold 2000*.

When I spoke to Mike Stabile of Kink.com in 2017 about the political climate and what that meant for his industry, he said, "right now,
given that [porn] scenes are largely distributed on the internet, it become
a little more difficult to make a community standards argument . . . [But]
there's a lot that you can do to enforce compliance or to get a population
to comply by going after a few select people. If you go after a clips producer who's doing something like making pissing videos, that person

doesn't have a huge amount to defend themselves. They're going to go under, they're going to fold, and they're going to settle, or they're going to go to jail. And anybody else who's doing that is probably going to stop doing it, even if it's unfair. And billing companies and credit card companies are going to pull out of that. You're going to lose your insurance. There's a lot of things that can happen with setting examples with one or two well-placed cases."

The future may be a bit murky at this point, but no matter what obstacles have set themselves up before pornography in America, I've come to appreciate the industry's unyielding will to not just live, but to thrive. I've been inspired by the passion and commitment of the people who are determined to keep making it, unapologetically, proudly, and much to the benefit of the rest of us. Technologically, legally, and sexually, we are all in debt to the individuals who do the work most of us are too afraid of, in the face of taboo, ridicule, the religiously fanatical, the sexually repressed, and sometimes the law itself. Our First Amendment rights in the US have been reinforced at nearly every turn by the refusal of pornographers to be silenced. Our sexual knowledge and freedom has deepened as we've watched their exploits and taken their teachings into our own bedrooms. And none of us can even fathom what state our technology would be in had porn not led the charge in every imaginable way.

Today, pornography has become more than a punch line in civilian conversations. It is a subject of academic and scientific study, a cultural touchstone for media-conscious Americans, and a vanguard of social justice for marginalized groups. Pornographers are taking to the podiums of workshops and lecture halls, the covers of magazines, the screens of online publications, the pages of books, the centers of documentaries, and even the halls of lawmaking bodies to advocate for their very existence. And the world is, finally, listening. As Jiz Lee wrote in their essay in *Coming Out Like a Porn Star*, "Where media outlets and public opinion continue to portray a negative, one-sided depiction of porn and its participants, our stories reveal a more honest depiction . . . May our words be stepping-stones for increased sexual awareness and nuances to come."

The public has taken a few steps into the void between "them" and "us," and I'm watching with glee as it fills up with willing participants in a conversation about sex, work, and entertainment. Fans are more interactive than ever, with webcamming, custom videos, and sexting apps providing a direct line to porn actors who were once positioned on the opposite side of a vast canyon. The Internet is picking away at my home, the middle ground, as sex workers and porn makers interact with and educate the public about their work and their lives, cutting directly across the ever-lower walls that once separated the two sides of the divide.

It's a bittersweet realization that, really, I'm no longer needed here. The people who do the *real* work—who hold the banners and ride into battle every day—are fully capable of telling their own stories, and it seems that at last there is a social landscape in which those stories are more valued than they've been before. I still gladly write about them and their work for several publications, and I doubt I'll ever totally break the habit. I'll always be interested in porn, but my relevance is fast diminishing in the face of the new guard.

And, you know, I think that's wonderful.

A Glossary of Porn Terminology

GOING TO A PORN website can be a bit overwhelming, and one might find oneself down an unexpected and possibly unwelcome rabbit hole, having cavalierly clicked on a thumbnail, word, or acronym that was unfamiliar. This kind of bold browsing can lead to amazing discoveries, but it can also end up killing your good time if you wander into territory that does not turn you on. So here's a short list you can refer to while perusing your favorite porn site—or the pages of this book—to clue you in on what these terms mean. (Please note that this is a very abbreviated list of primarily mainstream porn categorizations and terminology; the world of kinky porn is vast and would require a far longer list than I have room for here, not to mention a writer with more specialized knowledge than yours truly.)

(Please also note that I apologize to anyone who's easily shocked, and that I wonder why you picked up this book.)

Adult: In the porn community, "adult" is shorthand for the porn—or adult entertainment—industry.

Amateur: The word "amateur" in porn is nebulous at best. Most "amateur" videos that make their way onto porn sites are really not amateur at all, but rather filmed to look that way by professionals. However, with the rise of user-uploaded content on tube sites, the ratio is changing, particularly on free sites.

Analingus: Butt licking! Hooray!

ATM: Shorthand for "Ass to Mouth," which refers to a penis or a sex toy moving from one body cavity to another, either being shared between two recipients or simply by moving from one end of a person's body to another. (Note: This is a high-risk sexual activity, as fecal bacteria ending up in any other orifice can make you very sick. Actors who do this go through a thorough backdoor cleaning ritual beforehand. Do not attempt at home without serious preparation.)

Bareback: Sex with no condom. This term is often used in gay male porn.

BBC: Acronym for "Big Black Cock." As with the term "interracial," BBC most often applies to scenes in which the BBC in question is paired with one or several women of lighter complexion.

BBW: "Big, Beautiful Women." Refers to larger, curvier ladies.

BDSM: Not just a porn category by any means, BDSM is a sort of umbrella term for many kinky sexual and lifestyle practices that involve "Bondage, Dominance and Submission, and Sadomasochism."

BDWC: Another, more specific, term for interracial porn. Stands for "Black Dicks, White Chicks."

B/G: A "Boy/Girl" paring, referring to cisgender men and women. These letters can be rearranged to describe many scenarios: B/B/G, for instance, or G/G/G/G/B, G/G, etc.

Bisexual: In most porn, "bisexual" refers to bisexual cisgender men, as mainstream producers more or less expect women to be bisexual on camera. So if you're searching for bisexual porn, expect to see more penises than vaginas.

BJ: "Blowjob," which means fellatio, which means oral sex performed on somebody with a penis! Huzzah!

Blowbang: Multiple people being given blowjobs by one person—like a gangbang, but only featuring oral penetration.

Bukkake: A blowbang or gangbang that ends with everybody ejaculating on the center of attention. This usually means cis men ejaculating on cis women, but there are certainly variations—like bukkakes in which people with vulvas squirt on somebody—too.

Bull: The bull is the man brought into a sexual encounter to have sex with a woman (see: "hotwife") while her regular partner (see: "cuckold") watches. Bulls are usually extremely masculine in looks and demeanor.

Casting couch: The conceit of this genre is that a young, inexperienced performer comes in to be considered for a role and is recorded giving sexual favors to improve her standing, without getting paid and sometimes without her knowledge. The majority of these scenes are, in fact, paid, but they're based on unethical practices that many agree do go on in the industry. (An interesting side note: the "casting couch" trope goes all the way back to the early twentieth century in Hollywood. A soft-core erotic film called *The Casting Couch* was made in 1923 to play on the already-rampant advent of producers preying upon young actresses' desperation for roles. Joan Crawford played a small role in this film.)

Civilian: An industry term for someone who doesn't work in porn.

Creampie: An internal ejaculation. Usually the ejaculate is squeezed back out of whatever orifice it went into for the camera.

Cuckold: There's a large market for porn in which a man is either forced or chooses to watch his wife or girlfriend (see: "hotwife") have sex with another man (see: "bull").

Cumshot: The be-all, end-all of most porn scenes, when the person with the penis pulls out and ejaculates on camera. Also known as the "pop shot" or the "money shot."

Cumswap: A cumswap can take many forms, but the basic idea is that after a person with a penis has ejaculated, two or more performers find creative ways of exchanging the semen, usually from mouth to mouth—but other orifices are definitely on the table.

DA: Double anal penetration, usually with two penises.

DP: "Double Penetration." This can refer to a variety of sex acts that include two people penetrating another person. In straight porn it most often means a woman being penetrated anally and vaginally at the same time by two penises. (Note: By all accounts this is not as easy as it looks, so proceed with caution if you want to try this at home.)

DV: Double vaginal penetration, usually with two penises.

Eurogirls: European women, often portrayed as prostitutes.

Facesitting: Pretty much exactly what it sounds like, but possibly with less cunnilingus than you might expect. Facesitting videos are focused more on the power dynamic of a woman sitting on a partner's face than on sexual gratification.

Fauxcest: Simulated incest, almost always taking place between fully adult members of on-screen extended families. Probably the most common pairing is stepmom with stepson, but stepbrothers, stepsister, stepfathers, and so on are also popular. Also called "taboo relations."

Femdom: A woman in the dominant role in a BDSM scene. Also called "submale."

Fetish: A term that you'll see much more of in kink-specific circles, a fetish is a specific item or act that some folks need in order to feel sexually fulfilled. Fetishes can take almost any form, but the more common ones revolve around body parts (feet, for instance) or objects (stockings, balloons).

FFM: Two females, one male in a threesome.

Footjob: Exactly what it sounds like. Requires quite a lot of foot-eye coordination, I would imagine.

FTM: A term for a trans man—person who was designated female at birth who identifies as male, and who is usually transitioning (or has transitioned) to living as a male. (The inverse—MTF—could be applied to describe a trans woman, but isn't as commonly used.)

Gangbang: Multiple people having sex with one person, who's the center of attention.

Gay: In porn terminology, this word is almost never used to describe lesbians or others who fall under a six on the Kinsey Scale. It's applied almost exclusively to gay cisgender men.

GILF: "Grandmother I'd Like to Fuck."

Gokkun: Similar to bukkake, except after everybody has ejaculated, the recipient of their donations eats it all, usually out of a container of some kind.

Gonzo: An in-the-action genre of porn that usually eschews scripts and plot in favor of all-sex scenes, often filmed from the "POV" perspective and tending toward rougher sex.

Handjob: Manual stimulation of the penis.

Hentai: Japanese animated porn.

Hotwife: A woman who has sex with another man (see: "bull") for the edification, or humiliation, or both, of her lover (see: "cuckold").

IR: "Interracial." Usually refers to black men paired with light-skinned women—most often white women. (See also: "BBC" and "BDWC.")

Kink: A broad term that covers a huge variety of "atypical" sexual and sensual behaviors. For some, "kinky" means having sex on the living room couch instead of in bed. For others, kink sets in somewhere between the third and fourth milk enema.

Lesbian: Most mainstream porn labeled "lesbian" will feature straight or bisexual cisgender female performers who look classically "femme." A better term for this, which is often used instead, is "girl/girl" or "G/G."

Maledom: A man in the dominant role in a BDSM scene.

MILF: "Mother I'd Like to Fuck."

MMF: Two males, one female in a threesome.

Orgy: Multiple people having sex with one another (usually four or more). Not to be confused with a gangbang, in which everybody is having sex with one central person.

Partygirls: This is a chip off the *Girls Gone Wild* block. These videos are often portrayed as amateur, and it can be pretty difficult to tell whether that's true or not.

POV: Acronym meaning "Point Of View." This is a filming technique that makes it look as if the person holding the camera is the person having sex. Sometimes it is! But often it's filmed over that person's shoulder by a cameraperson or director.

Raw: See "bareback," but used more universally.

Selfsuck: People with penises and incredibly bendy spines can do this. Use your imagination.

Smothering: See: "facesitting," but with a bit more of a Dom/sub, kinky focus, as this smothering is a form of breath play. (Note: As with any form of erotic asphyxiation, smothering can be dangerous. Please be careful and do some research on the subject should you want to experiment with this.)

Str8bait: Straight cis men, usually masturbating for a presumably gay male audience (though lots of people who aren't gay men who love this genre).

Straight4Gay: A porn category in which a straight person is brought in to have sex with a gay person in order to "convert" them to straightness. In my opinion, this category ranges from fun to really, really awkward.

Tickling: There is a huge market for tickling videos. These rarely involve sex, and are often fully clothed, but they count as kinky porn because watching tickling gets lots of people off.

TS: Shorthand for "transsexual." Usually refers to trans women.

Watersports: Pee! Yippie!

Part of the crowd at the opening of "Consent" at apexart in March 2012
(PHOTO COURTESY OF APEXART)

Recommended Viewing
for the Feminist-Minded

So, YOU MIGHT WONDER: After all these years of watching porn professionally, what kind of smut *does* Lynsey G. recommend?

Well, my darlings, that's a difficult question to answer. Everyone has different tastes, different fantasies, different desires. And, as this book has begun to illuminate, there's porn out there for *all* of it. So what works for me might not do it for you, and it's up to you to go out and find your particular cup of tea. Surely, after reading about the evils of watching pirated porn, none of you want to go poking around on free tube sites! That is very, very sweet of you. But it leaves you in something of a conundrum when it comes to finding your ideal jerk-off material without hours of time and many dollars spent on research. So I'm providing you with a list of recommendations for ethically made porn that might tickle your fancy, or at least set you on a path toward finding something that you like.

Do bear in mind several things before you take off on your horny adventures: Many porn companies now use tube sites to advertise their content, and even pirated clips on those sites will often include performer names or other clues to who was involved in making the scenes. So if you *do* end up on a free porn site and find something that you like, *please* consider doing a teensy bit of work to find out who made it, then going to that performer's or producer's website and making a purchase. Remember, paying for your porn is the surest way to make sure that more of the stuff you like will get made! Also, if you spend a very short period of time on Google looking for the stuff that you're interested in rather than heading straight to a tube site, you'll soon find a website that *sells* that kind of fare. There's lots of free stuff to wade through, but I promise that if you look for a way to purchase that same stuff, you *will* find it!

Pink & White Productions. I can't recommend this company hard enough. Founder Shine Louise Houston and her team of delightfully pervy queers are behind one of the feminist porn world's most successful production companies. Pink & White runs several sites:

- **CrashPadSeries.com**, a series of sexy vignettes featuring solos, couples, and groups of queers getting it on in creative, delightful, and always ethical ways at "the Crash Pad," an apartment dedicated to voyeuristic pleasure;

- **HeavenlySpire.com**, a site dedicated to the erotic appreciation of masculinity in its many forms;

- **PinkLabel.tv**, a video-on-demand site that features videos from nearly every amazing indie porn producer on the feminist and queer spectrum. You'll find hot action featuring people of many backgrounds, body types, gender identities and expressions, and kinks, directed and produced by filmmakers whose work is exemplary but doesn't fit into the categories that more mainstream distributors are often looking for. Any filmmaker or performer whose work you find on PinkLabel is worth pursuing—find their websites, track them down on social media, and keep track of what they're doing.

MakeLoveNotPorn.tv. In case you hadn't picked up on the fact that I'm a huge fan of Cindy Gallop's mission to make sex a less contentious part of the cultural conversation, here's my direct endorsement. The site is super fun (most of the interface is SFW), and it's free to sign up. Then it's just a few bucks a pop to rent any real-world sex video that strikes your fancy! There's all kinds of hot material from all kinds of real-world people.

Lust Films was founded by Erika Lust in Barcelona. The company makes gorgeous erotic films and vignettes, all produced ethically and with a primarily female viewership in mind. Check out all of their feature-length films, and *definitely* visit sister site **xConfessions**, which is dedicated to cinematic vignettes based on the erotic confessions of fans and members of the site. The footage is beautiful, the sex is hot, and the storytelling aspect of these scenes adds a lot of depth to the experience.

TRENCHCOATx, an indie website co-created by performer-producers Stoya and Kayden Kross, is a new take on the production, distribution, and marketing of porn. With categories that eschew condescending and stereotypical language, the site allows members (who can sign up for free and only purchase the scenes they want) to compile their own lists of "squicks" and "squees," which help personalize the user experience and find the things that get them going. Dazzling performances from many sex-positive and feminist-minded actors, a wide variety of content ranging from vanilla to kinky, and gorgeous visuals from a wide variety of brilliant directors.

FoxHouse Films, founded by Mistress Alyx Fox, is filmed at a variety of locations, and has made some very dirty, very kinky, very sex-positive, decidedly hot porn.

A company founded and run by Jennifer Lyon Bell out of the Netherlands, **Blue Artichoke** has made award-winning feature films that prove that sex can be beautiful and dirty and thought-provoking all at once.

Ms. Naughty, an Australian filmmaker and the woman behind **BrightDesire.com,** has been in the online porn-for-women game for a long time, and has filmed some extraordinary work down under.

AORTA Films, a queer, feminist porn company out of New York City, offers an irreverent and gender-bending and beautifully shot take on experimental erotic film that I really enjoy.

Jacky St. James is a director who has worked extensively with Digital Sin and New Sensations, and is now writing and directing for Sweet Sinner. She recently headed up a Showtime original softcore series called *Submission*. Though her work doesn't often fall into the indie milieu that is often associated with "feminist" porn, her work is undeniably made ethically and with feminist ideals in mind. Oh, and it's super hot.

When it comes to feminist art porn, **Madison Young**'s level of commitment to feminism, indie ideology, sex-positivity, and boundless dedication to artistic expression through sex is simply astonishing.

Sssh.com, founded almost twenty years ago by Angie Rowntree, was one of the first websites dedicated to making and selling smut for women. Most of the performers on the site aren't dedicated porn professionals, and many are paired with their real-life partners for a more authentic feel.

Courtney Trouble's queer porn company, **TroubleFilms,** has produced a lot of hardcore content that brings queer sex acts into the light for the world to see. Explore the site for queer, kinky, hardcore action featuring people of many gender identities and predilections.

jessica drake's Guide to Wicked Sex series is sex education that's beautifully produced and stars some of the biggest names in the industry. Ms. drake is an outspoken feminist who has performed, written, and directed for Wicked Pictures, one of the oldest and most respected names in the mainstream industry, for years. She's always seeking to educate herself and then her viewers about sexuality.

Tristan Taormino's Expert Guides series, released by Adam and Eve, is educational, ethical, blatantly feminist, and extremely sexy. Many of my favorite performers have starred in these films, and Tristan's sexpert advice in between hot sex scenes is invaluable.

Belladonna is a legendary performer who moved behind the camera to direct numerous films for **Evil Angel**. I strongly recommend her work, if you are of a hardcore and kinky mindset. In fact, I recommend most Evil Angel fare. Although most of the content they put out leans to the weird and the hardcore, they are known in the industry for having high standards for establishing consent on set and providing performers with great working conditions.

Another note: Possibly the greatest way to find porn that works for you is to follow your favorite performer on social media. If someone has a look or a kink or a certain *je ne sais quois* on camera that mesmerizes you, track them down! Generally, the performers that get you going end up working with other performers and producers—or produce their own content— that will turn you on. You can also find out if they have a website or a clip store, or if they do cam shows or any other type of work that you can purchase from them directly. The more you can pay them for what they do, the more they'll get to do it!

Further Reading for the Curious

THIS BOOK IS BASICALLY a compendium of some of the experiences I've had, personally, and a smattering of the things I, myself, have learned. It barely begins to scratch the surface of this "multifaceted beast," as Kink.com's Mike Stabile once called the adult industry in our conversation. And, if you're like me, you may want to know more than these few pages can teach. For those whose curiosity has been piqued, I recommend any and all of the below resources, although of course this list is nothing like exhaustive. Some of these books are more focused on pornography, others on larger issues of sex, but all exist within a broader tradition of fascinating examinations of the things that get us going as humans. Spend some time at your local bookstore or library perusing the shelves around any of these titles, and keep an eye on the publishers who are listed here. I'm certain you'll come across more delectable reading matter to satisfy your needs.

Aimee, Rachel, Eliyanna Kaiser, and Audacia Ray, eds. *$pread: The Best of the Magazine that Illuminated the Sex Industry and Started a Media Revolution*. New York, NY: The Feminist Press, 2015.

Akira, Asa. *Insatiable: Porn—A Love Story*. New York, NY: Grove Press, 2014.

Bering, Jesse. *Perv: The Sexual Deviant in All of Us*. New York, NY: Scientific American/Farrar, Straus and Giroux, 2013.

Comella, Lynn. *Vibrator Nation: How Feminist Sex-Toy Stores Changed the Business of Pleasure*. Durham: Duke University Press, 2017.

Foucault, Michel, and Robert Hurley, trans. *The History of Sexuality*. Vol. 1-3. Camberwell, Vic.: Penguin, 2008.

Horn, Tina. *Love Not Given Lightly: Profiles from the Edge of Sex*. Berkeley, CA: ThreeL Media, 2015.

Knight, Tyler. *Burn My Shadow*. New York, NY: Rare Bird Books, 2016.

Lee, Jiz, ed. *Coming Out Like a Porn Star: Essays on Pornography, Protection, and Privacy*. Berkeley, CA: ThreeL Media, 2015.

Ley, David J. *Ethical Porn for Dicks: A Man's Guide to Responsible Viewing Pleasure*. Berkeley, CA: ThreeL Media, 2016.

Ogas, Ogi and Gaddam, Sai. *A Billion Wicked Thoughts: What the World's Largest Experiment Reveals about Human Desire*. New York, NY: Dutton, 2011.

Porn Studies. Vol. 1-4. New York, NY: Routledge, 2014-2017.

Pressick, Jon, ed. *Best Sex Writing of the Year 2015: On Consent, BDSM, Porn, Race, Sex Work and More*. New York, NY: Cleis Press, 2015.

Q., Siouxsie. *Truth, Justice, and the American Whore*. Berkeley, CA: ThreeL Media, 2016.

Roach, Mary. *Bonk: The Curious Coupling of Sex and Science*. New York, NY: W.W. Norton & Company, 2008.

Small, Oriana (a.k.a. Ashley Blue). *Girlvert: A Porno Memoir*. New York, NY: Rare Bird Books, 2011.

Taormino, Tristan, Celine Parreñas Shimizu, Constance Penley, and Merreille Miller-Young, eds. *The Feminist Porn Book: The Politics of Producing Pleasure*. New York, NY: The Feminist Press, 2013.

Tarrant, Shira. *The Pornography Industry: What Everyone Needs to Know*. New York, NY: Oxford University Press, 2016.

Young, Madison. *Daddy: A Memoir*. New York, NY: Rare Bird Books, 2013.

Zeischegg, Christopher (a.k.a. Danny Wylde). *Wolves that Live in Skin and Space*. New York, NY: Rare Bird Books, 2015.

Acknowledgments

I HAVE WANTED TO WRITE a book since I was about six years old, but I never thought that this would be my first. And yet here it is, in all its glory—the culmination of years of unexpected twists, turns, and misadventures. It's also the result of a surprising jumble of friendships, alliances, and support from wholly unanticipated quarters. I'd never have made it to this point without the people who pitched in along the way. And so I'm going to thank them, one by one, in exhaustive detail.

First, I must take a moment, or possibly several, to thank the many, many people in the adult entertainment industry who have good-naturedly allowed me to stick a recording device in their faces, given me the opportunity to get the curiosity and awkwardness that defines me out of my system, and invited me into their careers and lives and homes so that I could poke around. You have all taught me volumes about your industry, yourselves, and the depths of human patience. I'd like to say an especially fond thank you to Kelly Shibari, whose friendship and kindness have continuously astonished me. To Wolf Hudson, who's just absolutely the freaking coolest and who always makes me smile. To Joanna Angel for never being too cool for me, even when she's clearly too cool for me. To Jacky St. James for letting me pester her with questions at nearly any time. To Jiz Lee for being a porno deity who's always willing to help me out. To Madison Young for being a constant inspiration in every one of the many things at which you excel. To Annie Sprinkle and Nina Hartley for just existing—you two are both warrior princesses and I look up to you every day. To Mike Stabile and the others at the FSC who came roaring in at the eleventh hour to check my facts on testing and condoms for me. And to every other person I've ever interviewed or asked for help in this particular field of ours.

Lainie Speiser, Brian Gross, Erika Icon, Chris Fam, Nelson Ayala, Kelly Shibari (again), and all the other PR wizards who have helped me get my bearings at conventions, parties, and other places where an introvert like me is way the hell out of her comfort zone: Thank you. You've helped me stay sane in even the weirdest of circumstances. (And Brian, I'm still not convinced you're actually the only person in the adult industry, masquerading as multitudes.)

To all my friends and family who have supported my work, even when it was difficult for them to do so, I want you to know that I appreciate every ounce of effort you've put into trying to understand why I do and what I do. For those who don't care to find out, I thank you for reminding me that there are those out there who aren't as fascinated by all of this as I am. That's important, even if I don't get it. And thanks for being nice to me, although I freak you out.

Especially to the "Boner Beach" crew, thank you for introducing me to the wide world of porno, and then listening to me rant and rave and obsess about it for decades. You are the best humans. *The best*. I luf foo all!

To the "secret" PronInsider crew from the days of the Black Apartment—our project may not have gotten very far, but it gave birth to something even greater. And there was so much good wine along the way!

To Miss Lola Bastinado—You are a Queen. Thank You for all your help. We'll never be able to repay You, but at least we had some fun times.

To every single editor who took a chance on me over the years, *especially* John Warner at *McSweeney's*: You have made my dreams come true. "Thank you" doesn't begin to cover it.

And, with all my heart, to the several editors with whom I've been privileged to work at The Overlook Press: Allyson Rudolph, who "got" me from the moment we set eyes on each other and without whom this book would probably have a really terrible title; Vanessa Kehren, who saw me through some tough times; and Chelsea Cutchens, whose last-inning assistance has been invaluable. Also to Kelsey Osgood, whose friendship has kept me stable many times over the course of this bumpy ride. And, naturally, to the venerable Peter Mayer, to whose insatiable curiosity and generous succor this tome owes its very existence.

A really special thank-you must go out to Julia Knight, formerly of apexart and now of a forthcoming poster museum in New York City. Almost none of the last third of this book would have happened without you, and the book itself likely would not exist. Another thank-you goes to Steven Rand, still of apexart, for going out on a limb with an art show about porno, and even farther out on that limb with me as its curator.

To the cultured degenerates of the *WHACK!* crew: j. vegas, Maxxx Peters, Lolly Gagger, Christian Madsen, Swabbin DeBoner, Lexi Love (again), Leroy Bigguns, Norman Nailher, Rick Amortis, Lady Leik, Sophie Delancey, Janet Renho. You perverts all know that you were a part of something weirdly special, and your dedication to our raunchy cause makes me smile, even now. Those were some good old days, indeed.

To Ginn. My god. Dear Ginn. I don't even know how to express the gratitude I have for you just being you, and helping me be me. All I can say is thank you. Over and over, until the end of the earth.

To Jayel Draco, who met me at a very strange time in my life and refused to let any of what this book describes freak him out. You've only seen the weirdness deepen, and yet you stay. I can't ever thank you enough for putting up with me through this process, for moving to Montana with me to make it happen, and for loving me the whole time. I have not always been the easiest to get along with, and your patience means the world. Let's build more worlds!

And again, and again, and again, to j. vegas. Thanks, man. It's been realer than real, my friend. Without you, I literally don't know who or where or what I would be right now.

Bibliography

Abram, Susan. "Adult film company Vivid Entertainment wants quick resolution to condom law amid porn shutdown over HIV." LosAngelesDailyNews.com. August 22, 2013. http://www.dailynews.com/health/20130822/adult-film-company-vivid-entertainment-wants-quick-resolution-to-condom-law-amid-porn-shutdown-over-hiv.

Adam Grayson, qtd. by Barbara Herman. "Transgender Porn Is A Best-Seller, But Is It Good For Trans People?" *International Business Times*. July 29, 2015. http://www.ibtimes.com/transgender-porn-best-seller-it-good-trans-people-2028219.

Adult Performer Advocacy Committee. "APAC Takes Position on Racial Discrimination in the Adult Entertainment Industry." September 19, 2016. http://www.apac-usa.com/single-post/2016/09/19/APAC-Takes-Position-on-Racial-Discrimination-in-the-Adult-Entertainment-Industry.

Adult Video News. "FSC: AHF Uses Cal/OSHA Complaints to Harass Political Opponents." AVN.com. March 11, 2016. https://avn.com/business/articles/legal/Utah-Pols-Declare-Porn-a-Public-Health-Crisis-Um-Hooray-639670.html.

Adult Video News. "Transsexual Reps, AVN Meet to Discuss Award Show Issues." AVN.com. February 7, 2012. https://avn.com/business/articles/video/Transsexual-Reps-AVN-Meet-to-Discuss-Award-Show-Issues-463961.html.

Akira, Asa. *Insatiable: Porn – A Love Story*. New York: Grove Press, 2014.

Alptraum, Lux. "How a Cam Girl Conspiracy Theory Sparked Masturbation Innovation." *Motherboard*. April 15, 2016. http://motherboard.vice.com/read/how-a-cam-girl-conspiracy-theory-sparked-masturbation-innovation.

Alptraum, Lux. "How Sex Workers Get Paid." *Motherboard*. January 29, 2016. http://motherboard.vice.com/read/how-sex-workers-get-paid.

Alptraum, Lux. "Silicon Valley's Very Confusing Relationship with Sex."
    Motherboard. February 18, 2016. http://motherboard.vice.com/read
    /silicon-valleys-very-confusing-relationship-with-sex.

Alptraum, Lux. "Why sex toys controlled by smartphones are a bad idea."
    Fusion. April 18, 2016. http://fusion.net/story/290923/enough-with
    -the-sex-toy-apps/.

Andy. "Why Are Porn Performers Scared to Talk About Internet Piracy?"
    TF. April 13, 2014. https://torrentfreak.com/why-are-porn-perfomers
    -scared-to-talk-about-internet-piracy-140413/.

Andy San Dimas, interview by Lynsey G. "Andy San Dimas Interview—Part
    1." YouTube video, published by *WHACK! Magazine*, 6:50. Posted
    January 25, 2010. https://www.youtube.com/watch?v=o9bw2R
    xUYbQ.

Anonymous, interview by Lynsey G. January 12, 2011.

April Flores, interview by Lynsey G. January 18, 2012.

The Associated Press. "Some in porn business consider leaving Los Angeles
    after vote to require condoms for adult-film actors." NYDailyNews.com
    .January 18, 2012. http://www.nydailynews.com/news/porn-busines
    s-leaving-los-angeles-vote-require-condoms-adult-film-actors-article
    -1.1008399.

Auerbach, David. "Vampire Porn." *Slate*. October 23, 2014. http://www
    .slate.com/articles/technology/technology/2014/10/mindgeek_porn
    _monopoly_its_dominance_is_a_cautionary_tale_for_other_industries
    .html.

Augusta. "Cambria List." Everything2. August 30, 2002. http://everything2
    .com/title/Cambria+List.

AVN Staff. "Legal Panel 'When The Whip Comes Down' Discusses Impending
    Trump Era." AVN.com. January 20, 2017. https://avn.com/business
    /articles/legal/legal-panel-when-the-whip-comes-down-discusses
    -impending-trump-era-711469.html.

Ballotpedia. "Los Angeles Porn Actors Required to Wear Condoms Act,
    Measure B (November 2012)." Ballotpedia.org. https://ballotpedia.org
    /Los_Angeles_Porn_Actors_Required_to_Wear_Condoms_Act,_Measure
    _B_(November_2012).

Berlatsky, Noah. "The way to fix the world's porn 'problem'? Make more
    of it." QZ.com. March 11, 2016. http://qz.com/636771/the-way-to
    -fix-the-worlds-porn-problem-make-more-of-it/

Bilton, Nick. "Strippers Go Undercover on Snapchat." *The New York Times*.
    February 25, 2015. http://www.nytimes.com/2015/02/26/style/strippers
    -go-undercover-on-snapchat.html.

Black, Rosemary. "Prehistoric sex toy wasn't just a feel-god aid." NYDailyNews

.com. May 17, 2010. http://www.nydailynews.com/life-style/prehistoric -siltstone-phallus-world-oldest-sex-toy-tool-ignite-fires-article -1.447999.

Blue, Violet. "Are more women OK with watching porn?" Oprah.com via CNN.com. July 24, 2009. http://www.cnn.com/2009/LIVING/personal /07/24/o.women.watching.porn/.

Blue, Violet. "PayPal, Square and big banking's war on the sex industry." Engadget.com. December 2, 2015. https://www.engadget.com/2015 /12/02/paypal-square-and-big-bankings-war-on-the-sex-industry/.

Blum, Steven. "Rise and Grind: A Look at the Side Hustles of Porn Stars." *Broadly*. September 22, 2016. https://broadly.vice.com/en_us/article /rise-and-grind-a-look-at-the-side-hustles-of-porn-stars.

Brad Armstrong, interview by Lynsey G. "BRAD ARMSTRONG Pt. 2— 'Thankfully, everybody's horny. That's the thing that keeps us going!'" *WHACK! Magazine* via LynseyG.com. May 25, 2010. http://lynseyg .com/ivan-i-truly-dont-care-what-others-think-of-me/.

Brittany Andrews, interview by Lynsey G. January 22, 2012.

Buck Angel, interview by Lynsey G. "Interview with Adult Film Producer & Performer, and LGBT Icon—Buck Angel." *WHACK! Magazine*. February 24, 2013. http://whackmagazine.com/post/43893223375/interview -with-adult-film-producer-performer.

BusinessWire. "AHF: Breach of Porn Actors' Data Reveals Failure of AIM Clinic Testing Model." BusinessWire.com. March 31, 2011. http://www .businesswire.com/news/home/20110331006926/en/AHF-Breach -Porn-Actors%E2%80%99-Data-Reveals-Failure.

BusinessWire. "Free Speech Coalition: 'Measure B Decision Will Hurt Adult Performers.'" BusinessWire.com. December 15, 2014. http://www .businesswire.com/news/home/20141215006587/en/Free-Speech -Coalition-%E2%80%9CMeasure-Decision-Hurt-Adult.

Cadence St. John, interview by Lynsey G. "CADENCE ST JOHN—'I never had a problem with exposing myself!'" *WHACK! Magazine* via LynseyG.com. August 9, 2011. http://lynseyg.com/cadence-st-john-i -never-had-a-problem-with-exposing-myself/.

California v. Freeman. No A-602, U.S. 1989.

Capri Anderson, interview by Lynsey G. "Capri Anderson at AEE 2012!" YouTube video, published by *WHACK! Magazine*, 3:52. Posted on January 23, 2012. https://www.youtube.com/watch?v=W_a04aQjVns.

Carmon, Irin. "The Insider Take On Porn And Condoms." Jezebel.com. February 10, 2011. http://jezebel.com/5757027/the-insiders-take-on -porn-and-condoms.

Canham, Matt. "Next anti-smut bill? Measure would let Utahns sue makers of porn movies." *The Salt Lake Tribune.* December 31, 2016. http://www. sltrib.com/news/4768176-155/next-anti-porn-bill-measure-would-let.

Casey Calvert, interview by Lynsey G. February 6, 2016.

Centers for Disease Control. "Condom Fact Sheet In Brief." CDC.gov. http://www.cdc.gov/condomeffectiveness/docs/condomfactsheet inbrief.pdf.

Chen, Adrian. "Porn Star HIV Test Database Leaked." March 30, 2011. Gawker.com. http://gawker.com/5787392/porn-star-hiv-test-database -leaked.

Chivers, ML, G Rieger, E Latty, and JM Bailey. "A sex difference in the speci- ficity of sexual arousal." *Psychological Science* 115, no 11 (November 2004): 736–744 doi: 10.1111/j.0956-7976.2004.00750.x.

Christina Cicchelli, interview by Lynsey G. "CHRISTINA CICCHELLI— 'Being a pervert myself I was curious about the many ways people got their rocks off.'" *WHACK! Magazine* via LynseyG.com. April 27, 2010. http://lynseyg.com/christina-cicchelli-being-a-pervert-myself-i -was-curious-about-the-many-ways-people-got-their-rocks-off/.

Christopher Ruth, in private conversation with the author, January 21, 2016.

Cindy Gallop, interview by Lynsey G. February 11, 2014.

Cindy Gallop, interview by Lynsey G. "Cindy Gallop Sinterview, Pt. 1!" YouTube video, published by *WHACK! Magazine*, 11:58. Posted Au- gust 28, 2012. https://www.youtube.com/watch?v=md8cJA2G0-c.

Clark Matthews, interview by Lynsey G. "CineKink2013 / Krutch p3." YouTube video, published by Cinekink, 0:50. Posted April 9, 2013. https://www.youtube.com/watch?list=UUQTiH93_sqvjusk6SJfcbTw&v =nya2XTIJBK0.

Clark-Flory, Tracy. "Do Men Really Hate Condoms in Porn? An Investiga- tion." Vocativ.com. October 7, 2016. http://www.vocativ.com/365967 /men-condoms-porn/.

Clark-Flory, Tracy. "Exclusive: Accused Porn Star Breaks Silence Over Abuse Allegations." Vocativ.com. January 11, 2017. http://www.vocativ.com /392136/exclusive-accused-porn-star-breaks-silence-over-nikki-benz -abuse-allegations/.

Clark-Flory, Tracy. "One Year Later, James Deen's Career Is Still Going Strong." Vocativ.com. November 22, 2016. http://www.vocativ.com /377525/james-deens-career-sexual-assault-violence/.

Clark-Flory, Tracy. "Porn's taboo transsexual stars." *Salon.* February 12, 2012. http://www.salon.com/2012/02/12/porns_taboo_transsexual _stars/.

Clark-Flory, Tracy. "Study: Porn stars aren't 'damaged.'" *Salon.* November 28, 2012. http://www.salon.com/2012/11/28/study_porn_stars_arent _damaged/.

Clark-Flory, Tracy. "Would you watch porn for the plot?" *Salon*. April 11, 2015. http://www.salon.com/2015/04/11/would_you_watch_porn_for_the_plot/.

Cohen, Elizabeth. "Prevent STDs like a porn star." CNN.com. May 19, 2011. http://www.cnn.com/2011/HEALTH/05/19/std.protection.ep/index.html.

Corey Price, qtd. by Kimberly Truong. "Pornhub Might Be Your New Source For Sex Ed." *Refinery29*. February 1, 2017. http://www.refinery29.com/2017/01/138743/pornhub-sex-ed-site.

"COURTNEY CUMMZ—'I am the dirtiest whore in the adult business!'" *WHACK! Magazine* via LynseyG.com. June 1, 2010. http://lynseyg.com/courtney-cummz-i-am-the-dirtiest-whore-in-the-adult-business/.

Courtney Cummz. Interview by Lynsey G.

Courtney Trouble, interview by Lynsey G. February 3, 2011.

Cowart, Leigh. "How Porn Isn't Protecting Its Stars From HIV." TheDailyBeast.com. February 19, 2016. http://www.thedailybeast.com/articles/2016/02/20/how-porn-isn-t-protecting-its-stars-from-hiv.html.

Dan Reilly, interview by Lynsey G. January 10, 2012.

Danny Wylde, interview by Lynsey G. January 21, 2012.

Danny Wylde, interview by Lynsey G. "Danny Wylde: Probably the Most Articulate Artist and Porn Star You Know, Part II." LynseyG.com. August 22, 2011. http://lynseyg.com/danny-wylde-probably-the-most-articulate-artist-and-porn-star-you-know-part-ii/.

Danny Wylde, interview by Susannah Breslin. "A Male Porn Star Discovers Leaving Porn Is Harder Than You'd Think." Forbes.com. February 21, 2017. https://www.forbes.com/sites/susannahbreslin/2017/02/21/male-porn-star-retired/#25816bbd54d4.

Dave Navarro, interview by Lynsey G. "SINTERVIEW with DAVE NAVARRO: Measure B, Porn, Art and more." *WHACK! Magazine*. November 16, 2012. http://whackmagazine.com/post/35836149924/sinterview-with-dave-navarro-measure-b-porn-art.

Davenporte, Barbie. "Porn Wikileaks, AIM & You: The Facts & How to Protect Yourself." LAWeekly.com. April 8, 2011. http://www.laweekly.com/news/porn-wikileaks-aim-and-you-the-facts-and-how-to-protect-yourself-2531115.

De Cadenet, Amanda. "More Women Watch (and Enjoy) Porn Than You Ever Realized: A Marie Claire Study." MarieClaire.com. October 19, 2015. http://www.marieclaire.com/sex-love/a16474/women-porn-habits-study/.

Debi Diamond, interview by Lynsey G. "DEBI DIAMOND—'I had done everything with everybody, I was a true groupie porn slut!'" *WHACK! Magazine* via LynseyG.com. June 22, 2010. http://lynseyg.com/debi-diamond-i-had-done-everything-with-everybody-i-was-a-true-groupie-porn-slut/.

Desal, Miraj U. "Racism Against Asians And Asian Americans Is Prejudice You Can Still Get Away With." HuffingtonPost.com. September 23, 2015. http://www.huffingtonpost.com/miraj-u-desai/racism-against-asians-and_b_8185388.html.

Diaz, Jesus. "The Bizarre History of the Vibrator: From Cleopatra's Angry Bees to Steam-Powered Dildos." Gizmodo.com. May 13, 2012. http://gizmodo.com/5909857/the-bizarre-history-of-the-vibrator-from-cleopatras-angry-bees-to-steam-powered-dildos.

Dickson, EJ. "When porn stars become escorts: Lucrative new trend could also be risky." Salon. February 24, 2014. http://www.salon.com/2014/02/24/when_porn_stars_become_escorts_lucrative_new_trend_could_also_be_risky/.

DiVirgilio, Andrea. "Money In Pornography: One Of The Most Misunderstood Industries." TheRichest.com. December 1, 2013. http://www.therichest.com/expensive-lifestyle/money/money-in-pornography-one-of-the-most-misunderstood-industries/.

Downing, Martin J., Eric W. Schrimshaw, et al. "Sexually Explicit Media Use by Sexual Identity: A Comparative Analysis of Gay, Bisexual, and Heterosexual Men in the United States." Archives of Sexual Behavior (2016). Doi: 10.1007/s10508-016-0837-9.

The Economist. "Naked Capitalism." September 26, 2015. http://www.economist.com/news/international/21666114-internet-blew-porn-industrys-business-model-apart-its-response-holds-lessons.

FCSPass.com. https://fscpass.com/.

Federal Drug Administration. "APTIMA HIV-1 RNA Qualitative Assay." FDA.gov. http://www.fda.gov/downloads/BiologicsBloodVaccines/BloodBloodProducts/ApprovedProducts/LicensedProductsBLAs/BloodDonorScreening/InfectiousDisease/UCM149927.pdf.

The Feminist Porn Awards. "What is feminist porn?" FeministPornAwards.com.http://www.feministpornawards.com/what-is-feminist-porn-2/.

Finn, Holly. "Online Pornography's Effects, and a New Way to Fight Them." WSJ.com. May 3, 2013. http://www.wsj.com/articles/SB10001424127887323628004578456710204395042.

Fisman, Raymond, Sheena S. Iyengar, Emir Kamenica, Itamar Simonson. "Racial Preferences in Dating: Evidence from a Speed Dating Experiment." Review of Economic Studies 75 (2008): 117-132, doi: 0034-6527/08/0006011$02.00.

Flores, April. "April Flores, BBW Porn Performer, On Being A 'Fat Girl' And Loving It." XOJane.com. February 22, 2013. http://www.xojane.com/issues/my-history-with-the-word-fat-and-how-i-came-to-embrace-it.

Forbes, Sarah. *Sex in the Museum: My Unlikely Career at New York's Most Provocative Museum.* New York: St. Martin's Press, 2016.

Fox, Alyx, interview by PinkLabel.tv. "FOCUS ON: Alyx Fox on FOX-HOUSE Films and Filming Trans Women in BDSM Porn." PinkLabel.tv. February 26, 2016. http://www.pinklabel.tv/on-demand /foxhouse-films-trans-women-porn.

Frank, Cosmo. "The Tranny Awards Are Getting a Less Offensive Name." Cosmopolitan.com. March 10, 2014. http://www.cosmopolitan.com /entertainment/news/a21825/tranny-awards-becoming-transgender -erotica-awards/.

Free Speech Coalition. "Recent DPH Report Addresses Non-Compliant Out-of-State Shoot in September." FreeSpeechCoalition.com. December 30, 2014. https://www.freespeechcoalition.com/blog/2014/12/30/recent -dph-report-addresses-non-compliant-out-of-state-shoot-in-september.

Friday, Wednesday Lee. "The Long, Strange History of Sex Toys: Whether for fashion, décor, worship, or for fun, dildos are a part of human history." Kinkly.com via Alternet.org June 19, 2013. http://www.alternet .org/sex-amp-relationships/sex-toy.

Frontline. "American Porn." PBS.org. Accessed December 10, 2016. http://www.pbs.org/wgbh/pages/frontline/shows/porn/.

Fuller, Thomas. "Actors in Pornographic Films Fight Proposal to Enforce Safety Regulations." NYTimes.com. February 18, 2016. http://www .nytimes.com/2016/02/19/us/actors-in-pornographic-films-fight -proposal-to-enforce-safety-regulations.html.

Fusion. "Inside Miami's sex industry: Porn stars reveal how the internet is changing their business." *Fusion*. July 20, 2015. http://fusion.net/story /168910/miami-porn-industry-sex-workers/.

G., Lynsey. "After James Deen, How Can the Porn Industry Keep Performers Safe?" BitchMedia.com. December 14, 2015. https://bitchmedia.org /article/look-feminist-porn-and-consent-james-deen.

G., Lynsey. "Blowing the Budget." *Bitch Magazine*, no. 64 (Fall 2014): 45–49.

G., Lynsey. "The Conflicted Existence of the Female Porn Writer, Column 5: Schooled by the Stars, or What I Learned at the Porn Expo." *McSweeney's Internet Tendency*. December 16, 2009. https://www .mcsweeneys.net/articles/column-5-schooled-by-the-stars-or-what-i -learned-at-the-porn-expo.

G., Lynsey. "The Conflicted Existence of the Female Porn Writer: Column 10: The Smut Smorgasbord and Surreptitious Sex Habits." *McSweeney's Internet Tendency*. April 1, 2010. https:/ /www.mcsweeneys.net/articles /column-10-the-smut-smorgasbord-and -surreptitious -sex-habits.

G., Lynsey. "Consent." Apexart.org. March, 2012. https://apexart.org/exhibitions/lynseyg.php.

G., Lynsey. "THE CRASH PAD—'Some of them are covered in sweat by the time they're finished.'" *WHACK! Magazine* via LynseyG.com. March 2, 2010. http://lynseyg.com/the-crash-pad-these-ladies-are-so-dedicated-to-getting-each-other-off-that-some-of-them-are-covered-in-sweat-by-the-time-theyre-finished/.

G., Lynsey. "PayPal Is Bringing Sexy Back." *MEL Magazine.* July 27, 2016. https://melmagazine.com/paypal-is-bringing-sexy-back-3a12ee2d3114 #.fb0yn3maz.

G., Lynsey. "'Suitcase Pimps' in the Adult Industry: an informational essay." LynseyG.com. August 26, 2014. http://lynseyg.com/suitcase-pimps-in-the-adult-industry-an-informational-essay/.

G., Lynsey. "We Can—& Should—Learn From How The Porn Industry Deals With Rape." *Refinery29.* December 10, 2015. http://www.refinery29.com/2015/12/99292/james-deen-rape-feminism-debate.

G., Lynsey. "What Do Porn Directors Do When Somebody Farts on Set?" *MEL Magazine.* October 6, 2016. https://melmagazine.com/what-do-porn-directors-do-when-somebody-farts-on-set-93f8661ec462#.a91sywwcm.

G., Lynsey. "Who's Teaching the Next Generation of Pornographers?" *MEL Magazine.* December 2, 2016. https://melmagazine.com/whos-teaching-the-next-generation-of-pornographers-f037f1e6ad05#.9bizxzj7a.

G., Lynsey. "Yellowface Is a Problem, But It's Not THE Problem." LynseyG.com. February 3, 2013. http://lynseyg.com/yellowface-is-a-problem-but-its-not-the-problem/.

Gallop, Cindy. "Cindy Gallop: Make love, not porn." TED video, 4:30. Posted December 2, 2009. http://blog.ted.com/cindy_gallop_ma/.

Gen Padova, interview by Lynsey G. December 23, 2016.

Geuss, Megan. "Pornhub launches an all-you-can-watch subscription service for $9.99 a month." *Ars Technica.* August 6, 2015. http://arstechnica.com/business/2015/08/pornhub-launches-an-all-you-can-watch-subscription-service-for-9-99-a-month/.

Girl on the Net. "What the New British Porn Bill Means for You." Vice.com. November 23, 2016. https://www.vice.com/en_uk/article/non-conventional-sex-the-government-wants-to-block-perfectly-legal-porn-digital-economy-bill.

Goff, Keli. "Is the Porn Industry Racist?" TheRoot.com. April 3, 2013. http://www.theroot.com/articles/culture/2013/04/pornindustry_racism_whats_behind_it/.

Goodman, Lizzy. "Stoya Said *Stop.*" *New York Magazine.* June 27, 2016. http://nymag.com/thecut/2016/06/stoya-james-deen-c-v-r.html.

Griffith, JD, S Mitchell, CL Hart, LT Adams, LL Gu. "Pornography actresses: an assessment of the damaged goods hypothesis." *Journal of Sex Research* 50, no 7 (2013): 621–632 doi: 10.1080/0224499.2012 .719168.

Gross, Doug. "In the tech world, porn quietly leads the way." CNN .com. April 23, 2010. http://edition.cnn.com/2010/TECH/04/23/porn .technology/index.html.

Hay, Mark. "Datagasm." Aeon.co. July 14, 2016. https://aeon.co/essays /micro-targeted-digital-porn-is-changing-human-sexuality

Heitz, David. "Preventing the Spread of HIV in the Porn Industry." HIVequal.com. Febraury 28, 2016. http://www.hivequal.org/hiv-equal-on-line/preventing-the-spread-of-hiv-in-the-porn-industry.

Herman, Barbara. "In Bed With Porn Super Agent Mark Spiegler: 'It's Business, With Sex.'" *IBT*. January 23, 2015. http://www.ibtimes.com/bed-porn-super-agent-mark-spiegler-its-business-sex-1792720.

Herman, Barbara. "Women In Porn: They Direct, Win Awards, Control Their Careers; More Progressive Than Hollywood?" *IBT*. January 27, 2016. http://www.ibtimes.com/women-porn-they-direct-win-awards-control-their-careers-more-progressive-hollywood-1793950.

Hess, Amanda. "How Many Women Are Not Admitting to Pew That They Watch Porn?" *Slate*. October 11, 2013. http://www.slate.co6++++blogs /xx_factor/2013/10/11/pew_online_viewing_study_percentage_of _women_who_watch_online_porn_is_growing.html.

Hess, Amanda. "The Rise of VR Porn." *Slate*. January 21, 2016. http://www.slate.com/articles/technology/users/2016/01/vr_porn_is_he re_does_virtual_sex_really_feel_real.html.

Hill-Meyer, Tobi. "Where The Trans Women Aren't: The Slow Inclusion of Trans Women in Feminist/Queer Porn." *The Feminist Porn Book: The Politics of Producing Pleasure*. Tristan Taormino, Celine Parreñas Shimizu, Constance Penley, and Merreille Miller-Young, eds. New York: The Feminist Press, 2013.

Holmes, David. "Pornhub launches 'Netflix for porn' subscription service." *The Guardian*. August 6, 2015. https://www.theguardian.com/cul-ture/2015/aug/06/pornhub-launches-paid-subscription.

Houston, interview by Lynsey G. "HOUSTON—'Hello, my name is Houston and I am a porn superstar.'" *WHACK! Magazine* via LynseyG .com. July 20, 2010. http://lynseyg.com/houston-hello-my-name-is -houston-and-i-am-a-porn-superstar/.

Howard, Jacqueline. "Republicans are calling porn a 'public health crisis,' but is it really?" CNN.com. September 2, 2016. http://www.cnn.com /2016/07/15/health/porn-public-health-crisis/.

Hudson, David L. "Pornography and Obscenity." First Amendment Center. September 13, 2002. http://www.firstamendmentcenter.org/pornography -obscenity.

India Summer, interview by Lynsey G. "INDIA SUMMER—'I consider my-self an Orgasmonaut exploring the inner and outer space of my sexu-ality!'" *WHACK! Magazine* via LynseyG.com. September 13, 2011. http://lynseyg.com/india-summer-i-consider-myself-an-orgasmonaut -exploring-the-inner-and-outer-space-of-my-sexuality/.

Indo-Asian News Service. "30 percent of global web traffic is porn." Gadgets360. June 5, 2011. http://gadgets.ndtv.com/internet/news/30 -percent-of-global-web-traffic-is-porn-study-223878.

"Industry." Directed by Lynsey G. Published by apexart, 18:57. March 21, 2012. http://apexart.org/images/lynseyg/videos/INDUSTRY.m4v.

Instinct Magazine. "CDC Reveals Gay Porn Performer Transmitted HIV After Testing Negative." InstinctMagazine.com. February 16, 2016. http://instinctmagazine.com/post/cdc-reveals-gay-porn-performer -transmitted-hiv-after-testing-negative/.

Ivan, interview by Lynsey G. "IVAN—'I truly don't care what others think of me.'" LynseyG.com. May 25, 2010. http://lynseyg.com/ivan-i-truly -dont-care-what-others-think-of-me/.

Ivan, interview by Lynsey G. "Ivan at AEE 2011!" YouTube video, published by *WHACK! Magazine*, 8:47. Posted January 31, 2011. https://www .youtube.com/watch?v=NetFoIbcBQw.

James Darling, interview by Lynsey G. "A Long-Awaited Interview with James Darling!!!" LynseyG.com. June 11, 2013. http://lynseyg.com /a-long-awaited-interview-with-james-darling/.

James Deen, interview by Lynsey G. "JAMES DEEN—'I'm the luckiest boy alive.'" *WHACK! Magazine* via LynseyG.com. April 13, 2010. http://lynseyg.com/james-deen-im-the-luckiest-boy-alive/.

Javanbakht, Marjan, Pamina Gorbach, et al. "Adult Film Performers Trans-mission Behaviors and STI Prevalence." 2014 National STD Preven-tion Conference. June 9 – 12, 2014.

Jenna Haze, interview by Lynsey G. "JENNA HAZE—'I was like, "If you're gonna cum, just cum on her!"'" *WHACK! Magazine* via LynseyG.com. April 26, 2011. http://lynseyg.com/jenna-haze-i-was-like-if-youre -gonna-cum-just-cum-on-her/.

Jenna Haze, interview by Lynsey G. "JENNA HAZE—'She's not just a total slut like she is on camera. She's the kind of girl who you wouldn't know does porn!'" *WHACK! Magazine* via LynseyG.com. April 20, 2011. http://lynseyg.com/jenna-haze-shes-not-just-a-total-slut-like-she-is-on -camera-shes-the-kind-of-girl-who-you-wouldnt-know-does-porn/.

Jennifer Lyon Bell, interview by Lynsey G. May, 2011.

jessica drake, interview by Amanda Hess. "Talking to Porn Star jessica drake About the New Condoms In Porn Law." Slate.com. November 15, 2012. http://www.slate.com/blogs/xx_factor/2012/11/15/measure_b_ passed _porn_star_jessica_drake_on_the_new_condoms_in_porn_law.html.

jessica drake, interview by Lynsey G. January 20, 2016.

jessica drake, interview by Lynsey G. "jessica drake—'I'm so in love with my job and people can tell I'm not just going through the paces!'" WHACK! Magazine via LynseyG.com. April 6, 2010. http://lynseyg .com/jessica-drake-im-so-in-love-with-my-job-and-people-can-tell-im -not-just-going-through-the-paces/.

Jewell, Hannah. "Um, Look At This Actual 28,000-Year-Old Dildo." BuzzFeed .com. January 17, 2015. https://www.buzzfeed.com/hannahjewell/um -theres-currently-a-28000-year-old-dildo-in-london.

Juicy Jay, interview by Lynsey G. "JUICY JAY OF JUICADS.COM—'We have by far the easiest-to-use platform. And definitely the most seduc- tive!'" WHACK! Magazine via LynseyG.com. http://lynseyg.com/juicy -jay-of-juicyads-com-we-have-by-far-the-easiest-to-use-platform-and -definitely-the-most-seductive/.

Katsuni, interview by Lynsey G. "KATSUNI—'I love everything about sex. It's like having a great dinner!'" WHACK! Magazine via LynseyG.com. July 27, 2010. http://lynseyg.com/katsuni-i-love-everything-about-sex -its-like-having-a-great-dinner/.

Kaylani Lei, interview by Lynsey G. "KAYLANI LEI—'I love getting spun and thrown around!'" WHACK! Magazine via LynseyG.com. Novem- ber 9, 2009. http://lynseyg.com/kaylani-lei-i-love-getting-spun-and -thrown-around/.

Kelly Shibari, interview by Lynsey G. January 18, 2012.

Kerner, Ian. "Is there such a thing as 'good porn'?" CNN.com. November 7, 2016. http://www.cnn.com/2016/11/07/health/ethical-porn-ian-kerner/.

Kink.com. "About Us." http://www.kink.com/page/about-us.

Kristina Rose, interview by Lynsey G. "KRISTINA ROSE—'I think people connect with that realness. And I suck a mean dick.'" WHACK! Magazine via LynseyG.com. July 6, 2010. http://lynseyg.com /kristina-rose-i-think-people-connect-with-that-realness-and-i-suck -a-mean-dick/.

Kuepper, Michelle. "German Entrepreneur Fabian Thylmann Exits Online Porn Empire." Heureka. October 21, 2013. http://theheureka.com /fabian-thylmann.

Lance Hart, interview by Lynsey G. February 2, 2016.

Lawrence, Kelsey. "What Millenials' Favorite Porn Can Teach Us About Race in America." Mic.com. August 26, 2015. https://mic.com/articles/124368/what-millennials-favorite-porn-can-teach-us-about-race-in-america#.lVniibKDv.

Lee, Jiz, ed. "How to Come Out Like a Porn Star: An Introduction," in *Coming Out Like a Porn Star: Essays on Pornography, Protection, and Privacy*. Berkeley: ThreeL Media, 2015.

Lee, Jiz. "Fisting Day," in *Best Sex Writing of the Year: On Consent, BDSM, Porn, Race, Sex Work and More*, ed. John Pressick (New York: Cleis Press, 2015), 98.

Lennard, Natasha. "Can These Pornographers End 'MILFs,' 'Teens,' and 'Thugs'?" TheNation.com. September 29, 2016. https://www.thenation.com/article/can-changing-our-porn-vocabulary-change-porn-itself/.

Leue, Eric Paul. "Suing Porn Stars Will Not Lead to Less HIV." Advocate.com. August 17, 2016. http://www.advocate.com/commentary/2016/8/17/suing-porn-stars-will-not-lead-less-hiv.

Licensed Adult Talent Agency Trade Association. http://latata.org/about/.

Lolly Gagger, interview by Lynsey G. January 5, 2011.

Love, Sinnamon. "A Question of Feminism." *The Feminist Porn Book: The Politics of Producing Pleasure*. Tristan Taormino, Celine Parreñas Shimizu, Constance Penley, and Merreille Miller-Young, eds. New York: The Feminist Press, 2013.

Lux Alptraum, interview by Lynsey G. December 28, 2011.

Lux, Tori. "Tori Lux: James Deen Assaulted Me, Too." TheDailyBeast.com. November 29, 2015. http://www.thedailybeast.com/articles/2015/11/30/tori-lux-james-deen-assaulted-me-too.html.

Lux, Venus. "Venus Rising: Woman on Top." AIPDaily.com. May 17, 2015. http://aipdaily.com/author/venus-lux/.

MacMillen, Hayley. "My Boyfriend & I Have The Same Taste In Porn." *Refinery29*. April 20, 2016. http://www.refinery29.com/2016/04/108731/feminist-porn-for-women-problem.

Madison Montag, interview by Lynsey G. "MADISON MONTAG—'I love my dick too much to lose it to a knife!'" LynseyG.com. May 17, 2011. http://lynseyg.com/madison-montag-i-love-my-dick-too-much-to-lose-it-to-a-knife/.

Madison Young, interview by Lynsey G. October 22, 2011.

Maggie Mayhem, qtd. by Kitty Stryker, "Principled Pornography: How Queer/Indie Sites are Reframing the Industry." HuffingtonPost.com. April 19, 2012. http://www.huffingtonpost.com/kitty-stryker/principled-pornography-ho_b_1435614.html.

Mandy Morbid, interview by Lynsey G. "MANDY MORBID—'Bra size is 28FF or 28G/H depending on what time of the month it is, style, and amount of cleavage desired.'" *WHACK! Magazine* via LynseyG.com. http://lynseyg.com/mandy-morbid-bra-size-is-28ff-or-28-gh-depending-on-what-time-of-the-month-it-is-style-and-amount-of-cleavage-desired/.

Marie Madison, interview by Lynsey G. "MARIE MADISON—'I'm fucking the way I really enjoy fucking, and I think it shows.'" *WHACK! Magazine* via LynseyG.com. August 24, 2010. http://lynseyg.com/marie-madison-im-fucking-the-way-i-really-enjoy-fucking-and-i-think-it-shows/.

Marks, Andrea. "Fresh Flowers, Plenty of Lube: Inside the World of Feminist Porn." *Rolling Stone*. December 1, 2016. http://www.rollingstone.com/culture/features/fresh-flowers-plenty-of-lube-inside-world-of-feminist-porn-w452344.

Mark Spiegler, interview by Marc Palatucci. "The Consummate Professional—Mark Spiegler." *Office Magazine*. 2017. http://www.officemagazine.net/interview/consummate-professional-mark-spiegler.

Max Hardcore, qtd. in "Max Hardcore Speaks Out from the Can!" *WHACK! Magazine* via LynseyG.com. June 29, 2010. http://lynseyg.com/max-hardcore-speaks-out-from-the-can/.

May Ling Su, interview by Lynsey G. "An Interview with May Ling Su." LynseyG.com. March 18, 2011. http://lynseyg.com/an-interview-with-may-ling-su/.

McClintock, Pamela and Tim Appelo. "Where Are All the Black Actors?" HollywoodReporter.com. March 3, 2011. http://www.hollywoodreporter.com/news/are-all-black-actors-163464.

McCullough, Brian. "Chapter 6—A History of Internet Porn." *Internet History Podcast*. January 4, 2015. http://www.internethistorypodcast.com/2015/01/history-of-internet-porn/.

Merchant, Brian. "Your Porn Is Watching You." Motherboard.vice.com. April 6, 2015. http://motherboard.vice.com/read/your-porn-is-watching-you.

Michael Stabile, interview by Lynsey G. February 26, 2017.

Michael Stabile, qtd. by Mark Hay. "Datagasm: Ever-faster feedback loops and micro-targeted digital porn are pushing human sexuality into some seriously weird placesaeon.com. July 14, 2016. https://aeon.co/essays/micro-targeted-digital-porn-is-changing-human-sexuality.

Mickey Mod, interview by Lynsey G. November 16, 2016.

Miller, Daniel. "Inside the Risky Business of Porn Star Agents." *The Hollywood Reporter*. November 15, 2012. http://www.hollywoodreporter.com/news/porn-star-agents-inside-risky-390466.

Miller, Dan. "Kink, Evil Angel, Doc Johnson Take Stances on James Deen." AVN.com. November 30, 2015. https://avn.com/business/articles/video /Kink-Evil-Angel-Doc-Johnson-Take-Stances-on-James-Deen-614326.html.

Miller, Dan. "Live Cam Market Comes Out in Force at AVN Expo." AVN. January 22, 2016. https://avn.com/business/articles/technology/Live Cam-Market-Comes-Out-in-Force-at-AVN-Expo-620247.html.

Miller-Young, Mireille. "Porn isn't a public health hazard. It's a scapegoat." *The Washington Post*. May 23, 2016. https://www.washingtonpost .com/news/in-theory/wp/2016/05/23/porn-isnt-a-public-health-hazard -its-a-scapegoat/?utm_term=.a52de0d429b9.

Millward, Jon. "Deep Inside: A Study of 10,000 Porn Stars and Their Careers." JonMillward.com. February 14, 2013. http://jonmillward .com/blog/studies/deep-inside-a-study-of-10000-porn-stars/.

Milot, Stephanie. "Watch Pornhub and . . . Save the Whales?" *PC Magazine*. February 11, 2016. http://www.pcmag.com/article2/0,2817,2499163 ,00.asp.

Mireille Miller-Young, interview by Farai Chideya. "Sex Stereotypes of African Americans Have Long History." NPR.org. May 2, 2007. http://www.npr.org/templates/story/story.php?storyId=10057104.

Misti Dawn, interview by Lynsey G. "MISTI DAWN—'No one has sex on camera without being wired a lil' off!'" *WHACK! Magazine* via LynseyG.com. March 1, 2011. http://lynseyg.com/misti-dawn-no-one -has-sex-on-camera-with-out-being-wired-a-lil-off/.

"Morality." Directed by Lynsey G. Published by apexart, 17:02. March 21, 2012. http://apexart.org/images/lynseyg/videos/MORALITY.m4v.

Moreland, Rich. *Pornography Feminism: As Powerful as She Wants to Be*. Washington: Zero Books, 2015.

Morris, Chris. "Condoms in Porn? Just Another Day at Wicked Pictures." CNBC.com. January 15, 2013. http://www.cnbc.com/id/100359796.

Morris, Chris. "Meet the New King of Porn." CNBC.com. January 18, 2012. http://www.cnbc.com/id/45989405.

Morris, Chris. "Porn and Banks: Drawing a Line on Loans." CNBC.com. May 17, 2013. http://www.cnbc.com/id/100746445.

Morris, Chris. "Porn's dirtiest secret: What everyone gets paid." CNBC.com. January 20, 2016. http://www.cnbc.com/2016/01/20/porns-dirtiest -secret-what-everyone-gets-paid.html.

Morrissey, Tracie Egan. "*Walking Dead* Porn Parody Relies on Yellowface." Jezebel.com. January 31, 2013. http://jezebel.com/5980498/walking -dead-porn-parody-relies-on-yellowface.

Moye, David. "Donald Trump Appeared In A Playboy Softcore Porn Video." *The Huffington Post*. September 30, 2016. http://www.huffingtonpost .com/entry/donald-trump-playboy-porn_us_57eee2fbe4b0c2407cde0fd2.

Moye, David. "Porn Industry In Decline: Insiders Adapt to Piracy, Waning DVD Sales (NSFW)." *The Huffington Post*. January 19, 2013. http://www .huffingtonpost.com/2013/01/19/porn-industry-in-decline_n_2460799 .html.

Mr. Marcus, interview by Lynsey G. January 19, 2012.

Mr. Marcus, interview by Lynsey G. "MR. MARCUS—A Sit Down with a Stand-up Cocksman." *WHACK! Magazine* via LynseyG.com. September 15, 2009. http://lynseyg.com/mr-marcus-a-sit-down-with-a-stand-up-cocksman/.

Mycio, Mary. "The World's Oldest Pornography." *Slate*. February 14, 2013. http://www.slate.com/articles/health_and_science/science/2013/02 /prehistoric_pornography_chinese_carvings_show_explicit_copulation .html.

Nate Glass, interview by Lynsey G. January 21, 2016.

The National Sex Offender Website. "Facts and Statistics: Raising Awareness about Sexual Abuse." The National Sex Offender Public Website. https://www.nsopw.gov/en/Education/FactsStatistics.

Neal, Jarret. "Let's Talk About Interracial Porn," in *Best Sex Writing of the Year: On Consent, BDSM, Porn, Race, Sex Work and More*, ed. John Pressick (New York: Cleis Press, 2015), 146.

Nica Noelle, interview by Lynsey G. "NICA NOELLE ON THE APA—"We may not agree with other organizations on every issue, but we're not about competition or infighting!" *WHACK! Magazine* via LynseyG .com. September 27, 2011. http://lynseyg.com/nica-noelle-on-the-apa-we-may-not-agree-with-other-organizations-on-every-issue-but-were-not -about-competition-or-infighting/.

Nikki Benz, interview by Lynsey G. "NIKKI BENZ—'This is adult enter- tainment. I'm gonna keep it adult!'" *WHACK! Magazine* via LynseyG.com. July 19, 2011. http://lynseyg.com/nikki-benz-this-is -adult-entertainment-im-gonna-keep-it-adult/.

Nikki Darling, interview by Lynsey G. February 15, 2016.

Nina Hartley, interview by Lynsey G. "NINA HARTLEY—'It's nice to . . . get out of the "nipple ghetto."'" *WHACK! Magazine* via LynseyG.com. http://lynseyg.com/nina-hartley-its-exciting-to-get-out -of-the-nipple-ghetto/.

Nina Hartley, interview by Lynsey G. "Nina Hartley at AEE 2011!" YouTube video, published by *WHACK! Magazine*, 7:54. February 21, 2011. https://www.youtube.com/watch?v=lnxQ30d9mH8.

Nina Mercedez, interview by Lynsey G. "NINA MERCEDEZ—'I'm either going to do it all the way or I'm not even going to bother!'" *WHACK! Magazine* via LynseyG.com. August 23, 2011. http://lynseyg.com

/nina-mercedez-im-either-going-to-do-it-all-the-way-or-im-not-even
-going-to-bother/.

Nyomi Banxxx, interview by Lynsey G. January 19, 2012.

Nyomi Banxxx, interview by Lynsey G. "NYOMI BANXXX—'Honestly,
we all have a little freak in us!'" *WHACK! Magazine* via LynseyG.com.
February 8, 2011. http://lynseyg.com/nyomi-banxxx-honestly-we-all
-have-a-little-freak-in-us/.

Ogas, Ogi, and Sai Gaddam. *A Billion Wicked Thoughts: What the World's
Largest Experiment Reveals about Human Desire.* London: Dutton, 2011.

O'Neill, Stephanie. "Los Angeles Measure B: Mandating Condom Use in
Adult Films." Blogs.KQEDNews.org. October 12, 2012. http://blogs
.kqed.org/election2012/2012/10/12/los-angeles-measure-b-mandating
-condom-use-in-adult-films/.

Orenstein, Peggy. "When Did Porn Become Sex Ed?" *The New York Times.*
March 19, 2016. http://www.nytimes.com/2016/03/20/opinion/sunday
/when-did-porn-become-sex-ed.html.

Oriana Small, interview by Lynsey G. March 2, 2012.

Owen, Tess. "California Might Make Condoms, Goggles, and Dental Dams
Mandatory in Porn." News.Vice.com. February 18, 2016. https://news
.vice.com/article/california-might-make-condoms-goggles-and-dental
-dams-mandatory-in-porn.

Paige, interviewed by Lynsey G. January 15, 2012.

Pappas, Stephanie. "The Porn Myth: Uncovering the Truth about Sex Stars."
LiveScience.com. February 25, 2013. http://www.livescience.com/27428
-truth-about-porn-stars.html.

Pardon, Rhett. "FSC: Settlement Renders Measure B Unenforceable."
Xbiz.com. March 29, 2016. www.xbiz.com/news/206164.

Pardon, Rhett. "Q&A With Steven Grooby, Founder of Grooby Productions." Xbiz.com. March 29, 2015. http://www.xbiz.com/arti-
cles/192784.

Pardon, Rhett. "Updated: Calif. Officials Vote Against Condom Rules for
Porn Productions." Xbiz.com. February 18, 2016. http://www.xbiz
.com/news/204524.

Pearson, Jordan. "'Popcorn Time for Porn' Lets You Stop Giving Money to
Shady Tube Sites." *Motherboard.* June 8, 2015. http://motherboard
.vice.com/read/popcorn-time-for-porn-lets-you-stop-giving-money-to
-shady-tube-sites.

Ponti, Crystal. "Are the Republicans Coming For Your Porn?" *Paste Magazine.* December 1, 2016. https://www.pastemagazine.com/articles/2016
/12/what-the-republican-stronghold-means-for-porn.html

Pornhub Insights. "Pornhub's 2015 Year in Review." Pornhub.com. January 6, 2016. http://www.pornhub.com/insights/pornhub-2015-year-in -review.

Pornhub Insights. "Pornhub's 2016 Year in Review." Pornhub.com January 4, 2017. http://www.pornhub.com/insights/2016-year-in-review.

Pornhub Sexual Wellness Center. "Welcome to the Pornhub Sexual Wellness Center!" Pornhub.com. February 1, 2017. http://www.pornhub .com/sex.

Q., Siouxsie. "Authentically Yours: Feminist Porn Gets Political." SFWeekly .com. April 16, 2014. http://archives.sfweekly.com/sanfrancisco /authentically-yours-feminist-porn-gets-political/.

RadioLab. "The Greatest Hits of Ancient Garbage." RadioLab.org. http://www.radiolab.org/story/91516-detective-stories/.

Raven Alexis, interview by Lynsey G. "RAVEN ALEXIS—'Sex is one of the most empowering things in the universe.'" *WHACK! Magazine*, via LynseyG.com. August 3, 2010. http://lynseyg.com/raven-alexis-sex-is -one-of-the-most-empowering-things-in-the-universe/.

"Reality." Directed by Lynsey G. Published by apexart, 21:01. March 21, 2012. http://apexart.org/images/lynseyg/videos/REALITY.m4v.

Rivas, Jorge. "Porn Stars of Color Face Racial Inequality and Wage Gap Too." ColorLines.com. http://www.colorlines.com/articles/porn-stars -color-face-racial-inequality-and-wage-gap-too.

Roach, Mary. *Bonk: The Curious Coupling of Sex and Science*. New York: W.W. Norton & Company, 2008.

Romero, Dennis. "Adult Performer Nikki Benz Alleges She Was Assaulted on Camera During a Porn Shoot." *LAWeekly*. December 20, 2016. http://linkis.com/www.laweekly.com/new/H4Ayi.

RT.com. "LA porn condom law upheld, similar to G-string mandates for strippers." RT.com. December 17, 2014. https://www.rt.com/usa /215011-porn-condom-law-upheld/.

Rudo, Paul. "Ten indispensable technologies built by the pornography industry." EnterpriseFeatures.com June 5, 2011. http://www.enterprisefeatures .com/ten-indispensable-technologies-built-by-the-pornography -industry/.

Ryan Driller, interview by Lynsey G. January 22, 2016.

Sabrina Deep, interview by Lynsey G. "The Great Gangbang Interview with Sabrina Deep, Part I." LynseyG.com. January 25, 2011. http://lynseyg .com/the-great-gangbang-interview-with-sabrina-deep-part-i/.

Saint, Nick. "How Pornographers Invented E-Commerce." *Business Insider.* August 6, 2010. http://www.businessinsider.com/the-producer-of-middle -men-talks-to-us-about-how-pornographers-invented-e-commerce -2010-8.

Salmon, Felix. "How MindGeek transformed the economics of porn." *Fusion.* October 10, 2015. http://fusion.nct/story/212078/how-mindgeek -transformed-the-economics-of-porn/.

The San Diego Union-Tribune. "Prop. 60: Don't overregulate adult-film industry." *The San Diego Union-Tribune.* September 13, 2016. http://www .sandiegouniontribune.com/opinion/editorials/sdut-no-prop-60 -condoms-overkills-2016sep13-story.html.

Scarlet, Minnie. "How to Make Ethical Porn in and Industry Built on Racism and Fetishization." Vice.com. December 21, 2016. https://www.vice .com/en_ca/article/how-to-make-ethical-porn-in-an-industry-built-on -racism-and-fetishization.

Seymore Butts, interview by Lynsey G. "SEYMORE BUTTS—'I've always envisioned writing a book…so I felt like I'd start with the sex instruction guide.'" *WHACK! Magazine* via LynseyG.com. November 9, 2009. http://lynseyg.com/seymore-butts-ive-always-envisioned-writing -a-book-so-i-felt-like-id-start-with-the-sex-instruction-guide/.

Sheena Ryder, interview by Lynsey G. "SHEENA RYDER—'I consider myself not bi, but bi-furious!'" *WHACK! Magazine* via LynseyG.com. October 11, 2011. http://lynseyg.com/sheena-ryder-i-consider-myself -not-bi-but-bi-furious/.

Shibari, Kelly. "IT HAPPENED TO ME: I'm The First-Ever Plus-Size Model On the Cover of *Penthouse Forum.*" XOJane.com. May 5, 2014. http://www.xojane.com/it-happened-to-me/kelly-shibari-penthouse -forum.

Shibari, Kelly. "What It's Really Like to Be a Plus-Size Porn Model—(First Of All, It Won't Make You Rich)." XOJane.com. June 13, 2014. http://www.xojane.com/sex/kelly-shibari-porn-star.

Shira Tarrant, interview by Joe Pinsker. "The Hidden Economics of Porn: A gender-studies professor explains how the industry works." TheAtlantic.com. April 4, 2016. http://www.theatlantic.com/business/archive /2016/04/pornography-industry-economics-tarrant/476580/.

Sinnamon Love, interview by Lynsey G. January 4, 2012.

Small, Oriana. *Girlvert: A Porno Memoir.* Los Angeles: A Barnacle Book, 2011.

Sophia St. James, interview by Lynsey G. "SOPHIA ST JAMES—'Being queer means that I'm an equal opportunity lover!'" *WHACK! Magazine* via LynseyG.com. May 10, 2011. http://lynseyg.com/sophia-st -james-being-queer-means-that-im-an-equal-opportunity-lover/.

Snow, Aurora. "A Famous Porn Star Claims She Was Raped On Set. Will She Receive Justice?" *The Daily Beast*. December 25, 2016. http://www.thedailybeast.com/articles/2016/12/25/a-famous-porn-star-claims-she-was-raped-on-set-will-she-receive-justice.html.

Snow, Aurora. "Accuser: James Deen Had Help Raping Me." *The Daily Beast*. December 7, 2015. http://www.thedailybeast.com/articles/2015/12/07/accuser-james-deen-had-help-raping-me.html.

Snow, Aurora. "The Adult Industry Doesn't Pay! (As Much As You Think)." *The Daily Beast*. November 23, 2013. http://www.thedailybeast.com/articles/2013/11/23/the-adult-industry-doesn-t-pay-as-much-as-you-think.html.

Snow, Aurora. "Christy Mack: The Porn World Unites Over a Fallen Comrade." *The Daily Beast*. August 16, 2014. http://www.thedailybeast.com/articles/2014/08/16/christy-mack-the-porn-world-unites-over-a-fallen-comrade.html.

Snow, Aurora. "Interracial Sex Still Taboo for Many Porn Stars." *The Daily Beast*. March 5, 2013. http://www.thedailybeast.com/articles/2013/03/05/interracial-sex-still-taboo-for-many-porn-stars.html.

Snow, Aurora. "Two More James Deen Accusers Tell All: 'There Was So Much Blood.'" *The Daily Beast*. December 2, 2015. http://www.thedailybeast.com/articles/2015/12/02/two-more-james-deen-accusers-tell-all-there-was-so-much-blood.html.

"Society." Directed by Lynsey G. Published by apexart, 24:06. March 21, 2012. https://apexart.org/images/lynseyg/videos/Society.m4v.

Spataro, Joanne. "The New Porn That's Better for Your Health." Tonic.Vice.com. January 9, 2017. https://tonic.vice.com/en_us/article/the-new-porn-thats-better-for-your-health.

Spence, Todd. "Studies Finally Reveal What Kind of Porn Most Women Watch." Break.com. May 13, 2015. http://www.break.com/article/women-enjoy-group-porn-studies-show-from-pornhub-2856738.

Squires, Bethy. "Business is Still Thriving for James Deen Following Rape Accusations." *Broadly*. June 16, 2016. https://broadly.vice.com/en_us/article/business-is-still-thriving-for-james-deen-following-rape-accusations.

State of New Hampshire v. Robert Theriault. No. 2007-601, Supreme Court of New Hampshire, 2008.

Stewart, Dodal. "Porn Performers Agree: The Porn Industry Is Racist." Jezebel.com. April 5, 2013. http://jezebel.com/5993788/porn-performers-agree-the-porn-industry-is-racist.

Stormy Daniels, interview by Lynsey G. "Stormy Daniels at Exxxotica NJ 2011!" YouTube video, published by *WHACK! Magazine*, 4:57. Posted December 5, 2011. https://www.youtube.com/watch?v=9RaL7BFWLps.

Stoya. "So You Want to Perform In Porn." *Vice.* June 7, 2013. http://www
.vice.com/read/so-you-want-to-perform-in-porn.

Stoya. "Stoya on the Great Condom Debate." Vice.com. September 27,
2013. http://www.vice.com/read/stoya-on-the-great-condom-debate.

Strusiewicz, Cezary Jan. "5 Ways Porn Created the Modern World."
Cracked.com. December 11, 2010. http://www.cracked.com/article
_18888_5-ways-porn-created-modern-world.html.

Stryker, Kitty. "Principled Pornography: How Queer/Indie Sites are Reframing the Industry." HuffingtonPost.com. April 19, 2012. http:/
/www.huffingtonpost.com/kitty-stryker/principled-pornography-
ho_b_1435614.html.

Stryker, Kitty. "The Soapbox: How PayPal & WePay Discriminate Against
the Adult Industry." *The Frisky.* April 2, 2014. http://www.thefrisky
.com/2014-04-02/the-soapbox-how-paypal-wepay-discriminate-
against-the-adult-industry/.

Syd Blakovich, interview by Lynsey G. "Syd Blakovich is the Damn Coolest."
LynseyG.com. December 11, 2010. http://lynseyg.com/syd-blakovich
-is-the-damn-coolest/.

Taormino, Tristan, Celine Parreñas Shimizu, Constance Penley, and Merreille
Miller-Young, eds. *The Feminist Porn Book: The Politics of Producing
Pleasure.* New York: The Feminist Press, 2013.

Tarrant, Shira. *The Pornography Industry: What Everyone Needs to Know.*
New York: Oxford University Press, 2016.

Tee Reel, interview by Lynsey G. February 3, 2016.

Tempesta, Erica. "'We're not objects': Transgender porn stars detail the discrimination they face working in the adult film industry, as they claim
most people still see them as just a 'fetish.'" DailyMail.co.uk. December
11, 2015. http://www.dailymail.co.uk/femail/article-3354547/We-not
-objects-Transgender-porn-stars-discrimination-face-working-adult
-film-industry-claim-people-just-fetish.html.

Tibbals, Chauntelle. "A World without Free Porn?" *Men's Health.* June 24,
2015. http://www.menshealth.com/sex-women/world-without-free-porn.

Tibbals, Chauntelle. "There's a Serious Racism Problem in the Porn Industry." Mic.com. February 19, 2016. https://mic.com/articles/135555
/there-s-a-serious-racism-problem-in-the-porn-industry#.4KD2bzSOO.

Tierney, John. "Porn, the Low-Slung Engine of Progress." *The New York
Times.* January 9, 1994. http://www.nytimes.com/1994/01/09/arts
/porn-the-low-slung-engine-of-progress.html.

Tierney, John. "Single Female Seeking Same-Race Male." Tierney Lab via
The New York Times. April 13, 2007. http://tierneylab.blogs.nytimes
.com/2007/04/13/single-female-seeking-same-race-male/.

Tim von Swine, interview by Lynsey G. January 22, 2016.

The United States Department of Justice. "Citizens Guide to U.S. Federal Law on Obscenity." Justice.gov. Accessed December 10, 2016. https://www.justice.gov/criminal-ceos/citizens-guide-us-federal-law-obscenity.

Venus Lux, interview by Lynsey G. February 1, 2016.

Vid Tuesday, interview by Lynsey G. "Vid Tuessday: The Shy Queer Pornstar Web Comic Geek with a Deckle Fetish You Really Want to Know, Part I." LynseyG.com. July 13, 2011. http://lynseyg.com/vid-tuesday-the-shy-queer-pornstar-web-comic-geek-with-a-deckle-fetish-you-really-want-to-know-part-i/.

Wallace, Benjamin. "The Geek-Kings of Smut." *New York Magazine*. January 30, 2011. http://nymag.com/news/features/70985/.

Ward, Mark. "Web porn: Just how much is there?" BBC News. July 1, 2013. http://www.bbc.com/news/technology-23030090.

Warren, Peter. "Tony T., Ramon Nomar File Defamation Suit in Response to Nikki Benz Allegations." AVN.com. January 12, 2017. https://avn.com/business/articles/legal/tony-t-ramon-nomar-file-defamation-suit-against-benz-brazzers-708535.html.

Warzal, Charlie. "The Internet's Dirty Secret: Nobody Knows How Much Porn There Is." *BuzzFeed News*. May 15, 2013. https://www.buzzfeed.com/charliewarzel/the-internets-weirdest-secret-nobody-knows-how-much-pornthe?utm_term=.lw3oZ9zbl #.laQ2brBgo.

Wild, Chris. "c. 30,000 – 0 B.C.: Prehistoric sex toys: The 'ice-age baton' in all its glory." Mashable.com. January 13, 2015. http://mashable.com/2015/01/13/prehistoric-sex-toys/#1QQ4D4Lc5kq9.

Wilford, John Noble. "Full-Figured Statuette, 35,000 Years Old, Provides New Clues to How Art Evolved." *The New York Times*. May 13, 2009. http://www.nytimes.com/2009/05/14/science/14venus.html.

Will Ryder, interview by Lynsey G. "WILL RYDER—'I'd like to say to the industry: "You're welcome."'" *WHACK! Magazine* via LynseyG.com. March 12, 2011. http://lynseyg.com/will-ryder-id-like-to-say-to-the-industry-youre-welcome/.

Williams, Mitchell. "How a Straight Adult Performer Convinced Me That Condoms Are Useless in Porn." HuffingtonPost.com. November 21, 2012. http://www.huffingtonpost.com/mitchell-williams/how-a-straight-adult-performer-convinced-me-that-condoms-are-useless-in-porn_b_2165066.html.

Woollaston, Victoria. "The sex toys dating back 28,000 years: Ancient phalluses made from stone and dried camel dung started trend for sex aids." DailyMail.co.uk. January 13, 2015. http://www.dailymail.co.uk /sciencetech/article-2908415/The-sex-toys-dating-28-000-years -Ancient-phalluses-stone-dried-camel-dung-started-trend-sex-aids.html.

Wylde, Danny. "An Apology." TrveWestCoastFiction.blogspot.com. February 1, 2013. http://trvewestcoastfiction.blogspot.com/2013/02/an-apology .html?zx=fb0c9fca7e764807.

Yamato, Jen. "Joanna Angel Opens Up About James Deen's Alleged Abuse: 'He Really Is a Scary Person.'" TheDailyBeast.com. December 2, 2015. http://www.thedailybeast.com/articles/2015/12/02/joanna-angel-opens -up-about-james-deen-s-alleged-abuse-he-really-is-a-scary-person.html.

Young-Powell, Abby. "Students turn to porn for sex education." *The Guardian*. January 29, 2015. https://www.theguardian.com/education /2015/jan/29/students-turn-to-porn-for-sex-education.

Zywicki, Todd. "Operation Choke Point." *The Washington Post*. May 24, 2014. https://www.washingtonpost.com/news/volokh-conspiracy/wp /2014/05/24/operation-choke-point/.